A Guide to

Funding from Government Departments & Agencies

second edition

Susan Forrester
Anthony Stenson

Supported by the government's
Active Community Unit

DIRECTORY OF SOCIAL CHANGE

Published by
The Directory of Social Change
24 Stephenson Way
London NW1 2DP
Tel. 020 7209 5151; Fax 020 7209 5049
e-mail info@dsc.org.uk
from whom further copies and a full publications list are available.

Directory of Social Change is a Registered Charity no. 800517

First published 1998
Second edition 2001

ISBN 1 900360 79 9

British Library Cataloguing in Publication data
A catalogue record for this book is available from the British Library

Text design by Lenn Darroux
Cover design by Russell Stretten
Typeset by Linda Parker
Printed and bound by Antony Rowe, Chippenham

Other Directory of Social Change departments in London:
Courses and conferences tel. 020 7209 4949
Charityfair tel. 020 7209 1015
Charity Centre tel. 020 7209 1015
Marketing and research tel. 020 7209 4422

Directory of Social Change Northern Office:
Federation House, Hope Street, Liverpool L1 9BW
Courses and conferences tel. 0151 708 0117
Research tel. 0151 708 0136

Contents

Information about this Guide

Its scope

This guide describes the funding to the voluntary sector **within England only** during 2000/01 from central government departments and their agencies. These agencies include the 'arms length' governmental bodies known as NDPBs (Non-Departmental Public Bodies) and voluntary organisations administering delegated funds for government departments. It also covers those departments with a UK-wide remit, such as Defence, the Foreign Office and the Department for International Development.

The book serves a number of roles:

- as a basic guide for fundraisers (particularly newcomers);
- as a comparative resource to other government departments;
- as a broad survey of tranches of finance to which the voluntary sector has access.

This guide cannot be definitive – developments and changes inevitably occur during and after publication. Some programmes included in the book are nearing their conclusion, others may be in the pipeline, or may not. However the information provided offers a thorough overview to enable the reader to ask further questions and to track the new sources.

Our definition of 'voluntary organisation' is inclusive, from major national bodies to local community groups. The common factors are that they are independent and self-governing, non-profit-making (any profits are ploughed back), and voluntary, i.e. receiving considerable voluntary help whether from donations, public support or unpaid trustees – though many have a mainly salaried workforce.

We have aimed to outline the range of ways in which the voluntary sector receives financial support covering:

- funding programmes directed specifically at voluntary and community organisations;
- funding programmes, often from NDPBs, covering a wider constituency than the voluntary sector alone;
- grant-in-aid to individual voluntary organisations on an annual review basis;
- special departmental initiatives to tackle a problem and to test and pilot new approaches/methods;
- service contracts.

(Service contracts occur most extensively at local authority level.)

In addition funding may become available through taking part in area-based and partnership initiatives. Central government has set up a number of programmes.

The guide does not cover:

- the National Lottery (though the New Opportunities Fund is covered because of its closer direction from government);
- European funding;
- local authority funding (although some time-limited exploratory programmes with a central government dimension are included.)

It only lightly touches upon the arts programmes.

How the guide is organised

The guide maps out the funding sources within each of the departments. These are followed by the funding programmes of 'Related Agencies', the NDPBs grant-aided by those departments and other organisations disbursing government funding.

The contents list on pages 41–8 shows the running order in its entirety. In addition there are individual contents lists at the beginning of the sections for each department.

Indexes

Readers are strongly advised also to use the indexes to track all the funding sources that could be of interest to their area of activity. The subject index should be particularly helpful in this respect.

The entries

The names of the directorates, divisions and units, etc. within departments have been given in full to help newcomers develop a 'feel' for the department and its internal structure. An awareness of this kind can help trace new potential contacts and other sources of funding. Use the *Civil Service Yearbook* and *Vachers* to help in this respect (see Appendix 2). It needs to be appreciated that the titles of divisions and units, etc. are frequently changed.

Contact names and telephone numbers

Readers must not be surprised if these prove to be out-of-date. Personnel changes are frequent and have occurred within the course of this research. Despite this the information provides a valuable trail which enables the current contacts to be found if sensible questions are asked.

Asking questions

Be clear about the questions you want to have answered. Civil servants reply helpfully to the questions asked, but rarely offer information. The replies you get depend on the questions you ask. Sometimes their understanding of their own department, let alone their division, may be limited. If the person you are talking to can't help, for whatever reason, and you want greater clarification, ask for an officer with a wider brief. As a general rule it is better to start at a higher staffing level than lower (but not too high).

Administration and assessment

Always be aware of the autonomy of government departments and agencies. Each operates individually and the arrangements for grant programmes vary also. There are considerable administrative differences in the processing of applications. Each will function according to the scope, size and purpose of its grant programmes.

Many NDPBs (e.g. the Countryside Agency, English Heritage and English Nature) devolve funding work to their regional offices where staff members can develop closer working relationships with local applicants.

Treasury Rules

The strictures for public accountability under Treasury Rules are common to all: the annual round of the financial year (April to March); accounting requirements; financial monitoring; annual clawback of funding.

The annual funding cycle

Many grant programmes run to this timetable:

Sept/autumn	Closing date for applications
Jan	Notification of awards to applicants
Feb/Mar	Programme of work agreed with applicants

Table 1 (Annual application deadlines for grant schemes) covers those schemes where deadlines were clear at the time of editing. It shows that whilst deadlines vary, in general they are in early autumn.

New programmes and opportunities

Grant-making programmes usually inform their own constituency of voluntary organisations about new application rounds and new arrangements. Do not assume, however, that this will be the case. Be sure to keep in touch to try to find out when new annual programmes are likely to start, so that you can plan you own work schedule more effectively.

Organisations new to certain fields of work must be sure to get on the mailing lists relevant to them.

In addition organisations should be alert to announcements about other opportunities to work with departments on matters of mutual concern to them. These announcements are made in the specialist press and also at times in the national press.

On occasions respected national voluntary organisations with a good practical track record can reach funding arrangements to explore their interest/proposals if they are important areas in line with government policy.

Table 1 Annual application deadlines for grant schemes (as at autumn 2000)

(months of the year January to December)

	J	F	M	A	M	J	J	A	S	O	N	D
Education												
Work-Life Balance Fund							•					
UK online Capital Modernisation Fund					•							
Early Education/Section 64 (Early Years)										•	•	
National Childcare Strategy											•	•
Environment												
Darwin Initiative												•
Environmental Action Fund									•	•	•	
Special Grants Programme									•			
Health												
Minority Ethnic Health Grants										•		
Section 64 Grants									•			
Shared Training Programme						•						
Opportunities for Volunteering General Fund									•			
Home												
Probation Unit Grants											•	
Active Community Grants										•	•	
ACU Capital Modernisation Grants				•								
Connecting Communities							•					
Family Support Grant												•
RDS Innovative Research Challenge Fund			•									
International Development												
Charity Know How	•			•			•		•			
Development Awareness Fund											•	
Enterprise Development Innovation Fund			•					•				
Innovations Fund				•					•			
Youth												
Commonwealth Youth Exchange Council										•		
National Voluntary Youth Organisations										•		
Local												
Greater Manchester Grants	•				•				•			
West Yorkshire Grants								•				

The Programmes and Key Developments

Main funding programmes

National voluntary organisations and others may receive funding from the central government department, or agency, to which their work is related. Most central government departments have a funding programme open to voluntary organisations with a *national* remit, or to *initiatives of national significance.* The work they support would, of course, be expected to be within and supporting governmental policies in that area of interest. (These programmes, one of the largest of which is the Section 64 programme within the Department of Health, are listed in Table 2, page 20.) Their programmes are open to annual application and their criteria may change from year to year.

A number of departments, the Ministry of Defence, the Foreign Office, Social Security and Trade and Industry, do not have designated funding programmes, but support is given to the voluntary sector through their direct funding relationships with certain organisations carrying out work close to its interests, or on its behalf. These grants may be open to annual review but are not part of a competitive round and are mostly in the form of grant-in-aid.

Changes and developments in programmes

Voluntary organisations should be alert to developments in structures and remits within departments. Invariably the relevant voluntary bodies will have taken part in consultations and discussions before the introduction of initiatives which could affect them but newcomers should realise that programmes are not written in stone – every year changes may occur.

Some sectors within departments have adopted new names displaying a new bias of interest – the Non-Governmental Unit of the Department for International Development has become the Civil Society Department administering a Civil Society Challenge Fund focusing on projects developing civil society and empowerment and open to a broader range of non-profit organisations and alliances including unions and churches. In addition Partnership Programme Agreements are being drawn up with major development NGOs formerly supported year on year with block grants.

Since the last edition of this guide new units have been created within, for example, the Home Office where the Family Support Unit and the Racial

Equality Unit both run funding programmes open to the voluntary sector. The latter, called Connecting Communities, is open to public agencies as well as the voluntary sector

New programmes are drawn up. This is on an irregular basis, and not part of a regular schedule. (Of course there may well be minor changes made within a programme from year to year, and applicants need to be alert to these.) The Active Community Unit at the Home Office totally revised its grant-making criteria for 2001/02. Its Active Community Grants are accompanied by a completely new scheme, Capital Modernisation Grants, which aim to encourage voluntary and community groups to pool their resources and develop jointly run public bases.

The role of the Active Community Unit

It is worth giving a brief note on this unit which has a central role in taking a national overview of the voluntary and community sector and in supporting its development. The unit is currently based within the Home Office although this is not inevitable – its equivalent has previously been placed within the then Department of National Heritage. Its location depends on the assignment of ministerial responsibilities. There were two ministers with joint responsiblities for the unit in autumn 2000, Lord Falconer of the Cabinet Office and Paul Boateng of the Home Office.

The changes in the unit's name gives some indication of its developing role over recent years, from Voluntary Services Unit (VSU) to Voluntary and Community Unit (VCU) to Active Community Unit (ACU). The ACU has a wider role and a higher profile than its precursors. Its aim is not merely to support the sector but to stimulate its growth – to 'create a step-change in voluntary and community involvement' with two central objectives 'to promote increased voluntary and community involvement' and 'to support the development of active communities'. All sorts of voluntary and volunteering activity are promoted including employer-supported community involvement within business. Traditionally the unit has supported key infrastructure organisations whose remits are wider than any single department which its current policy provides for through its new 'strategic grants'. The unit, and its funding programmes, places particular emphasis on the development of work with black and minority ethnic communities.

The ACU has taken the lead role in the work on the Compact on Relations between Government and the Voluntary and Community Sector, and the mutual undertakings regarding independence, funding, policy development and consultation, and the specific codes, such as the Funding Code of Good Practice. It is also supporting the drive for local authorities to develop such local Compacts.

Funding to local groups

Whilst, as has been stated, as a general rule central government departments support national work and leave the funding of local and community activities to local government, in recent years a number of time-limited programmes have been initiated by departments, administered on their behalf by agencies 'closer to the ground':

- Community Resource Fund, administered by community foundations for the Active Community Unit;
- Neighbourhood Support Fund, administered for the Department for Education and Employment (DfEE) by Community Development Foundation, National Youth Agency and Youth Alliance;
- Community Champions Fund, delegated from the DfEE to the Government Offices for the Regions (GORs) and then to local administrators;
- Adult and Community Learning Fund, administered for the DfEE by two national agencies.

These programmes have varied greatly in size. The largest, the Neighbourhood Support Fund, has made no less than £60 million available over three years.

These precede major interdepartmental initiatives of great importance for the voluntary and community sector which will be coming on stream during 2001.

- The Children's Fund will release £70 million of its allocation to be adminstered by and for local voluntary and community groups over a period of three years.
- The Neighbourhood Renewal Fund, as part of the National Strategy for Neighbourhood Renewal, is expected to help fund capacity building and fund additional training of key individuals as well as community chests to assist local communities.

Funding may also be available to enable community inputs to Local Strategic Partnerships (LSPs). At the time of writing the details about this had not been announced. Certainly LSPs in the most deprived areas will receive start-up funding through the New Deal for Communities to help empower local people and communities to play their part in setting local priorities and determining local action for their neighbourhoods. Funds should help cover the cost of residents' and groups' participation, and allow LSPs to use 'innovative approaches to involving local people', alongside funding for small 'community chests'.

In addition the partnership and area-based initiatives (see Regional Section) may run their own local community funds, but the decision to do so varies.

The Active Community Unit in the Home Office is taking the leading role with an inter-departmental working group on resourcing community capacity building. Part of its role is to look at the different departmental initiatives and to consider how to develop a more cohesive approach to the resourcing of local voluntary and community groups.

Joined-up thinking

The Social Exclusion Unit within the Cabinet Office has been a key player in the government's drive to achieve more cooperative working between departments on cross-sectoral issues and has taken a major part in the thinking behind the development of the two new funding streams mentioned above.

This has been accompanied by a marked growth of inter-departmental initiatives. Specific inter-departmental units which have been established include Sure Start, Rough Sleepers, New Deal for Disabled People, New Deal for Lone Parents, and Connexions. The Neighbourhood Renewal Unit will coordinate the work of the various departments and agencies concerned with the National Strategy for Neighbourhood Renewal and should become operational from April 2001.

Partnerships and special initiatives

There has been a proliferation of area-based initiatives over recent years. Through these central government has sought to stimulate new initiatives and cooperative work at the local level through the development of a variety of partnerships across all sectors, public, private and voluntary/ community. Certain areas, localities, or zones, have been selected in areas of particular need to receive additional funding for innovative approaches. They include Health Action Zones, Education Action Zones, New Deal for Communities, and Sure Start. Sure Start aims to meet targets in selected districts and builds on the Early Years Development and Childcare Partnerships conducted by all local authorities. More recently the Legal Services Commission (successor to the Legal Aid Board) has been developing Local Legal Services Partnerships throughout the country. Whilst these initiatives do not operate as specific funding programmes, voluntary organisations may be funded for an agreed activity or service which forms part of a wider strategic plan.

(Local voluntary and community groups within the location of a special initiative should be alert to the possibility of that initiative having decided to provide a community fund in their area. Some HAZs and other partnership programmes have done so.)

The plethora of partnerships has led to a new community planning duty by which service providers across the country are being encouraged to establish Local Strategic Partnerships i.e. a 'single coordinating partnership for an area [...] linking the neighbourhood to the regions, coordinating across and between partnership activity'.

Regionalisation

A cross-departmental unit, the Regional Coordination Unit, has been set up to give more coherence to the work of the GORs. A particular aim will be to introduce better coordination of area-based initiatives many of which, at the time of writing, overlap and make competing demands on local partners.

The introduction of Regional Development Agencies (RDAs) has added an important new dimension to government. Voluntary groups have formed into regional networks to be able to make an input into their decisions which will increasingly affect their work. The agencies have called for freedom from restricted budgets and power to decide their own spending priorities according to regional needs as expressed in their strategic plans. As a result the Single Regeneration Budget, the massive fund jointly supported by many departments, particularly the Department of Environment, Transport and the Regions (DETR), the Department of Trade and Industry (DTI) and the DfEE, will not continue, after a transition year. From 2002/03, this funding will go directly to each RDA into their 'single spending pot'.

Agencies

It is not possible to estimate the amount devoted by Non-Departmental Public Bodies (NDPBs)to the voluntary sector. They support a mix of activities from the public, private, voluntary/community sectors in their funding programmes. Moreover, they are also able to raise support additional to their grant-in-aid from government. The Countryside Agency, for instance, which assumed responsibilities from the former Countryside Commission and parts of the work of the former Rural Development Commission, administers the Local Heritage Initiative, jointly funded by the agency, the Heritage Lottery Fund and the Nationwide Building Society. It also administers another programme launched in 2000, Walking the Way to Health, which it funds along with the New Opportunities Fund and the British Heart Foundation.

New Opportunities Fund (NOF)

This massive programme will absorb, from 2001, after the demise of the Millennium Commission, a third of all National Lottery funding for good causes. It has been included because its policies and initiatives are closely controlled by government and it has been set up as an NDPB.

It works with a range of partners. For UK online, the UK network of online centres, NOF funds related operational costs through its CALL programme, whilst capital costs are funded by the DfEE. Its Green Spaces programme is to be administered on its behalf by a range of agencies, both voluntary sector organisations and NDPBs.

Analysis of Funding

Background

The guide covers the funding to the voluntary sector in England from 11 government departments, and from nearly 60 agencies related to them.

We have taken the opportunity to look at the funding we have identified and to make some observations to give the voluntary sector some ideas about the relative scale of funding to different areas of work.

Funding by grant programmes targeted specifically at the voluntary sector

The total funding in England can be split into three broad sectors. Figure 1 shows how funding from the Housing Corporation still accounts for the lion's share (nearly two thirds) of the total funding. This, however, is a drop from 78% in the previous edition. Whereas in the previous edition of this guide the funding for 'All other grants' and the Arts Council of England was similar (11% for each), this edition shows 'All other grants' at 23%, and the Arts Council of England at 15%. In addition the arts figure is inflated as it includes the administrative costs of the Arts Council of England and the other agencies it funds, especially the ten Regional Arts Boards.

Figure 1 Funding schemes open only to the voluntary sector 2000/1 (Total: £1.299 billion)

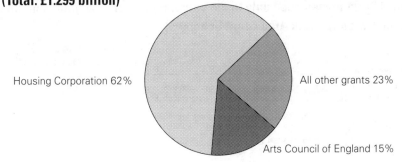

Housing Corporation 62%
All other grants 23%
Arts Council of England 15%

Figures 2 and 3 make a comparison between the years 2000/01 and 1998/99 (the year used in the previous edition) of the funding schemes only open to the voluntary sector (excluding the Housing Corporation, the Arts Council of England and the metropolitan areas). They show an increase of £89 million. All but £14 million of this increase is accounted for by an additional £35 million to the voluntary sector from the

Department for International Development (DfID), £20 million from the Neighbourhood Support Fund by the Department for Education and Employment (DfEE) and £20 million from the Rough Sleepers Unit by the Department of the Environment, Transport and the Regions (DETR).

Figure 2 breaks down 'All other grants', as shown in the pie-chart, *by percentage*. Figure 3 analyses 'All other grants' this time in terms of the *actual totals* contributed by each department.

Figure 2 Programmes open only to the voluntary sector – by percentage (excludes Metropolitan Area Grant Schemes)

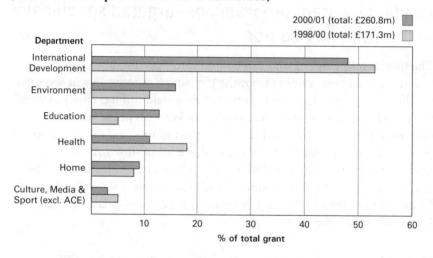

Figure 3 Programmes open only to the voluntary sector – by grant amount (excludes Metropolitan Area Grant Schemes)

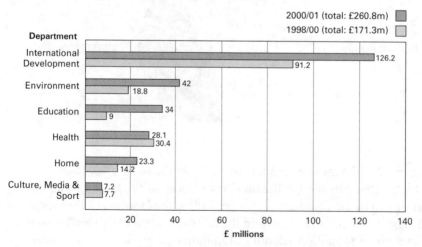

The main change is that the Department of Health's contribution has been overtaken by the DETR and the DfEE in each analysis.

Whilst a cursory glance at the percentages in Figure 2 might suggest a drop in the the funding from the DfID and the Department for Health, Figure 3 shows a considerable increase in the total sum given by DfID, and that the drop in funding to the voluntary sector from the Department of Health is not as great as might be suggested.

Figure 3 shows that most departments have increased their spending directed at the voluntary sector, with the exception of the Department of Health and the Department of Culture, Media and Sport.

The detailed figures are shown overleaf.

Note: Significant funding omitted from Figures 2 and 3 and Table 2:

- NDPBs with grant programmes supporting a wide range of beneficiaries often in the public as well as the private sectors could not be included in this analysis as their proportion of grant-aid to the voluntary sector was not consistently supplied. Such major NDPBs/ agencies include: English Heritage; the British Council; the Countryside Agency; English Nature; the Forestry Commission; the Employment Service; the Prison Service.
- Annual grant-in-aid to certain key voluntary sector organisations, many originally set up via governmental initiatives (see Table 3 and Figure 4 below).
- Major regional and area-based partnership programmes (see Regional Section).

Table 2 Grant programmes specifically for voluntary organisations – 2000/01 (agency-administered schemes excluded)

	£'000	%
Department for International Development	**126,176**	**43**
Civil Society Challenge Fund (UK)	20,100	
Conflict and Humanitarian Affairs Department (UK)	100,750	
Development Awareness Fund (UK)	5,000	
Charity Know How (UK)	326	
Department for Education and Employment	**34,075**	**12**
Early Education Grants	1,825	
Section 64 – Early Years Division	776	
SEN Small Programmes Fund	1,000	
Adult and Community Learning Fund	5,000	
National Voluntary Youth Organisations	4,000	
Citizenship Education Grants	474	
Neighbourhood Support Fund	20,000	
Community Champions Fund	1,000	
Department of Health	**28,100**	**10**
Section 64 (health and personal social service)	21,000	
Opportunities for Volunteering Scheme	6,600	
Black and Minority Ethnic Anti-Drug Grants	500	
Home Office	**23,333**	**8**
Active Community Unit:		
Active Community Grants (UK)	18,000	
Capital Modernisation Grants (UK)	2,333	
Family Support Grant	3,000	
Department of Environment, Transport and the Regions	**42,025**	**14**
Housing Management and Tenant Participation – Section 16	5,975	
Environmental Action Fund	4,212	
Special Grants Programme, regeneration/housing	1,440	
Housing Corporation Resettlement of Single and Homeless People	9,000	
*Rough Sleepers Unit	20,398	
Local Heritage Initiative	1,000	
(plus an extra £3 million from Nationwide Building Society and Heritage Lottery Fund)		
Culture, Media and Sport	**7,193**	**2**
New Partners, Arts & Business	3,500	
Sportsmatch Scheme	3,373	
Visiting Arts	320	
Metropolitan Area Grants	**31,960**	**11**
Greater Manchester Grants Scheme	2,800	
London Borough Grants	28,000	
West Yorkshire Grants	1,160	
TOTAL	**292,862**	**100**

*This is one-off funding and will not be available in following years

Figure 4 Ongoing annual grants to individual organisations – 2000/01

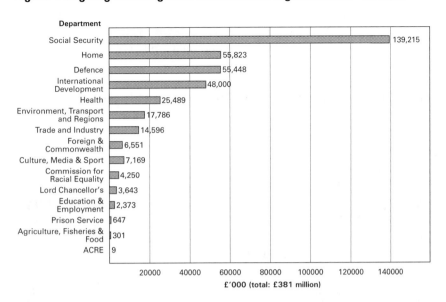

£'000 (total: £381 million)

Annual grants-in-aid to voluntary organisations outside competitive programmes

It is also of interest to look at those grants to voluntary organisations made on a regular, annual review basis outside the competitive arrangements for funding programmes. These totalled over £381 million in 2000/01 (£88 million more than the competitive funding programmes listed above).

These awards are generally referred to as grants-in-aid. The distinction between grants and grants-in-aid is not always clear even within the Civil Service. Grants-in-aid tend to be on a continuing basis to bodies towards their operational costs. These organisations are closely linked to particular government policies and interests and many have owed their genesis as voluntary organisations to joint initiatives arising between government departments and/or their agencies and voluntary sector interests.

Figure 4 shows this by department and Table 3 gives a detailed breakdown of the grant recipients. Over a third of the total amount (34%) was given as grant-in-aid to the Independent Living Fund by the Department of Social Security (£131 million). Other major grants-in-aid were awarded to the Army Cadet Corps by the Ministry of Defence (£40 million) the Family Fund Trust by the Department of Health (£25 million), Victim Support by the Home Office (£18 million) and the National Association of CABx by the Department of Trade and Industry (£14 million).

Much of this funding is given to the work of organisations which are themselves funding bodies, providing financial and other support to people and young children with physical problems, such as the Independent Living Fund, Motability and the Family Fund Trust.

Table 3 Grant-in-aid outside funding programmes and special initiatives – 2000/01

Department/section	£'000
MAFF	**301**
Family and Wildlife Advisory Group	265
National Federation of Young Farmers' Clubs	36
DCMS	**7,169**
Governing Bodies of Sport	7,169
Defence	**55,448***
(including Army Cadet Corps – £40,079)	
DfEE	**2,373**
Trident (work experience)	30
National Mentoring Network	600
Basic Skills and Adult Further Education	597
(7 organisations including National Institute	
for Adult Continuing Education – 445)	
Access and Participation in Further Education:	
SKILL	92
View	4
Learning Alliance	850
NACRO	
Rathbone Community Industry	
CSV	
YMCA	
Voluntary Sector National Training Organisation	200
DETR	**17,786**
Encams (Tidy Britain Group/Going for Green)	3,763
Groundwork	7,500
Mobility for disabled and elderly:	
Community Transport Association	70
Mobility Choice	70
RoSPA	408
DfID	**48,000**
Partnership Programme Agreements	48,000
Foreign	**6,551***
Foreign Policy Grants	6,551
Health	**29,600**
Family Fund Trust	25,360
Women's Aid Federation Helpline	49
British Fluoridation Society	80

International Disability Action:
    Disability Awareness in Action   41
    Royal Association for Disability & Rehabilitation   26
    British Council of Disabled People   8
    UK Disability Forum for Europe   10
Sexual Health Promotion   2,100

Home   **55,823**
Refugee Integration   2,100
    (including Refugee Council – £1,374
    Refugee Action – £550)
Refugee Reception and One Stop Services   14,000
Refugee Council Panel of Advisers for Unaccompanied Minors   805
Refugee Legal Centre and Immigration Advisory Service   18,000
Crime Concern core funding   750
Reducing Burglary Initiative: Crime Concern and NACRO   573
Victim Support   18,300
SAMM   100
NACRO Mental Health Unit   196
Family Support:
    National Family and Parenting Institute   666
    Parentline   333

HM Prison Service   **647**
National Association of Prison Visitors   11
Prisoners Abroad   85
NACRO Prisons Link Unit   226
NACRO core funding   175
CSV: Offenders Pre-release Voluntary Work   150

Commission for Racial Equality   **4,250**
Racial Equality Councils   4,520

Lord Chancellor's   **3,643***
Funding for Marriage Relationship Support   3,643

Regional/Zone-   **3**
ACR   3

Social Securit   **139,21**
Increasing the Independence of Disabled People
    Independent Living Fund   131,30
    Motabilit   7,90
    BLESM   1

Trade and Industr   **14,59**
RoSP   18
National Association of Citizens Advice Bureau   14,41

Tota   **385,44**

*The breakdown for these grant totals from the Ministry of Defence, the Foreig Office and the Lord Chancellor's Department is given in the entries. Many of thei large grants are made on a regular annual basis whilst others are contractua arrangements. However in the case of these departments funding programmes a such are not set up and most grants appear to be made as a result of individual approaches.

Understanding the Funder's Perspective

Advice from John Marshall, head of grants and funding policy at the government's Active Community Unit in the Home Office.

It is clear from the hundreds of applications we receive each year that not enough organisations take the trouble to find out about funders' objectives and expectations. Time spent on clarifying funders' needs will save you time and hopefully increase the chances of your application clearing the first fence.

Government grants are primarily designed to meet departmental policy objectives and programme outcomes. These should of course be reflected in the published criteria for grant. Applications are, therefore, expected to demonstrate clearly how they will help departments achieve their objectives. Too many applicants seem to assume that the core work of their organisation is reason enough to secure government grant. I am afraid that no matter how effective or important the work of your organisation, you need to show how it meets the objectives of the funder.

Whenever you apply for government grants it is worth reflecting on the financial regime within which civil servants operate. Departmental grant funding is discretionary, which means it is subject to annual Parliamentary approval and allocations are decided by the relevant ministers. It is public money, which can only be disbursed in furtherance of government policies and in ways which maximise the efficient and effective use of such funds.

When considering applications government officials are concerned with a number of factors which help us determine whether or not a grant should be recommended, including:

- assessing the impact on the achievement of policy objectives (this includes evidence of the previous track record of the organisation);
- weighing the size of investment against the potential return (organisations invariably over-bid against our budgets);
- looking for evidence that the organisation has the capacity to undertake the project without affecting its core activity;
- ensuring that any risks, in terms of operation or funding, are identified in advance.

Departments increasingly rely on formal evaluation of programmes and activities to provide evidence to Parliament on whether policy outcomes are being achieved. This process also informs future policy development.

In turn, funders look for evidence in grant applications that organisations have self-evaluation systems, where users, partners and stakeholders are regularly consulted. This should also include realistic appraisal of funded activities and outcomes and their relation to policy objectives. Funders will, therefore, expect organisations to make an evidence-based case for the activities for which funding is sought.

Securing a grant is challenging enough, but sustaining the funding once it has been allocated is just as much of a challenge. Departments have finite budgets and are cautious about committing expenditure beyond a fixed period. The funding relationship should perhaps be more of a priority for departments and funded organisations than it often is in practice. I encourage all our funded organisations to maintain regular contact with us, sharing information from any key meetings or achievements and working for openness in all our dealings.

When things go wrong, as they inevitably do from time to time, it is the organisations which have kept us informed throughout that we are able to help. My advice is 'Do not assume the worst. A government grant is an investment that departments will want to protect. It is in everyone's interests, therefore, to discuss difficulties openly and seek a resolution together.'

The Compact *Code of Good Practice on Funding*, published in 2000, is a helpful source of further information on the funding relationship between government and the voluntary and community sector. A copy of the code is available on the Home Office website: www.homeoffice.gov.uk/acu/codes.htm

---

In the following section we reproduce a guide to *Making Partnerships Work*, based on a research report funded by the Joseph Rowntree Foundation.

Making Partnerships Work: a practical guide for community and voluntary groups

This guide is designed to meet the needs of community and voluntary groups, at local and regional levels, who wish to become involved in cross-sectoral partnerships. Its aim is to help groups to negotiate better partnerships with the public and private sectors.

The guide is based on a research report, undertaken for the Joseph Rowntree Foundation by the Ashridge Centre for Business and Society, that involved in-depth investigations of 12 different kinds of partnerships that were widely seen as 'successful', and interviews with almost 60 partners and observers from all sectors.

The advice given within this guide is based on the observations and experience of the interviewees and it covers a number of issues, particularly the decision about whether to opt into a partnership and the development of positive relationships with other partners, the management of the partnership, and the implementation of partnership projects.

Community and voluntary groups can play a number of roles within partnerships: these include being 'lead partners', being partners alongside others, being members of steering or consultative committees, being deliverers of partnership projects under contract, or being beneficiaries of partnerships' activities. However, the ability of local groups to make a real contribution depends to a great extent on the willingness of the other partners to include them at all levels of the partnership. As a result, local groups must make informed decisions about the costs and benefits of participating.

What is a partnership?

Three or more organisations – representing the public, private and voluntary sectors – acting together by contributing their diverse resources to pursue a common vision with clearly defined goals and objectives. The objective of a partnership should be to deliver 'more than the sum of the individual parts'.

Why work in a partnership?

There are a number of reasons behind the growing numbers of cross-sectoral partnerships. Firstly, central government funding regimes have required bidders to form cross-sectoral initiatives. Secondly, the notion of partnership fits in with increasing demand from the public for a greater say in the design and provision of local services. This fits in with concepts of the 'stakeholder society'. Thirdly, there is a widening perception that partnerships between organisations in different sectors can be more efficient in tackling social and economic needs and allocating public funds.

Ashridge interviewees repeatedly stressed the point that multi-agency and multi-faceted responses are required because most social and economic problems have complex and multiple causes. The majority of them believe that partnerships are the best way to tackle these issues in a fundamental and holistic way.

They agreed that partnerships should aim to bring about permanent changes in social, economic and environmental conditions, and thought that right from the start, partnerships should make it clear that they are trying to build structures, attitudes and values that will last a long time. This means encouraging all the partners, stakeholders and members of the wider community – including young people – to grow in confidence, ability and expertise, and to move beyond small local projects to tackle bigger, more substantial programmes of change.

Most interviewees felt that partnerships should seek to empower the local community to act for itself and should build the capacity of local people to engage with the change process. They believed that if the aim was to create change that outlived the partnership, community involvement, consultation and participation should be an unbroken 'golden thread' throughout the partnership's lifetime. Communities and local groups should be involved in financial and management roles as well as in policy-making in order to enhance their ability to contribute at all stages in the process.

However, many interviewees stressed that partnership is not a panacea. Groups who are considering joining one or setting one up should ask themselves if it is the most appropriate solution to the issues they are trying to address.

Is membership of a partnership appropriate for you?

Will a partnership with other sectors be the most effective way of delivering the results you want? There are a number of issues to consider.

1 Are your aims compatible with those of other partners? Does your purpose as a group tie in with their aims and objectives? At a general level, will there be 'added value' for you from working jointly with them? If the links and overlaps are difficult to spot, will membership of the partnership be worthwhile for your group? More specifically:

   - If you are a deliverer of services, will the partnership benefit the communities you exist to serve, or will it divert you from your core aims?
   - If you hold contracts or service level agreements with some of the other partners, will both you and they be able to keep the different relationships separate?
   - If you are a campaigning group, will your ability to campaign be compromised by entering a partnership with the other organisations concerned?

2 Is there time for a 'period of courtship' between the partners, during which relationships can form properly, and partners can get to know each other and understand each other's aims, aspirations and constraints? Or is this a swift response to an opportunity or a crisis that is not backed by any real desire to work together? The first kind will probably be more stable and satisfactory for your group than the second.

3 Do you believe that a real sense of joint purpose and endeavour can be created between your group and the other partners? Can sufficient common ground be agreed? Are the other partners willing to take on board your interests and concerns, and to find ways to cater for the people you represent? Are the other partners prepared to negotiate with you, or do they expect you to fall in with their priorities and plans?

4 Partnership means the presentation of a united front, despite any internal disagreements. Respondents said it is essential to focus on 'the 90% on which you can all agree, not the 10% where you're never going to see eye-to-eye'. This requires compromise on the part of all the partners. Partnerships are like marriages, in that they require give and take, equal treatment, respect and

commitment from all the partners. Does this partnership have the potential to develop these qualities and values?

5 What will your group gain from joining the partnership? Is it worthwhile for you and your members to invest time and energy in the initiative? The benefits can be in a number of forms: influence on policy; access to decision-makers; advantages for your users and members; new opportunities or facilities for the community; funding or in-kind resources for your group or your beneficiaries; new knowledge and skills. What will be the benefits of joining the partnership, and do they justify your investment of time and energy?

6 Do you have sufficient resources and time to engage in this initiative? Will you be drawn away from your main area of business? On a practical level, does your constitution permit you to work on these subjects, in this geographical area, and with these intended beneficiaries, and does it allow you to take part in a joint venture with other organisations? If you are a membership organisation, do your members endorse the decision to invest the group's time and resources in a partnership?

7 Are you willing to cope with the factors that are outside your control, such as local politics and the criteria of external funders? Which goal posts can be moved, and which cannot? Make sure you know and are prepared to deal with the practical details.

8 It is legitimate for other partners to ask you what contribution you can bring to the joint initiative, as all the partners should bring positive inputs to the initiative. You may be able to offer matching funding, but your knowledge, insights, skills, resources and contacts can be even more valuable. Can you help to open out the partnership to the wider community? Think through and explain what benefits you could bring to the partnership.

Which type of partnership is most suitable for you?

Partnerships exist on a spectrum between the 'strategic' and the 'project specific'. At one end of the spectrum is the high-level campaign, for instance the city-wide 'liaison group' that creates a broad framework for the partners' regeneration activities. Another example is a coalition between agencies to lobby on behalf of an area, a theme or group of people (for example the homeless or refugees). These are often loose federations that do not employ staff but devolve all action to the separate member organisations.

At the other end of the spectrum, the partnership sets up a permanent mechanism in order to manage and deliver a particular long-term service – for example, the management of a housing estate or a community facility. In this instance, the partnership needs to own and control capital resources, generate revenues to fund its activities over the longer term and set up a permanent legal vehicle to deliver its work. Development trusts fall into this category.

The majority of partnerships are probably in the middle of this spectrum, creating and then managing finite projects that will achieve the goals on which the partners have agreed to collaborate. Partners agree a method of delivering the projects: they may create a joint agency that controls the resources used to deliver the projects, or they may agree that each partner will deliver separate parts of the programme. The partnership will probably be time-limited by the funds available.

Voluntary and community groups are increasingly getting involved in all these types, but are much less likely to be invited to join 'strategic level partnerships' unless they are themselves 'strategic' or umbrella organisations. Sometimes, voluntary and community groups are in the lead, inviting partners from other sectors to join an initiative they have devised. More often, the public sector is in the lead, and takes responsibility for inviting partners from private and voluntary/ community sectors to join the initiative.

Your decision about whether to join a partnership depends on the type of initiative that is being established and its suitability as a vehicle to help you achieve your aims and objectives.

Can you secure respect from the other partners?

The positive finding from the Ashridge research was that all the respondents who were questioned wholly agreed that the community should benefit from partnership activity and supported the involvement of community and voluntary groups.

However, in some of the study areas, voluntary sector respondents said they had found it hard to break into the 'inner circle' and overcome their disadvantage with the other partners. They suggested a number of strategies they had used to address this problem.

- They sought opportunities to meet and talk to other partners in order to break down others' assumptions that they were less professional and less competent than organisations in other sectors. They worked with other colleagues in the sector to present a more united front.

- They spent time exploring what other partners were trying to achieve and why, and explained how their own aims and objectives dovetailed. They explained what they could contribute and how appropriate their skills and abilities were to the partnership.

- They had to convince partners they were representative of other residents and stakeholders and were not just 'local activists' who spoke only for themselves (which was the underlying assumption of many other partners). They also suggested ways in which the partnership could strengthen community representation through forums, elections and capacity building.

- They showed that they too wanted to see some action and results that would prove the worth of the partnership, and they made concrete proposals that helped to crystallise ideas and accelerate the pace of development.

- They persuaded other partners to participate in consultative meetings, workshops, discussion groups, retreats and awaydays that would break down the barriers to cooperation, and they pressed for training courses that would equip the sector to play a greater role in the partnership.

- They built relationships with individuals who could help to counteract old conflicts and disagreements between their organisations.

The increasing involvement of community and voluntary sectors

Partnerships should be expected to make a thorough assessment of their 'stakeholders' and the local community in order to establish the informal and formal groups that should be involved. Although many partnerships still see voluntary and community organisations as lesser partners, there are growing numbers that believe in equal access and status for community and voluntary groups. Despite this, there is much less agreement on when, where and how this involvement should be organised.

However egalitarian the partnership aims to be, it is inevitable that different stakeholders will be involved at different levels in the partnership, and will play different roles. Another factor for community and voluntary groups to consider is the type of role they wish to play in the partnership, and the type of role it is appropriate for them to play, given their aim, remit, size and resources.

What kind of role is most appropriate for your group?

Partner

A limited number of organisations can become formal partners in the initiative; that is, members of the governing body or steering group that has ultimate responsibility for the performance of the partnership. Publicly-funded partnerships often have a 'lead partner' (the 'accountable body'), and this role can be taken on by organisations in any sector.

Consultee

Many more organisations will become involved in the consultative forums and committees that are established to give a voice to the 'stakeholders' and beneficiaries who are affected by the work of the partnership.

Delivery agent

Some organisations can find a suitable role as delivery agents for the partnership. In some cases this is because all the partnership's work is done through intermediaries. In the majority of cases, this role will be undertaken on a contract basis, usually after a tendering process.

Beneficiary

Many organisations will be beneficiaries of the partnership. Activities are often organised around existing agencies, and this can attract investment for new facilities and services into those groups. Many partnerships give small grants to local groups to help increase levels of 'community activity' or to encourage participation by disadvantaged groups.

Informed

Other groups will just be given information about the work of the partnership. Ideally those groups that are simply kept informed are happy to have a 'hands-off' relationship with the partnership, but in practice many of the groups in this category will be striving for a more direct relationship with the partnership, probably inhibited in part by the large number of other community and voluntary groups that are also lobbying for better links and more influence.

What level of commitment are you prepared to make?

These roles offer different rewards and demand different levels of commitment for local community and voluntary groups, and before opting for the most senior levels of representation groups should work out what benefits they seek from the relationship and what kind of contribution they are prepared to make.

How are partnerships organised?

The 12 partnerships studied by Ashridge have a variety of structures and organisational forms, but the most common organisational structure is one which comprises three elements:

- the governance function – the board or executive arm of the partnership;
- the management function – the individual or team that implements the partnership's activities;
- the consultative function – the various committees, subcommittees and steering groups that offer stakeholders the opportunity to contribute and that report to the executive body.

Governance – being a board member

The role of the board is typically to:

- set the parameters for the initiative;
- define the vision and mission of the partnership;
- form policy and ensure accountability;
- determine, approve and endorse key programmes and activities to ensure they meet the strategic objectives;
- review progress and performance and decide corrective action;
- plan the long-term development of the partnership, including planning a suitable exit strategy.

Operating an effective board

Interviewees made a number of observations about the operations of an effective board.

- There should be a maximum of 10–14 members.
- The board should be selected or elected to ensure that all the key interest groups and stakeholders are represented in a balanced way at the 'top level' of the partnership.

- Despite disparities in power and influence outside the partnership, the board members should treat each other as equals and find ways to make decisions in an equitable and consensual way. Methods included ensuring representatives of the community had an absolute majority on the board so that decisions could not be forced through against the wishes of the community, or refusing to take votes so that if a consensus could not be reached, there was effectively a veto.
- The board should be composed of individuals and organisations that can make a real contribution to the work of the partnership; ideally, a board should contain no 'passengers'. Board performance should be regularly reviewed: induction and ongoing training should be provided for its members.
- Each individual board member must be capable of committing his or her organisation and rallying its support for the initiative. They should understand how their organisation works and be able to explain and negotiate its internal politics for others.
- Board members should act democratically and be willing to be accountable to the partnership's stakeholders. The partnership should establish structures and processes that ensure that board members from all sectors can speak for their colleagues. This could include an election process for board members in some or all sectors (not just the community representatives).
- Governance and management functions should usually be kept separate. Only in the smallest partnerships should the board become involved in management supervision. But boards should realise that they (and not the management team) have responsibility and decision-making powers.

Management – running the partnership's activities

The size of the management team within the 12 partnerships studied ranged from one person to 12. The role of the management team is to:

- implement the agenda set by the partnership board by translating policies into specific programmes and actions;
- coordinate the work of the agencies that are acting for the partnership;
- plan, appraise and project manage activities;
- let and manage contracts;
- manage partnership resources;
- monitor and assess progress, and report to the board.

Managing the partnership effectively

Interviewees made comments about effective partnership management.

- Management teams should be seen as impartial and independent rather than being perceived as 'puppets' of one of the partners because of their location, employment situation or funding arrangements.
- Management teams should not usurp the board's functions through setting the agenda for their meetings, presenting proposals in certain ways and taking actions on the ground without reference to the board. They should be clear about boundaries in duties and precisely what has been delegated, and they should make the division in roles clear to others in the community.
- Some interviewees suggested the management team should also be acting as honest broker, facilitator or intermediary between partners.

Consultation – being a stakeholder on committees or forums

Partnerships almost invariably set up a series of standing committees through which they can communicate with stakeholders and beneficiaries. These groups can be organised by theme, by sector, and/or on a geographical basis. They are called by a variety of different names: committees, subcommittees, forums, assemblies or working groups. Membership may be confined to individuals, or to groups, or to a combination of both.

Because these groups have very different functions and levels of influence in different partnerships, their roles are the most difficult to define. Basically, their role is to provide a forum in which particular aspects of the partnership's agenda can be considered in greater detail.

At the most nominal level, they may be used simply to give information about planned or completed activities to the stakeholders and beneficiaries.

When the partnership believes stakeholders should have some influence in decision-making, committees or forums are consulted about the options and may be asked for suggestions and proposals. They may also get the opportunity to comment on performance and progress.

Where they have most power and influence, they are: asked to assist with the preparation of the vision and mission statement; invited to identify issues and priorities; play a role in setting the partnership agenda; in a position to affect the strategic direction of the partnership.

Making the consultative process effective

Ashridge interviewees made a number of observations about what made the consultative process effective, and readers may find these suggestions useful in their negotiations with their local partnerships.

- **The starting point influences speed of progress**
  The speed with which effective consultative arrangements can be put in place depends to a great extent on whether community involvement is accepted locally as the legitimate style for getting things done. In areas where partnerships are able to build on previous community development activity, far higher levels of involvement and representation can be achieved. In previously 'unorganised' communities, higher levels of investment and time will be required.

- **Membership should be based on 'stakeholder analysis'**
  Groups should ask if the partnership has undertaken a 'stakeholder analysis' to identify the individuals and organisations that have a legitimate claim to be involved in the consultative arrangements: those who will be affected by the initiative, either positively or negatively; the intended beneficiaries and users of services; those who could be needed as a resource, including experts, practitioners and delivery agents; and those whose fortunes will affect or be affected by the partnership, can all legitimately call themselves 'stakeholders'.

- **Consultation takes time**
  Partners need to face the fact that involving more people in a wider consultative process necessarily slows down the decision-making process. Groups should also point out that their sector has more limited time and resources available than other sectors and that, as a result, it will usually take longer for them to organise proposals or responses to proposals.

- **Action 'versus' thinking**
  Groups should stress that partnerships must try to balance means and ends in implementing their policies. Some partnerships take their time consulting, gathering views and making joint decisions on priorities; others go much more quickly for an action-orientated approach. Clearly a partnership that achieves very little

cannot be said to be successful, but at the other extreme an initiative that produces real change without the support and involvement of all sectors cannot be truly described as a partnership.

- **The ability to make informed decisions**
  Groups should stress that in order to be effective, members of consultative groups should have access to adequate information about the partnership and its work, and be able to discuss this information in time to make an informed input into the decision-making process.

- **The skills to participate effectively**
  Groups should ask for early and ongoing training to develop their capacity to operate effectively in committees and forums. This can include confidence-building and assertiveness skills; as well as practical issues like running meetings and understanding policies and procedures.

- **Investment in capacity building**
  Groups should ask for support from skilled community forum workers to help build their capacity to contribute, but should also stress that all the partners and managers must recognise the importance of community involvement and make resources available to encourage fuller participation.

- **Removing practical barriers to involvement**
  Levels of community participation are significantly affected by the timetables set by the partnership itself and its external funders and by practical factors like the location and timing of meetings, the availability of childcare, transport or translation facilities, willingness to cover expenses of participants and indeed the use of jargon and the style of the meetings.

- **Linking nominated representatives to the wider community**
  Community representatives who operate at board level or are members of select consultative committees should be effectively linked into wider groups of stakeholders and beneficiaries in ways that enable them to speak with authority on behalf of the wider community.

Many interviewees were worried about the ability of individuals to represent 'the community'. The answer to this lies with the partnership and the arrangements it puts into place to support the community representatives in their role as spokespeople. Representatives need to be part of a broader consultation and participation process for local stakeholders.

- **Ethical use of informal channels**
  Groups must recognise that the formal consultation and decision-making processes are frequently accompanied by private conversations and telephone calls between partners, staff, community representatives and others before meetings. As a result, many decisions are taken outside the formal frameworks. There was a strong pragmatic view among interviewees that these informal relations could build trust and confidence, avoid open conflict and work up compromises that all could accept. This can obviously lead to 'fixing', 'politicking' and the concentration of power in the secretive hands of a small group of insiders unless the 'shadow structure' is open and accessible to all and is used to build the positive relationships within the partnership.

- **Opening access to all areas of partnership activities**
  If groups want to continue to develop their role and their level of responsibility within the partnership, they need to become familiar with the whole round of activities undertaken within the partnership. This includes policy-making and strategy development, management, financial management, implementation and evaluation. The most robust initiatives ensure all the partners are familiar with the full range of skills and activities involved in running an effective partnership.

- **The range of skills to be developed**
  Groups should press for resources and look for opportunities to develop the ability to:
  - analyse and define the areas and issues to be addressed by the initiative;
  - prioritise needs;
  - develop visions and a mission statement;
  - understand the system (know where grants come from and how to access funding and support);
  - design programmes of action and the appropriate management structures to support them;
  - implement, monitor and assess programmes;
  - review and recreate the long-term strategic direction of the initiative.

Are you interested in short-term or long-term goals?

Ashridge interviewees said partnerships have to find the right balance between short-term goals that demonstrate quick results and are more motivational, and longer-term goals (for example job creation) that have bigger impacts but are far harder to achieve.

However, interviewees believe that the most significant challenges for partnerships are to take a longer-term strategic view of the future, and to create fundamental changes for the good in local circumstances. They said this could only be achieved by changing the hearts and minds and developing the skills of the people working with the partnership in the community. They stressed the importance of encouraging and enabling 'the community' to contribute to the change process.

This widely held perception gives voluntary and community groups a significant opportunity to influence the partnership agenda. By encouraging all the partners, stakeholders and members of the wider community to grow in their confidence, ability, expertise and experience, and by encouraging young people to become involved, the 'golden thread' of community involvement and participation can remain intact in the longer term.

Weigh up the short-term and long-term costs and benefits

The decision about whether or not to become involved in a local partnership may involve an assessment of the longer-term benefits of opting in. Short-term advantages may be the important factor for many groups, but if you can afford to take a longer-term view it may be worth thinking more strategically about whether sustained involvement could bring about real cultural change among all the partners and substantial improvements in local circumstances for the whole community.

Note: The Joseph Rowntree Foundation funded the research report *Making Partnerships Work* written by Andrew Wilson and Kate Chariton of the Ashridge Centre for Business and Society. This short guide based on these findings has been prepared under Ashridge direction by Caroline Clark of the Civic Trust Regeneration Unit. We warmly thank the foundation for allowing us to reproduce this very useful short guide.

The full report is available from: York Publishing Services Ltd, 64 Hallfield Road, Layerthorpe, York YO3 7XQ. Tel: 01904 430033. Price £9.95 plus £1.50 postage and packing. ISBN 1 89998739 8

Detailed Contents

(Grant-in-aid in italics)

Ministry of Agriculture, Fisheries and Food (MAFF)

Nobel House
17 Smith Square
London SW1P 3JR

Tel: 020 7238 3000
Fax: 020 7238 6241
E-mail: helpline@infomaff.gov.uk

Website: www.maff.gov.uk

Contents

(Grant-in-aid in italics)

The Ministry of Agriculture, Fisheries and Food (MAFF) supports a small number of national voluntary bodies with concerns close to its own objectives.

Conservation Management Division
Farming and Wildlife Advisory Group (FWAG)

Grant-in-aid: £265,000 (2000/2001); £259,000 (1999/2000)

A number of FWAG's farm conservation advisers are supported with services in kind including professional advice, and free office accommodation in addition to core funding grant-aid and an annual subscription.

Budget officer: Stephen Cane, Room 111 Tel: 020 7238 5668; Fax: 020 7238 6126

Conservation Grant Schemes

Grant total: £111,899,000 (2000/01); £94,688,000 (1999/2000); £72,472,000 (1998/99)

These substantial schemes are directed mainly, but not exclusively, at farmers. Charities and voluntary bodies which own and maintain farmland could be eligible to apply to them. The relative size of grant schemes (1999/2000) is shown below.

	£'000	% of total
Environmentally Sensitive Areas	39,078	41.3%
Countryside Stewardship	29,605	31.3%
Nitrate Sensitive Areas (NSAs)*	6,200	6.6%
Farm Woodland Premium	5,212	5.5%
Habitat Scheme: Water Fringe and Saltmarsh	1,920	2.1%
Organic Aid Scheme	11,800	12.5%
Moorland Scheme*	230	0.3%
Farm Waste Grant Scheme	61	0.1%
Countryside Access Scheme*	82	0.1%
Arable Stewardship*	500	0.6%

*Schemes now closed or closed to new applicants.

Environmentally Sensitive Areas (ESAs)

To encourage the adoption of agricultural practices that help to protect and enhance the environment in England's 22 ESAs. Funds are also available for public access and some capital works.

Countryside Stewardship

To conserve and enhance some key English landscapes, features and habitats, and, where appropriate, public access to them. Includes the Arable Stewardship Pilot Scheme, currently running in East Anglia and the West Midlands and designed to benefit wildlife and encourage the return of declining species on arable land. The scheme was also revised in 2000 to incorporate the erstwhile Habitat Scheme.

Organic Farming Scheme

Aid for farmers who want to convert to organic farming methods.

Farm Woodland Premium Scheme

To encourage the planting of new woods. This is in addition to the Forestry Commission's Woodland Grant Scheme (see separate entry).

Rural Enterprise Scheme

Takes over from the Objective 5b programme which closed at the end of 1999. Among other things, the scheme aims to: renovate and develop villages; protect and conserve rural heritage; protect the environment in connection with agriculture, forestry and landscape conservation; and improve animal welfare. Excludes Cornwall, Isles of Scilly, Merseyside and South Yorkshire where equivalent schemes operate under the Objective 1 programme.

Farm Waste Grants in Nitrate Vulnerable Zones

For the upgrading of waste storage and handling facilities in designated Nitrate Vulnerable Zones.

Conservation Training Activities

Aid for vocational conservation training for people involved in agriculture and forestry activities. Free conservation advice is available to all English farmers and a farm visit will be made on request by a conservation adviser either from the Agricultural Development Advisory Service (ADAS) or FWAG. Advice includes information on possible sources of grant aid. Free visits are not available to farmers who have received free advice on the same subjects from either ADAS or FWAG within the previous three years, or for land which is within an ESA or Countryside Stewardship Agreement.

E-mail: helpline@inf.maff.gsi.gov.uk

For more information on these schemes or to apply for a free conservation visit contact your local MAFF Regional Service Centre.

Cambridge – Beds, Cambs, Essex, Herts, Norfolk, Suffolk
Tel: 01223 462727; Fax: 01223 455652

Carlisle – Cumbria, Lancs, Northumberland, Tyne & Wear
Tel: 01228 523400; Fax: 01228 640205

Nottingham – Derby, Leics, Lincs, Northants, Notts, Rutland
Tel: 0115 929 1191; Fax: 0115 929 4886

Reading – Berks, Bucks, E & W Sussex, Hants, Isle of Wight, Kent, Gtr London, Oxon, Surrey
Tel: 01189 581222; Fax: 01189 392198

Bristol – Bath, Dorset, Somerset, Wilts
Tel: 0117 9591000; Fax: 0117 9505392

Crewe – Cheshire, Gtr Manchester, Merseyside, Shrops, Staffs
Tel: 01270 754000; Fax: 01270 669494

Exeter – Devon, Cornwall, Isles of Scilly
Tel: 01392 447400; Fax: 01392 410936

Northallerton – Cleveland, Durham, Humberside, Yorks
Tel: 01609 773751; Fax: 01609 780179

Worcester – Gloucs, Herefordshire, Worcs, Warwicks, W Midlands
Tel: 01905 763355; Fax: 01905 763180

Agricultural Resources and Better Regulation Division
National Federation of Young Farmers' Clubs

Grant-in-aid: £36,000 (2000/2001 and in previous year)

An annual grant towards its agricultural education activities.

Applications: Voluntary bodies should contact the MAFF division relevant to their work about potential funding where there is mutual benefit. This should be done at least nine months in advance of the time when a grant is required.

Budget officer: Geoff Webdale, Room 718 Tel: 020 7238 5755; Fax: 020 7238 6553

Department of Culture, Media and Sport

2–6 Cockspur Street
London SW1Y 5DH

Tel: 020 7211 6000
Fax: 020 7211 6032
E-mail: enquiries@culture.gov.uk

Website: www.culture.gov.uk

Contents

Related Agencies

Related Funding

See **Regional Section** for: Regional Arts Boards; Regional Cultural Consortiums: Area Museums Councils

See **International Section** for: British Council: Visiting Arts

The department is responsible for government policy on the arts, sport, the National Lottery, libraries, museums and galleries, broadcasting, film, the music industry, press freedom and regulation, the historic environment and tourism. It is also responsible for taking forward cross-cutting policy on social inclusion, access, education and local, regional and international issues. The following are the department's structural links with organisations of particular interest to this guide.

- **Education, Training, Arts and Sport Directorate**
  Arts Division responsibilities include sponsorship of the Arts Council of England, support to the regional arts boards, and arts development including links with Arts & Business. The Sports and Recreational Division is responsible for the funding of UK Sport, Sport England and Sportsmatch.
- **Museums, Galleries, Libraries and Heritage Directorate**
  Responsibilities include: sponsorship of the British Library and Resource (the new museums, archives and libraries council); sponsorship of the national museums including the British Museum, Tate Modern, National Gallery and the V&A; educational matters including Area Museums Councils; independent and university museums; and volunteering.
- **Creative Industries, Broadcasting and Media Directorate**
  Media Division responsibilities include grant-in-aid to the National Film and Television School and the Film Council.
- **Regions, Tourism, Millennium and International Policy Directorate**
  Responsibilities include development of the eight Regional Cultural Consortiums, covering the arts, built heritage, sport, tourism, museums and libraries. See separate entry for details of consortiums. The directorate also sponsors and develops policy on the National Lottery Charities Board and the New Opportunities Fund Unit.
- **Strategy and Communications Directorate**
  The Social Policy and Statistics Unit takes forward the department's responsibilities on access, social inclusion, women, older people and disability.

Related Agencies

The Arts Council of England

14 Great Peter Street
London SW1P 3NQ

Tel: 020 7333 0100
Fax: 020 7973 6590
E-mail: information.ace@artsfb.org.uk
Website: www.artscouncil.org.uk

Contact: Information Officer

Grant-in-aid: £338 million (2003/04); £298 million (2002/03);
£253 million (2001/02); £238 million (2000/01) from Department for
Culture, Media and Sport.

The Arts Council of England (ACE) is the national funding body for the
arts in England. It is responsible for fostering the arts across the nation
through the distribution of public money from central government and
revenue generated by the National Lottery (some £250 million in
1998/99). As the above figures show, public funding is to rise by some
£100 million over three years to 2003.

ACE has the following objects:

- to develop and improve the knowledge, understanding and practice
  of the arts;
- to make the arts more accessible to the public;
- to advise and cooperate with central government departments, local
  authorities, the Arts Councils of Scotland, Wales and Northern
  Ireland and other bodies on any relevant matters.

ACE distributes part of its annual grant-in-aid directly and part through
the 10 Regional Arts Boards (RABs) with which it works closely and
which receive about a third of its funding (£79 million in 2000/01). The
RABs are independent organisations responsible for developing the arts in
their area. Together ACE and the RABs make up the integrated system for
arts funding and development in England.

Excluding the funding to the RABs, the major part of the council's grant-
in-aid (some 90%) is devoted to a group of organisations funded on a
regular or fixed-term basis. However, development funds are also available
to support the production, distribution and development of specific
projects, and research. A general leaflet about these programmes is
available from the Library and Information Service.

Resource: The Council for Museums, Archives and Libraries
(amalgamated former Museums and Galleries Commission and Libraries and Information Commission)

16 Queen Anne's Gate
London SW1H 9AA

Tel: 020 7273 1444
Fax: 020 7233 3686
Website: www.resource.gov.uk

Contact: Chris Alexander

Grant-in-aid from DCMS: £16,884,000 (2000/01)

Total grant expenditure: £17,105,000 (2000/01) (Resource received almost £5 million from other sources)

Resource is the new council for museums, archives and libraries. It was formed through the amalgamation of the old Museums and Galleries Commission with the Library and Information Commission.

Resource grants fund many non-national museums. Some grants are administered directly, others at arm's length through the Area Museum Councils, the Science Museum and the Victoria and Albert Museum. Resource also provides revenue funding for 7 Area Museum Councils (see separate entry).

Resource/V&A Purchase Grant Fund

Grant total: £1 million (2000/01)

This fund, administered by the Victoria and Albert Museum on behalf of Resource, helps with the purchase of objects relating to the arts, literature and history priced at £500 or over by non-national museums, art galleries, libraries and record offices. The maximum grant is 50% of the purchase price up to an annual limit, currently £80,000.

Applications: Contact Resource/ V&A Purchase Grants Fund, V&A Museum, London SW7 2RL Tel: 020 7938 9641

Preservation of Industrial and Scientific Material (PRISM)

Grant total: £250,000 (2000/01)

This fund, administered by the Science Museum on behalf of Resource, aims to further the preservation of material relating to the history and development of science, technology, industry, medicine and natural history. The fund awards grants towards the cost of acquisition and conservation of such material. All museums registered with Resource can apply. At the fund's discretion, applications can also be accepted from other charitable or public bodies engaged in the preservation of eligible material. Maximum grant is 50% of project costs for acquisition, and 70% for conservation. All grants are limited to a minimum of £500 and a maximum of £20,000 on any one item or project. Aggregated grants to any one institution are limited to a total of £20,000 in any one financial year.

Applications: Contact the Manager, PRISM Grant Fund, The Science Museum, South Kensington, London SW7 2DD Tel: 020 7938 8005; Fax: 020 7938 9736

Designation Challenge Fund

Total funding: £6 million (2001/02); £6 million (2000/01); £3 million (1999/2000)

This fund is aimed at displaying and publicising top collections and improving storage. Sixty-two awards were made in May 2000 to organisations mainly outside London, ranging from £36,000 to £300,000. This programme is finishing. The final application deadline was February 2001.

Contact: Yvette Burrows Tel: 020 7273 4200

Resource/DCMS IT Challenge Fund

Total funding: £500,000 (1999/2000–2000/01)

The aim of this fund is to enable museums to work together in developing projects that will show how IT can contribute to access, education and innovation in museums. Eleven grants were awarded under this fund in January 2000. The fund is now closed.

Contact: David Dawson Tel: 020 7273 8757

Education Challenge Fund

Total funding: £500,000 (1999/2000–2000/01)

This fund helps smaller volunteer-run museums to improve education and access standards, and runs up until April 2001. It was not known at the time of writing whether the fund would be renewed after that date.

Contact: Sue Wilkinson Tel: 020 7273 8711

Share the Vision

Total funding: £200,000 (2000/01)

Share the Vision is a consortium of various groups concerned with visual impairment who aim to improve access to library and reading services for the blind and visually impaired. The fund is not open for bids but some voluntary organisations have been funded to provide services, such as RNIB, the National Library for the Blind and HumanITy.

Contact: Isabel Thompson Tel: 020 7233 4200

Sharing Museum Skills Millennium Awards

Total funding: £600,000 (2000/01)

This scheme provides funding for secondments for people working and volunteering in this sector.

Contact: Catherine Atkinson Tel: 020 7273 1406

24-Hour Museum

Funding: £110,000 (2000/01)

A grant of £110,000 was given to the Campaign for Museums to set up an 'internet museum'.

Arts & Business

Nutmeg House
60 Gainsford Street
Butlers Wharf
London SE1 2NY

Tel: 020 7378 8143
Fax: 020 7407 7527
E-mail: head.office@AandB.org.uk
Website: www.AandB.org.uk

Contact: Richard Wilkinson/ Rebecca Rickard

Chief Executive: Colin Tweedy

Arts & Business promotes and encourages partnerships between business and the arts to their mutual benefit and to the benefit of the community at large. It originally focused on arts sponsorship but now promotes a wider range of partnerships – hence the change of its name (from Association for Business Sponsorship of the Arts) in 1999.

New Partners

Grant-in-aid from Arts Council: £7 million (2000/01–2001/02)

New Partners has taken over from the Pairing Scheme as the government-funded programme aimed at encouraging links between business and the arts. Whereas the Pairing Scheme was concerned only with business sponsorship of the arts, New Partners has a wider remit. The stated goal of New Partners is to increase business investment in the arts, but 'encouraging sponsorship alone is no longer the most effective method of doing this' – although sponsorship agreements are still eligible, as long as the business is sponsoring the arts for the first time. Arts & Business have given suggestions for the kind of projects they will fund: Arts-based training for businesses; Art collections; Art commissions; Artists in residence; Arts clubs: Forum theatre: 'Out-of-the-box experiences'; Performances and exhibitions on site; Sponsorship; Staff involvement and volunteering. The website gives further details of these possible ventures. Note that these are only suggestions and that Arts & Business are keen to consider novel ideas. Through New Partners, Arts & Business say they want to 'help business try something new with the arts'.

Financial levels: For any particular project, Arts & Business will make a grant to the arts organisation to complement the investment of the business. During 2000/01 these levels applied:

- The total amount of New Partners money available to an arts organisation in one financial year is £50,000. An organisation can apply for as many awards as they wish up to this limit. The money is always paid to the arts organisation.
- The business must invest at least £1,000.
- The minimum single award to the arts organisation from Arts & Business is £500 and the maximum £25,000.
- Businesses may apply to the scheme as many times as they wish.

Applications: Initial proposals are considered first by a regional panel which decides whether they go forward to the second stage. At stage two, proposals are worked up into full applications and put in front of a national panel. If an application is successful, there will then be a formal contract between Arts & Business, the arts partner and the business partner. Unsuccessful applications can be resubmitted at subsequent meetings.

There are no formal submission deadlines for proposals, but if a project or idea needs to happen at a certain time applicants should consider when they need a final decision and plan accordingly.

Information should be obtained from and contact maintained with the relevant offices – either the head office, noted above, or the regional offices listed below.

Director of Operations: Russell Jones

Regional Offices

Arts & Business London
Nutmeg House, 60 Gainsford Street, London SE1 2NY
Tel: 020 7378 8143; Fax: 020 7407 7527; E-mail: london@AandB.org.uk

The Sponsors' Club for Arts & Business (Northern)
c/o The Community Foundation, Cale Cross House, 156 Pilgrim Street,
Newcastle upon Tyne NE1 6SU
Tel: 0191 222 0945; Fax: 0191 230 0689;
E-mail: dh@communityfoundation.org.uk

Arts & Business North (Yorkshire)
Dean Clough, Halifax, West Yorkshire HX3 5AX
Tel: 01422 367860; Fax: 01422 363254; E-mail: north@AandB.org.uk

Arts & Business North (North West)
Room 413, 4th Floor, St James's Buildings, Oxford Street, Manchester
MI 6FQ
Tel: 0161 236 2058; Fax: 0161 236 2068;
E-mail: manchester@AandB.org.uk

Arts & Business Midlands (West)
Suite 16–18, 21 Bennetts Hill, Birmingham B2 5QP
Tel: 0121 248 1200; Fax: 0121 248 1202; E-mail: midlands@AandB.org.uk

Arts & Business Midlands (East)
Carlton Studios, Lenton Lane, Nottingham NG7 2NA
Tel: 0115 964 5648; Fax: 0115 964 5488;
E-mail: nottingham@AandB.org.uk

Arts & Business East
Hoste House, Whiting Street, Bury St Edmunds IP33 1NR
Tel: 01284 702242, Fax: 01284 702992, E-mail: east@AandB.org.uk

Arts & Business South East
4 Frederick Terrace, Frederick Place, Brighton BN1 1AX
Tel: 01273 738333; Fax: 01273 738666; E-mail: south.east@AandB.org.uk

Arts & Business South
The Point Dance and Arts Centre, Leigh Road, Eastleigh, Hampshire
SO50 9DE
Tel: 023 8061 9170; Fax: 023 8061 9173; E-mail: south@AandB.org.uk

Arts & Business South West
This office has still not been set up. Enquiries should be made to Arts &
Business Head Office – address as London;
E-mail: head.office@AandB.org.uk

The National Heritage Memorial Fund

7 Holbein Place
London SW1W 8NR

Tel: 020 7591 6000
Fax: 020 7591 6001
E-mail: enquire@hlf.org.uk
Website: www.hlf.org.uk

Contact: Andrea Wiggins, Information Officer

Grant total: £4 million (2000/01); £3 million (1999/2000); £2 million (1989/99)

The National Heritage Memorial Fund (NHMF), funded annually by the Department of Culture, Media and Sport, was initially funded by the sale of land compulsorily purchased for military reasons in wartime. The fund's role is to protect land, buildings, objects and collections which are of outstanding interest and are important to the national heritage, as a memorial to those who have given their lives for the country in war.

The NHMF became the national distributor of the Heritage Lottery Fund which transformed this small organisation in terms of its size, powers and responsibilities. Now the two operations are more clearly divided. The NHMF still carries out its original functions and is able in an emergency to move with great rapidity. The government's grant-in-aid has reduced considerably over the past years from £12 million for most years before 1996/97.

Grants and loans are provided for buying items which:

- are at risk of being sold abroad, developed, damaged or lost;
- have a clear memorial link.

Funding has been provided for land, buildings, works of art, museum collections, manuscripts and items of transport and industrial history. It also provides grants and loans to maintain and preserve most of these items. Applications should only be made as a last resort, after all other possible sources of funding have been tried. The fund will only pay for the total cost of a project in exceptional cases.

Projects, whether large or small, must fulfil all of the following conditions to be considered:

- they must be aimed at buying, maintaining or preserving land, buildings, objects or collections of outstanding interest and importance to the national heritage;
- they must be based in the UK;

- they must already have received financial help from other sources of funding but need more money to be finished off, or there must be no other available funding;
- they must give access to the public, unless this might reduce the value of the item;
- they must be financially secure in the long term;
- there must be a genuine worry that the item is otherwise going to be lost or damaged.

Examples of projects supported in 1998/99 included:

- *National Trust:* for survey and management of Orford Ness in Suffolk as a nature reserve (£38,890);
- *Imperial War Museum:* for preparation of a computerised database for the National Inventory of War Memorials (£37,752);
- *Brooklands Museum Trust:* for acquisition and transport of a Hawker Hurricane aeroplane from St. Petersburg to Brooklands Museum (£7,101).

Exclusions: Private individuals and businesses. Grants to repair or restore buildings. For such assistance contact English Heritage or the relevant local authority.

Applications: These should be made in writing and sent to the head of the fund, signed by the chairman, director or chief executive, and with a full justification of the need for help from the fund including:

- the reason for the grant;
- a full description of the project;
- photographs of the item, and for land and buildings, a map showing exactly where the property is and a site plan;
- full financial details, including an account of the money already raised or promised from other sources;
- formal valuation of the item, where appropriate;
- a description of the body applying for assistance, its finances, and plans to care for/manage the project in the future.

Applications are usually acknowledged within three working days. If the proposal meets all the conditions for applying for grants or loans, the applicant will be informed of the date when the trustees meet.

English Heritage

23 Savile Row
London W1X 2HE

Tel: 020 7973 3000
Fax: 020 7973 3146
Website: www.english-heritage.org.uk

Grant schemes: £35.1 million (1999/2000); £35.5 million (1998/99); £36.5 million (1997/98)

English Heritage (EH) is the national body created by Parliament in 1984 and charged with the protection of the country's historic environment and with promoting the public's access to, and enjoyment and understanding of it. It is the government's official adviser on all matters concerning heritage conservation and is funded by the Department for Culture, Media and Sport (DCMS) to run its grant programmes. EH assumed responsibility for the Heritage Grant Fund, formerly administered by the DCMS, in April 2000. English Heritage has a number of grant-giving programmes.

Historic Buildings, Monuments, Parks and Gardens Grant Scheme

The Scheme is offering £40 million over three years from 1999 and extends the previous scheme to include historic parks and gardens for the first time. This scheme is aimed at the country's most important historic properties and historic parks and gardens. Grants are considered towards major urgent repairs to grade I or grade II* listed buildings or scheduled monuments within the next two years or towards work required to prevent the loss of important historic landscape features. Funding priorities under this scheme for 1999–2002 cover:

- grade I or grade II* buildings included or eligible for inclusion on EH's Buildings at Risk register;
- scheduled monuments at risk;
- landscape features at risk within parks and gardens registered at grade I or grade II*;
- larger privately owned houses with associated contents;
- smaller country houses in the same family ownership for not less than 30 years where the project principally involves roof repairs;
- projects involving grade I or II* properties or scheduled monuments which can demonstrate significant social and economic regeneration benefits.

London Grants Scheme

A special grant scheme operates in London concentrating on repairs to grade II listed buildings at risk.

Emergency Works Grants and Advice Scheme
During 1998 a new 'fast track' and emergency works grant schemes was introduced. These target resources at smaller historic buildings needing strategic repairs and those that have suffered from disasters such as fire and flood.

Joint Grant Scheme for Churches and Other Places of Worship
This scheme, launched in 1996, is run jointly with the Heritage Lottery Fund to help with repair to historic religious buildings used for public worship by any denomination. The criteria for funding again rely on historic importance, urgency and financial need. Some improvements such as lighting, heating and toilets may be eligible in certain circumstances. Where funding is sought for other than structural works, some benefit to the wider public normally has to be shown. In addition to the Joint Grant Scheme for Churches and other Places of Worship, English Heritage gives grants to cathedrals each year.

Cathedrals Grants Scheme
Cathedral grants are normally made available for major fabric repairs, but sometimes other projects such as archiving, surveys and fire protection systems are also grant aided.

War Memorials Grant Scheme
This small scheme is running for an initial two-year period from 1999, in association with Friends of War Memorials, to assist with repairs and reinstatement of lost features to grade II listed war memorials situated in conservation areas.

Archaeology Commissions
The Archaeology Commissions Programme is a central strategic grant budget that enables English Heritage to fund important archaeological activities and strategic initiatives, to fulfil its remit under the 1983 National Heritage Act. The programme is explicitly linked to the agenda Exploring our Past 1998 Implementation Plan, with an emphasis on strategic national or regional research, management objectives, and projects that respond to the variety of threats to the archaeological resource that lie outside planning.

Applications: Applications are made through nine regional offices. Information on grants and application forms can be obtained by calling the relevant regional office telephone number listed below. Please check for application deadlines. The annual report, other literature and information on national programmes are available on the English Heritage website or from customer services.

Contact: Customer Services Tel: 01793 414910

Website: www.english-heritage.org.uk

or regional offices listed below.

Regional Offices
North East Region
Bessie Surtees House, 41–44 Sandhill, Newcastle upon Tyne NE1 3JF
Tel: 0191 261 1585

East of England Region
62–74 Burleigh Street, Cambridge CB1 1DJ
Tel: 01223 582700

North West Region
Canada House, 3 Chepstow Street, Manchester M1 5FW
Tel: 0161 242 1400

South West Region
29 Queen Square, Bristol BS1 4ND
Tel: 0117 975 0700

Yorkshire Region
37 Tanner Row, York YO1 6WP
Tel: 01904 601901

South East Region
Eastgate Court, 195–205 High Street, Guildford GU1 3EH
Tel: 01483 252000

East Midlands Region
44 Derngate, Northampton NN1 1UH
Tel: 01604 735400

London Region
23 Savile Row, London W1X 1AB
Tel: 020 7973 3000

West Midlands Region
112 Colmore Row, Birmingham B3 3AG
Tel: 0121 625 6820

Sport England

Governing Body Services
16 Upper Woburn Place
London WC1H OQP

Tel: 020 7273 1618
Fax: 020 7383 5740
Website: www.english.sports.gov.uk

Contact: Fabian Adams-Sandiford, Senior Policy Manager

Governing Bodies of Sport

Total grant: £7,169,000 (1998/99)

English or British governing bodies of recreational activities recognised by Sport England are eligible to apply for Exchequer grant aid. There can be only one governing body for each sport. In order to apply for Exchequer funding, each one must have a development plan that sets out a vision for the future of the sport, identifies the specific aims the governing body wants to achieve, and details how those aims are to be achieved. Sport England offers as much help as possible with the production of development plans. The grant-aid programme is intended to invest in elements of development plans that contribute directly to:

- business/organisational infrastructure;
- equal opportunities;
- youth development programmes;
- coach and officials education and training programmes;
- support for the development of clubs, community sport programmes and volunteers at all levels;
- programmes for the development of excellence that do not secure funding from the World Class lottery-funded programme.

Although there is no hard and fast rule about the term of a development plan, grant aid is usually made against a four-year plan. A firm offer is usually made for the first year with an indication of the likely level of support for the following three years of the plan. The programme only supports activities in England. Great Britain/United Kingdom governing bodies need to identify those elements of their development plans that relate to England only. The grant-aid programme complements other Sport England funding programmes provided under the Lottery Sports Fund. Awards are discretionary.

The following are some of the governing bodies funded during 1999/2000:

- *All England Netball Association* (£456,500);
- *Rugby Football League* (£368,250);

- British Cycling Federation (258,500);
- Football Association (£174,000);
- Royal Yachting Association (£125,000);
- British Mountaineering Council (£80,347);
- British Fencing Association (£45,000);
- English Karate Governing Body (£31,250);
- National Ice Skating Association (£22,917);
- British Handball Association (£7,000).

Some bodies also received capital lottery awards.

Institute of Sports Sponsorship

Warwick House
25–27 Buckingham Palace Road
London SW1W OPP

Tel: 020 7233 7747
Fax: 020 7828 7099
E-mail: info@sportsmatch.co.uk
Website: www.sportsmatch.co.uk

Contact: Mike Reynolds, Director

Sportsmatch Scheme

Total funding: £3,425,000 (2001/02); £3,373,000 (2000/01); £3,373,000 (1999/00)

Note: the above figures include administrative costs.

Sportsmatch is the business sponsorship incentive scheme for amateur sport, administered by the Institute of Sports Sponsorship and funded by the Department for Culture, Media and Sport, through Sport England. Sportsmatch gives sports organisers a better 'selling position' with potential sponsors. It matches a sponsor's investment in grass roots sports on a £ for £ basis from a minimum of £1,000 to a maximum of £50,000. Most awards are for less than £10,000. For schools the minimum award is £500. The sponsorship must represent new money, either as first time sponsorship or increased sponsorship. Sports organisers and potential sponsors are expected to work together to develop a joint proposal. National schemes can qualify provided they benefit sport at grass roots level. Eligible programmes are those that increase widespread amateur participation and/or improve skills.

Youth development programmes and those aimed at the disabled and other disadvantaged groups are prioritised. Support covers revenue activities or essential capital equipment directly related to the activities, e.g. nets, bats, balls, canoes and so on. A capital project is only permitted a total budget of less than £5,000.

For the period 1 July–31 December 2000, 183 awards were made totalling £1.52 million. These included:

- *English Federation of Disability Sport,* for a football development programme (£50,000);
- *Sports Aid Trust,* for a series of 'come and try' days (£30,000);
- *Royal Yachting Association,* for the 'Yachtingskool' video (£17,220);
- *Birmingham Federation of Clubs for Young People,* for a sports and activity development officer (£10,000);
- *British Tennis Foundation,* for a junior tennis coaching programme (£6,000);
- *Preston Basketball Forum,* for the development of basketball for boys and girls (£3,000);
- *Lord Cobham Youth Cricket Trust,* for a cricket coaching programme (£1,000).

Exclusions: Individuals and professional sporting events, although professional coaching services for amateurs are eligible.

Applications: Applications must be made jointly by the organisers and the sponsors. Full information, a newsletter and an application form are available from the above address, and advisers are always happy to discuss eligibility criteria with potential applicants. The independent awards panel meets every six weeks.

Ministry of Defence

Main Building
Whitehall
London SW1A 2HB

Tel: 020 7218 9000

Grants to Voluntary Organisations

Total funding: £15,368,905 (1999/2000)

Funding to voluntary organisations derives from as many as eight differing areas of the Ministry of Defence and the Armed Services. There is no general fund to which voluntary organisations may apply and in most cases an initial approach will be made by the Ministry. In 1999/2000 a large proportion of the funding (over £6 million) was paid to five voluntary organisations for 'services rendered' for welfare work for service personnel and their families. These were:

- *The Soldiers, Sailors, Airmen and Families Association – Forces Help* (SSAFA – FH) (£2,979,971);
- *Women's Royal Voluntary Service* (£1,969,397);
- *Service Hospitals Welfare Department,* managed by the Joint Committee of the British Red Cross and the Order of St John of Jerusalem (£949,323);
- *Pre-School Learning Alliance* (£241,049);
- *Relate* (£132,000).

Other grants were given to:

- *Sea Cadet Corps* (£6,536,109);
- *Combined Cadet Force* (£1,486,857);
- *Help Information Volunteer Exchange* (£246,100);
- *Home Start* (£218,000);
- *Royal British Legion,* for relief of Polish ex-servicemen and women (£184,700) and for war widows' pilgrimages (£125,000);
- *Council for Voluntary Welfare Work,* a consortium furthering HM forces' Christian work (£92,000);
- *Army Families Federation* (£58,000);
- *Victoria Cross & George Cross Association* (£39,000);
- *Youth Services* (£37,000);
- *Volunteer Cadet Corps* (£27,640);
- *Airwaves –* channel of communication for RAF families (£25,000);
- *Sea Scouts* (£15,307);
- *Community Relations Fund* (£4,689);
- *North British Housing Association* (£1,763).

There was also a grant made to the Army Cadet Corps, but the amount was not known at the time of going to press. Many grants are recurrent.

Contact: Howard G Reynolds, SP (Pol) 2B–1, Room 5/68, Metropole Building, Northumberland Avenue, London WC2N 5BL
Tel: 020 7218 9618; Switchboard: 020 7218 9000; Fax: 020 7218 9626

Department for Education and Employment

Main offices

Sanctuary Buildings **(S B)**
Great Smith Street
London SW1P 3BT

Caxton House **(C H)**
Tothill Street
London SW1H 9NF

Moorfoot **(M)**
Sheffield S1 4PQ

Main switchboard Tel: 020 7925 5000
Information office Tel: 020 7925 5189

Website: www.dfee.gov.uk

Other offices are situated in Darlington and Runcorn but they
do not feature in this guide.

Contents

(Grant-in-aid in italics)

Related Funding

See **Regional Section** for: Childcare Unit's Early Years Development and Childcare Partnerships, Sure Start; Connexions; Community Champions Fund; Education Action Zones; Neighbourhood Support Fund

See **International Section** for: Connect Youth International (formerly Youth Exchange Centre); Commonwealth Youth Exchange Council

Early Years Division (C H)
Early Education Grants
Grant total: £1,825,000 (2000/01)

These grants are available to national/umbrella organisations in the voluntary sector, and help to promote the government's policies for young children. They support projects and activities to improve the quality of, or disseminate good practice in, early years education. In the 2000/01 financial year, grants were made to seven voluntary organisations:

- *British Association for Early Childhood Education,* for staff costs and to assist the development and dissemination of good practice in early years education (£90,000);
- *Milton Keynes Pre-School Learning Alliance,* to improve support for children with special educational needs in pre-schools (£59,000);
- *National Children's Bureau,* to investigate and disseminate good practice in self-assessment by early education practitioners (amount to be agreed at time of writing);
- *World Association for Early Childhood Education (OMEP),* to support the OMEP World Presidency, currently held by the UK, and to provide assistance with overseas conferences and other costs (£15,400);
- *National Playbus Association,* to support the development of early years educational provision in playbuses (£48,606);
- *Playgroup Network,* to provide a training programme to raise awareness of good practice among development workers and local playgroup organisations (£12,086);
- *Pre-school Learning Alliance (PLA),* to support the PLA's training infrastructure (£1,600,000).

Grants can form 100% of total project costs and are normally between £10,000 and £100,000.

Contact: Linda Duberry Tel: 020 7273 5676; Fax: 020 7925 5079

Section 64 Grants
Grant total: £776,500 (2000/01)

The division assumed responsibility for the Section 64 grants to under 5s from the Department of Health in 1998. Grants are given to national voluntary organisations providing, promoting, publicising or advising on registered day care services. The grants have five objectives:

- supporting and promoting good quality early education and day care;
- promoting the training and development of early childhood workers;

- raising the quality of care;
- making childcare more accessible;
- making childcare more affordable.

Organisations receiving grant in 2000/01 include:

– *Pre-School Learning Alliance,* towards staff costs at head office and regional centres (£450,000);
– *National Childminding Association,* for three projects: to develop and produce new quality standards based on the NCMA Quality Childminding Charter; for a campaign to promote childminder registration and the taking up of the Working Families Tax Credit; and for a childminding helpline (£151,000);
– *National Children's Bureau,* to help towards the HQ expenses of the NCB's Early Childhood Unit (£40,000);
– *National Early Years Network,* to cover central administrative costs (£20,000);
– *Caroline Walker Trust,* to produce a training pack on 'eating well for under 5s in child care' (£16,000).

To win funding, bids have to show robust evidence of need, give clear and measurable outcomes and milestones, be consistent with other national activities and policies and demonstrate good value for money.

Applications: Applications for Early Education Grants, Section 64 Grants and the National Childcare Strategy (see separate entry) are dealt with in a combined exercise. Applications are invited annually, normally in the autumn. Details are sent to a wide range of voluntary organisations, inviting them to submit proposals for projects that meet stated objectives.

Contact: Charles Fuller Tel: 020 7273 5712

Powers: Regulation 15, Education (Grants) Regulations 1990; Section 64, Health Services and Public Health Act 1968

Early Excellence Centres

Total funding: £30 million (1999/2000–2001/02)

These 'one-stop' centres, of which there are 29 across the country, bring together nursery education, childcare and other services for the under fives and their families. They typically cover the 0–5 years age group in disadvantaged communities. Some centres are led by voluntary sector organisations, and most involve the voluntary sector to some degree or other.

Contact: Bharati Stubbs Tel: 020 7273 5855;
E-mail: bharati.stubbs@dfee.gov.uk

Children and Young People's Unit (C H, 4E)
Children's Fund

Total funding: £100 million (2001/02); £150 million (2002/03); £200 million (2003/04)

The Social Exclusion Unit's Policy Action Team (PAT) on Young People highlighted the need for improved preventative services for young people, and advocated increased support for families and a new preventative budget to promote effective cross-cutting interventions for young people facing the most acute risks. The Children's Fund, announced in the July 2000 Spending Review, builds on this.

A new Cabinet Committee on Children and Young People's Services has also been established. Chaired by the Chancellor, it will coordinate policies on government services for tackling poverty and disadvantage among children and young people. The committee is supported by the new cross-cutting Children and Young People's Unit, located in the Department for Education and Employment. The unit operates across departmental boundaries, and will include qualified people from across the civil service, the wider public sector and the voluntary and private sectors. The unit reports to Paul Boateng, who has been appointed as Minister for Young People, with the Secretary of State for Education and Employment retaining ultimate accountability to Parliament. The remit of the unit includes supporting ministers in developing, refining and communicating the government's overarching strategy for children and young people. The unit will maintain an oversight of services for vulnerable children and young people, help to improve services and develop, implement and manage the Children's Fund.

The Children's Fund will make available £380 million to develop services to identify children who are showing early signs of difficulty and provide them and their families with the support they need to overcome barriers and disadvantage. Local partnerships will be invited to draw up proposals showing how they can use money from the fund to expand preventative services in their area. Proposals will need to show how services will be delivered and how providers will work together. In the first instance, chief executives of local authorities will be invited to draw together key local providers and identify which partnership can best plan for and manage services to be funded. The voluntary and community sectors, children and their families will be key partners in local partnerships.

By April 2004, the fund will support some activity in all areas of England; the first year of funding, however, will focus on those areas in England with the highest levels of need and disadvantage amongst children and young people. In February 2001 the first 40 local authority areas to take part in the programme were announced.

The Local Network

Total funding: £70 million over three years – £10 million (2001/02); £20 million (2002/03); £40 million (2003/04)

Funding will be distributed directly to local voluntary and community groups through a network of local funds, administered by voluntary organisations with experience in grant administration. The Local Network will cater for children of all ages and will focus on helping local and community groups to provide local solutions to the problem of child poverty. It will include a strong emphasis on children and young people's own aspirations and views. The Network will consist of around 50 local funds covering the whole of England and will roll out gradually from April 2001.

Grants will be made under four themes:

- economic disadvantage – imaginative schemes to enable families to improve their living standards;
- isolation and access – prevention and crisis work with hard-to-reach groups;
- aspirations and experiences – bridging the gap between the childhood experiences of children in poverty and their contemporaries;
- children's voices – giving children a chance to articulate their own needs.

Local community groups who want to do something under these four themes will be able to apply to their local fund for a grant. No final decisions have yet been taken on the size of grants to be awarded. However, most grants are likely to be small, in the hundreds and thousands of pounds.

Community Foundation Network with its member community foundations has been appointed to administer the Local Network of Children's Funds. They will be working in partnership with other voluntary organisations such as Rural Community Councils, Councils for Voluntary Service and grant-making trusts, to provide a fund administrator in each local network area. Details of the location and local administrator for each local fund will be announced by the end of March 2001.

Contact: Community Foundation Network Tel: 020 7422 8617; E-mail: smcdougall@communityfoundations.org.uk

Further information: Website: www.dfee.gov.uk/childrensfund or Children and Young People's Unit Tel: 0207 273 5692.

Schools Plus Division
Education–Community Links (S B)

Total funding: £250,000 (1999/2000 and 2000/01)

Funding is available to projects that focus on developing school/community links in order to motivate pupils and raise standards of achievement. The department is both proactive and responsive in its selection of initiatives, but all are expected to have a national relevance. Organisations that received funding in 1999/2000 included:

- *Education Extra,* for a holiday family learning project aimed at fostering better understanding, communication and support within the family framework (£12,500);
- *The Community Education Development Centre,* for the expansion of the National School and Community Network, which helps schools work effectively in developing partnerships with their communities (£23,500);
- *Total Learning Challenge,* towards work on its handbook *Action on Disaffection,* which sets out the good practice TLC has developed over the past five years (£12,163);
- *National Children's Bureau,* for a pump-priming project that carried out preliminary work in preparation for a larger-scale project to develop a national Schools Council Network (£5,000);
- *Liverpool Hope,* for 'Reachout to Parents', a pilot project in London involving courses on parenting issues and skills (£3,000).

Contact: Sarah Wainer Tel: 020 7925 6034; Fax: 020 7925 5629; E-mail: sarah.wainer@dfee.gov.uk

Education–Business Links (S B)

Total funding: £244,000 (2000/01); £244,000 (1999/2000)

The department aims to improve the quality and coherence of education business link activities and to disseminate good practice through its support for a range of national bodies, projects, events and publications. Support is given to school business link activities that help raise standards of education, tackle underachievement and disaffection and ensure that young people have the necessary skills to take advantage of the opportunities they will meet in adult and working life. Voluntary sector organisations receiving grants in 1999/2000 included:

- *Business in the Community* (£144,000);
- *Understanding Industry* (£30,000);
- *Science Engineering Technology Mathematics Network* (SETNET) (£20,000).

Contact: Laura Cunningham Tel: 020 7925 6098;
E-mail: laura.cunningham@dfee.gov.uk

Stephen Stanton Tel: 020 7925 6324; Fax: 020 7925 5629
E-mail: stephen.stanton@dfee.gov.uk

Trident (work experience) (S B)

A single grant (£30,500 in 2000/01) is also awarded annually to Trident, which introduces schoolchildren to the world of work through quality work experience. This funding supports the development and training of its staff, most of whom are seconded from industry. It also supports the development of new materials for schools, employers and students aimed at making its work experience and Skills for Life programme more relevant to the current curriculum and needs of pupils and employers.

Note: Exchequer funding for voluntary organisations involved in study support ceased in 2000, principally because £225 million of lottery money has been made available for study support through the New Opportunities Fund (NOF) – see Appendix 1. Voluntary groups are eligible for this money as long as they are acting in partnership with a particular school (see separate entry on NOF). The new Exchequer-funded Study Support Standards Fund is providing £20 million in 2000/01 and £60 million the following year for study support, but this money is only available to schools through their LEAs. Responsibility for funding to voluntary organisations for parental involvement has moved to the Parental Involvement in Children's Education Team – see below.

Applications: Organisations seeking support in the areas listed above should contact the appropriate officer to discuss their proposals. Funds will normally only be allocated to national organisations or projects with a national, or potentially national, relevance. There are no fixed deadlines for the above funds; applications are processed as and when they are made.

Contact: Dawn Jukes Tel: 0114 259 4754; Fax: 0114 259 3847;
E-mail: dawn.jukes@dfee.gov.uk

Powers: Regulation 15 of the Education (Grant) Regulations 1990

National Mentoring Network (M)

Total grant-in-aid: £600,000 (2000/01)

The network receives funding for the salary of a national coordinator and contribution towards running costs. The National Mentoring Network (NMN) was set up in 1994 and is funded by membership fees and support from business and government departments, particularly the Department for Education and Employment with some support also from the Home Office. Its 700+ member organisations include schools, colleges, universities, education business partnerships, career services, businesses, TECs, voluntary and community groups and mentoring practitioners.

For two years starting in 1998, NMN was funded by the DfEE to manage a bursary programme to support the growth and development of mentoring in schools. Some 60 projects in England and Wales were supported and included a number of charitable organisations such as Age Concern, Stockport; Full Circle Arts, Manchester; and the African and Caribbean Finance Forum. For 2000/01 the DfEE and NMN have reviewed the projects to see which approaches were successful. Examples of good practice will be promoted. Mentor Points (or centres) will be piloted in three of the Excellence in Cities areas. These will help recruit and train volunteers.

For further information contact: Karen Evans, National Mentoring Network, First Floor, Charles House, Albert Street, Eccles M30 0PD Tel: 0161 787 8600; Fax: 0161 787 8555; E-mail: natment@globalnet.co.uk

Website: www.nmn.org.uk

Contact in DfEE: Leila Seals Tel: 01142 594742; Fax: 0114 259 3847; E-mail: leila.seals@dfee.gov.uk

Parents and Performance Division (S B, Room 2.54)
Parental Involvement in Children's Education
Total funding: £420,000 (2000/01); £350,000 (1999/2000)

Funding for parental and wider family involvement in children's education is a result of the government's commitment to encouraging greater involvement by parents in supporting children's learning.

Funds are not restricted to the voluntary sector, but voluntary organisations are welcome to apply. Proposals should aim to enhance or develop one or more of the following:

- increased involvement of parents and the wider family in children's learning;
- increased effectiveness and efficiency of family and parent support organisations through evaluation of performance, encouragement of moves towards self-sufficiency or developing national structures;
- increased quality and quantity of partnerships between schools, parents and the wider family through provision of advice, information and training or dissemination of best practice via conferences, workshops and publications.

Funds will normally only be allocated to national organisations or projects with a national, or potentially national, application. Funding given is 'pump-priming', for projects which are usually one-off or of limited duration. Grants must be matched by funding from other sources, such as the private sector, voluntary organisations, charitable trusts, other government departments, and so on.

Organisations that received funding in the financial year 1999/2000 included:

- *Community Education Development Centre*, for trialling materials for supporting parents in helping key stage 3 children with early reading, writing and mathematics (£44,000);
- *Parentline Plus*, for a feasibility study into a new service for parents and the family to enable them to support their children with homework (£35,000);
- *Advisory Centre for Education*, for its general education helpline (£20,000).

Applications: Standard application forms are available from the PICE team. Applications that meet the criteria cannot be guaranteed funding; overall availability of funds and the relative merits of competing bids may affect the decision.

Contact: Ms Grainne McQuillan Tel: 020 7925 5503; Fax: 020 7925 5179; E-mail: grainne.mcquillan@dfee.gov.uk

Powers: Regulation 15, Education (Grant) Regulations 1990

Special Educational Needs Division (SEN)
Small Programmes Fund (S B)
Grant total: £1 million (2000/01 and 2001/02)

The fund supports grants to the voluntary sector and bids to fund research projects. In allocating resources it seeks to provide funds to those projects that most clearly reflect its own priorities, i.e. those that:

- demonstrate a practical and positive impact on what happens in the classroom;
- encourage a whole school approach to inclusion;
- encourage a 'joined-up' approach to help redress the variations in the way the system provides for pupils with learning difficulties.

It was not possible, at the time of writing in summer 2000, to give examples of activities supported by this fund. Grants to organisations to which funding had already been committed were also made in 2000/01 but they are not necessarily representative of the new criteria (these included grants to I-Can, National Parent Partnership Network, Dyslexia Institute, KIDS, British Association of Teachers of the Deaf). Organisations which have previously received funding are eligible to apply again to this programme if their projects meet current criteria.

Applications: Prior to 2000/01 grants had been made to selected voluntary organisations. Now the funding programme has been opened up to a wider range of voluntary organisations. Applications forms and guidelines are available. Maximum grants are £50,000. The application deadline for 2000/01 was mid-September, but is likely to be earlier in subsequent years.

Contact: John Smyth Tel: 020 7925 5524; E-mail: john.smyth@dfee.gov.uk
Maggie Scott Tel: 020 7925 7379; Fax 020 7925 5920
Mike Diaper, Team Leader Tel: 020 7925 5281

Youth Service Unit (S B)
Grants to National Voluntary Youth Organisations (NVYOs)
Grant total: £12 million (1999/2000–2001/02)

These grants support the development and provision of planned programmes of informal, personal and social education for young people.

Priorities for funding: The two main objectives of the 1999/2002 scheme are:

- to combat social exclusion and inequality through targeting priority groups such as the disadvantaged (especially in inner cities, on run-down housing estates or in rural areas); the disaffected or at risk of drifting into crime; minority ethnic communities; and young people with disabilities;
- to raise the standard and quality of youth work by, for instance, training programmes for youth workers and volunteers, and increasing young people's participation in management and decision-making.

Programmes for young people aged between 11 and 25 are eligible, but 13–19 year olds are prioritised. Joint working and partnerships among NVYOs are particularly encouraged and resources were earmarked specifically for such work. Most grants are between £10,000 and £100,000 a year and do not exceed 50% of the total cost. Funding is given for core activities but this funding cannot exceed 30% of the total grant sought. A total of 84 projects were funded in the 1999/2002 programme, of which nine were joint programmes. Examples of organisations supported in the 1999/2002 programme include:

- *Youth Clubs UK,* to promote social inclusion for a wide range of young people via a range of products, activities and pilot projects taking place across England (£238,000 per year);
- *Endeavour Training,* to work in partnership with schools to address underachievement and non-participation among young people in the last two years of their schooling (£175,000 per year);
- *Duke of Edinburgh's Award* (Year 1: £130,000; Year 2: £110,000; Year 3: £100,000); Youth Access, for a range of measures to improve the quality of youth work (£100,000 per year);
- *Leap Confronting Conflict Programme,* for their work educating disadvantaged young people in conflict-related issues (Year 1: £65,000; Year 2: £63,000; Year 3: £62,000);
- *National Association of Youth Theatres,* for a regional development programme (£37,000 per year);
- *The Quakers/Leaveners,* for work countering bullying; to improve the quality of youth work; and for the Quaker youth theatre (Year 1: £24,000; Years 2 & 3: £20,000 per year);
- *Boys' Brigade,* to raise the standard of youth work within the brigade (Year 1: £19,000; Years 2 & 3: £18,000 per year);
- *African-Caribbean Evangelical Alliance,* for work with young black people and to train those working with young people in black majority churches (£10,000 per year);
- *International Voluntary Service,* to set up a mentoring scheme and to encourage young volunteers from disadvantaged and ethnic minority communities to join IVS work camps (£8,000 per year).

Two examples of joint programmes are:

- *Outward Bound Trust and Trident Trust,* to develop a programme to promote personal and social education for disaffected young people in South Yorkshire (Year 1: £35,000; Years 2 & 3: £50,000 per year);
- *Youth Hostels Association/RSPB/Youth Clubs UK,* for the further development of the Peer Education Environment Programme (Year 1: £17,000; Year 2: £23,000; Year 3: £26,000).

Exclusions: Youth exchanges, holiday playschemes, vocational preparation or volunteering for its own sake.

Applications: All organisations applying for grant have to be registered with the department as a NVYO. In order to join the register, organisations must offer evidence that:

- they operate in several areas of England;
- the organisation, or a clearly-defined part of it, has as its primary purpose the provision of planned personal and social education to significant numbers of young people, particularly those in the age range of 13–19, through activities that are educative, participative and enabling;

- they are a properly constituted organisation;
- they operate a sound financial management system and receive financial support of at least £5,000 a year from sources other than government grant.

The register is likely to be reviewed in early 2001 in preparation for a new scheme beginning in 2002.

Grant schemes run on a three-yearly basis and the current scheme runs from 1999/2002. Applications for grants under the 1999/2002 scheme were called for by 12 October 1998. Successful applicants were offered grant for the financial year 1999/2000, together, if appropriate, with indicative levels of grant for the following two years. Grant in these years depends on the outcome of monitoring and evaluation. Advice and full guidance notes can be obtained directly from the Youth Service Unit.

Contact: Tessa Thorns Tel: 020 7925 5266; Fax: 020 7925 6954; E-mail: tessa.thorns@dfee.gov.uk

Individual Learning Division
Adult and Community Learning Fund (M, East 8d)

Funding: £20 million (1998/99–2001/02)

This fund was created to sustain and encourage new schemes locally that help men and women gain access to education, including literacy and numeracy. Support is available to community-based organisations, working in partnership with others, combining learning opportunities with other activities relevant to local people, e.g. environmental projects, tenants' associations, childcare, crime prevention, arts, health. The aim is to draw in new and non-traditional learners, especially people who are disadvantaged and isolated. The fund seeks to make a lasting impact on individuals and communities by equipping people to improve their own lives, progress to further learning, engage with others and make a greater contribution to their neighbourhood. The fund is managed on behalf of the DfEE by two organisations: the National Institute of Adult Continuing Education and the Basic Skills Agency (addresses below). Around £5 million has been allocated each financial year until March 2002. The government established the fund with the aim of matching it with equivalent contributions from other sources.

A number of voluntary groups were successful in the fourth bidding round. They included:

– *Centrepoint*, for providing English language tuition and support for refugees and other homeless people in Centrepoint's central London premises (£77,946);

- *Hull Chinese Cultural Centre*, for working with Beverley College to develop a programme of practical learning in citizenship and health for the Chinese community in Hull (£55,812);
- *Girls' Friendly Society*, for piloting a health and basic skills programme for young women (£85,998);
- *Wessex Foundation*, for an organic farm-based programme developing agricultural, personal and social skills among young people (£76,000);
- *Manchester and Salford FSU*, for developing learning opportunities for families involved in community holiday clubs, homework activities and so on (£53,697);
- *Yorkshire Arts Circus*, Castleford, for work with families in writing community books for adults and children (£33,027);
- *Castlepoint Citizens Advice Bureau*, Essex, for planning a programme of training for part-time CAB volunteers in basic skills for CAB enquiries (£27,625);
- *Somali Womens Support*, for building the capacity of Somali parents in North Hammersmith to enable them to support children's learning at home and school (£9,930).

Applications: The deadline for the fifth round of funding was 30 September 2000, with the fund due to finish at the end of March 2002. At the time of writing, the DfEE was considering whether to issue further calls for new bids. The addresses of the two organisations administering the ACLF are:

Basic Skills Agency, 7th Floor, Commonwealth House, 1–19 New Oxford Street, London WC1A 1NU

Contact: Andrea Mearing Tel: 020 7405 4017; Fax: 020 7404 5038; E-mail: andream@basic-skills.co.uk

National Institute of Adult Continuing Education (NIACE)
21 De Montfort Street, Leicester LE1 7GE

Contact: Sue Cara Tel: 0116 204 4200; Fax: 0116 285 4514; E-mail: suec@niace.org.uk

DfEE contact: Jonathan Webster Tel: 0114 259 4199; Fax: 0114 259 3236; E-mail: jonathan.webster@dfee.gov.uk

Website: www.lifelonglearning.co.uk

UK online Capital Modernisation Fund (M, Room N908)

Total funding: £252 million (2000/01–2001/02)

This fund exists in parallel with the Community Access to Lifelong Learning (CALL) programme of the New Opportunities Fund (NOF – see Appendix 2). UK online is the government's programme to ensure that everyone in the UK has access to the internet. The difference between the two funds is simply that the Capital Modernisation Fund is for the capital funding of 700 new 'UK online centres' throughout the UK, while the NOF money – some £155 million for England – is for revenue funding. UK online centres are being set up in disadvantaged areas and aimed at groups of people whose access to information and communication technology (ICT) would ordinarily be limited. The following categories have been targeted:

- the 2000 most disadvantaged local authority wards;
- rural areas with significant transport and deprivation problems;
- small areas of deprivation within more prosperous areas;
- centres working with disadvantaged client groups, such as lone parents, ethnic minorities, the unemployed, people with disabilities and the over 60s.

Eligibility: For a project to be eligible, it must come under one of these categories. The government wants UK online centres to be developed, organised and operated according to the needs of the local community, and sees community involvement in the planning and use of the centres as vital. As community and voluntary organisations tend to be closer to local people, the government is particularly encouraging their involvement. However, a wide range of organisations may be involved, including libraries, museums and sports associations. Some applications will be from partnerships with private companies, local authorities and colleges. The size and location of centres will be determined according to local needs, and could range from community centres and libraries to football clubs and even pubs. Innovation in terms of location is seen as a key factor in reaching new learners who have become disaffected by traditional approaches. However, projects do not have to be of the single, local type and applications are also welcome for national projects targeting specific types of deprivation. Some examples of projects from the pilot phase of the programme were:

- *Burnley Football Club Adult Learning Centre*, encouraging older workers and the unemployed to improve their ICT skills;
- *Walthamstow Age Concern*, using laptops to bring ICT to over 50s;
- *Stourbridge College Centre*, a mobile learning centre bringing ICT to those, such as small business men and women, who find it hard to take time out to learn away from the business;
- *The Learning Freeway*, Romford, involving a local house on a housing estate providing ICT training to people who feel unable to get into ICT;
- *NACRO Services*, Sussex, a mobile centre to visit ex-offenders and their families to provide basic skills training.

Five national projects were announced in autumn 2000. These included:

- *The Foyer Federation,* in partnership with two companies, ICL and NTL, to provide internet facilities, computer courses and other forms of training in a network of 45 foyers (£6,500,000);
- *The BBC;*
- *Deafax;*
- *The Council for Ethnic Minority Voluntary Organisations;*
- *TS2K.*

Details of the latter four projects, and funding levels, were not available when going to press. This also applied to the over 150 local schemes that were announced through the Government Offices for the Regions. Funding levels will vary widely as online centres are expected to take a variety of forms. Private sector support must be a substantial feature of any bid for over £500,000 and is strongly encouraged for smaller ones.

Applications: These are being invited for the online centres programme in a number of calls over two years. The deadline for phase three of the programme is 4 May 2001. A joint application form for capital and revenue funding is available for organisations and partnerships that want to be involved in both the creation of online centres and the delivery of ICT services. For single, local projects, applications are processed through local government offices for the regions.

Contact for national projects, application forms and guidance notes: Sally Bullement, Room N908 Tel: 0114 259 4879; E-mail: ict.learningcentres@dfee.gov.uk

Website: www.dfee.gov.uk/ukonlinecentres/index1.htm

Millennium Volunteers Unit (M, Room N2)
Millennium Volunteers

Total funding: £15 million (2002/03) (forecast); £15 million (2003/04) (forecast); £15 million (2001/02) (forecast); £15 million (2000/01) (budgeted); £4 million (1999/2000)

Note: The above figures do not include a total of £12.75 million from the Windfall Tax which has been made available as start-up funding for the programme in England over the lifetime of the parliament that began in 1997. Including this figure, the programme in England has been funded with a total of £77.75 million.

The Millennium Volunteers (MV) programme promotes and recognises a sustained commitment by young people aged between 16 and 24 to voluntary activity that benefits the community. It aims:

- to increase the number and range of volunteering opportunities and organisations offering such opportunities;
- to encourage and support young people to take up MV opportunities;
- to benefit both the community, through projects, and young people, through personal development and the acquisition of new skills.

The MV Award of Excellence gives young volunteers national recognition. The programme is delivered through national and local voluntary organisations who run specific projects. Organisations must make bids in order to be awarded a contract to run a project. All bidders have to provide evidence that they meet the priorities for support, which are:

- to fill in the gaps in existing MV provision across England;
- to focus on government priorities, particularly in education, health, safer communities and rebuilding local communities (particularly the most deprived local authority districts and those involved in New Deal for Communities);
- to open up opportunities to more community-based and local voluntary organisations.

Bidders also have to meet the criteria for running MV projects that were detailed in the second bidding round. These criteria are that:

- projects must meet the key principles of MV;
- bidders must be able to work in partnership with young people and recognise them as equal stakeholders;
- bidders must have the management capability to run a MV project (including marketing and promotion of MV, monitoring of progress and ensuring compliance with relevant legislation).

Examples of projects under the MV programme are:

- *Salford Millennium Volunteers:* offers young people the opportunity to participate in a wide range of volunteering, particularly for people with disabilities. Volunteers are involved with such activities as supporting mountain rescue, designing leaflets and a website, teaching music and dance to children, and prison visiting.
- *Citizens' Advice Bureaux:* the National Association for CABx is funded to provide training in advice, administration, reception, IT support and local information for volunteers in many of their bureaux around the country.
- *George House Trust:* involves young volunteers in HIV support and advice in Manchester. Volunteers help to design publicity, befriend and counsel people with HIV, and support an advice and information line.
- *BTCV Staffordshire:* volunteers receive training in practical conservation, environmental education, sustainable development, green projects, environmental art and habitat restoration. BTCV has MV projects in most areas of the country.

- *Poole Council for Voluntary Service:* a helpline provides reliable and accurate information on a wide range of issues to young people in Poole. The aim is to encourage and enable volunteers to take over the running of the helpline.
- *Birmingham Focus:* provides support and a range of services for people with sight loss, such as escorting visually impaired people to take part in leisure activities and helping them to access new technologies.
- *Community Service Volunteers:* numerous projects around the country. Because funding is provided by way of contracts rather than grants, we were not able to obtain financial details of individual projects.

Financial criteria: Funding is provided for up to three years and up to 100% of costs. Projects are limited to a maximum of £500,000 over three years. All funding is provided under contracts for services rendered and as reimbursement for approved expenditure (normally quarterly or monthly in arrears). Advance funding may be agreed exceptionally where organisations with limited income may face cash flow difficulties in meeting the initial start-up costs.

Applications: At the time of writing (summer 2000), the two bidding rounds that launched the programme had finished, and bids were only being sought for projects that filled gaps in existing MV provision. The MV Unit invited organisations who had shown previous interest in MV to make bids, and advertised for further targeted gap-filling in the autumn of 2000.

Applications are assessed against the priorities for support, the total funding available, and the value for money provided by the project. Successful applicants are invited to negotiate on a contract, but this is not a guarantee either that a contract will be awarded or of how much money will be made available.

Contact: Phil Naylor Tel: 0114 259 4146; Fax: 0114 259 4510; E-mail: millennium.volunteers@dfee.gov.uk; Helpline: 0800 917 8185

Website: www.millenniumvolunteers.gov.uk

Powers: Employment and Training Act 1973

Strategy and Funding Division
National Training Organisations (M, Room E4C)

National Training Organisations (NTOs) are employer-led bodies responsible for the development of skills to meet the needs of the UK's employment sectors. Most are established as limited companies and many are applying for charitable status. The sectors themselves fund the running of their NTO but the Department for Education and

Employment (DfEE) provides funding for particular initiatives or activities such as workforce analysis, developing training pathways, monitoring skill needs and shortages and representing the views of employers to government. The NTO network was launched by the Secretary of State for Education and Employment in 1998. It brings together over 180 Industry Training Organisations, Lead Bodies and Occupations Standards Councils. Most NTOs cover a particular industry, commercial sector or public service, although a few, known as 'all-sector NTOs', cover broad occupational groups, such as management and administration. NTOs are recognised by the Secretary of State for a period of three years. By April 2000, 76 NTOs had been recognised by the Secretary of State, covering 94% of the workforce.

The Voluntary Sector National Training Organisation (VSNTO)

Funding: about £200,000 (2000/01)

The VSNTO is run by the National Council for Voluntary Organisations with the Scottish Council for Voluntary Organisations and the Welsh Council for Voluntary Action. It gained recognition as an NTO late in 1997 and will be considered for re-recognition early in 2001. The DfEE funds the VSNTO to run national projects aimed at improving skills and training in the voluntary sector.

Contact: Ben Kernighan, National Council for Voluntary Organisations, Regent's Wharf, 8 All Saints Street, London N1 9RL Tel: 020 7713 6161; Fax: 020 7713 6300

DfEE contact: Linda Pannell, NTO4, Room E4c, Moorfoot, Sheffield Tel: 0114 259 3925; Fax: 0114 259 4482

LEA Adult Education and Family Learning Team
Lifelong Learning Grants (C H, Level 1F)

Total grant-in-aid: £597,000 (2000/01)

Grants are awarded annually to seven national associations whose purposes include education. They each submit a work programme of educational activities for grant. Grants in 2000/01 were:

– *National Institute of Adult Continuing Education* (£445,000);
– *Pre-Retirement Association* (£79,550);
– *National Association of Women's Clubs* (£21,400);
– *National Federation of Women's Institutes* (£19,900);
– *Townswomen's Guilds* (£13,500);
– *Educational Centres Association* (£11,250);
– *National Women's Register* (£6,400).

Contact: Michelle Phipps Tel: 020 7273 4789; Fax: 020 7273 5124

Powers: Regulation 11 of the Education (Grant) Regulations 1990

Youth Support Services Implementation Division (M)
New Start

Total funding: £10 million

New Start is a service for 14–17 year-olds who have either dropped out of learning or are in danger of doing so. It aims to increase their participation in and motivation for learning, and thereby improve their employability. It does this by providing a wide range of support, which may include individual assessment and mentoring (often through a personal adviser/mentor), work experience, college tasters, outward bound courses, basic skills training, and so on.

The initiative is delivered by local partnerships, some of which feature voluntary sector organisations as partners. Other voluntary organisations may then receive funding from partnerships to provide the services mentioned above.

New Start will run concurrently with Connexions (see Regional Section) until the latter strategy has been extended across the country as a whole. The provision currently under New Start will form part of the whole Connexions strategy. Groups interested in providing services under New Start should first contact their regional Government Office (see separate entry for address).

Contact: Mark Kaczmarek Tel: 0114 259 3399

Website: www.dfee.gov.uk

Standards Quality and Access Division
Access and Participation in Further Education (S B, 1F/18)

Two annual grants-in-aid are made:

- *Skill: National Bureau for Students with Disabilities,* for its work in developing opportunities for students with disabilities and learning difficulties in post-16 education, training and the transition to work (£92,000 in 2000/01; £88,000 in 1999/2000);
- *VIEW: the Association for the Education and Welfare of the Visually Handicapped,* to support the Piano Tuners' Diploma of the Piano Tuners' Examination Board (£4,000 pa).

Contact: Jane Ashworth Tel: 020 7925 5915; Fax: 020 7925 5454

Resource and Contract Management Division (M)
Training for Adults and Young People with Special Needs

The department contracts with the four members of the Learning Alliance – NACRO, Rathbone Community Industry, CSV and the YMCA – for project-based work. Funding is available up to a total of £850,000 per year. This arrangement commenced in 1998 and runs up to the end of the 2001/02 financial year. The fundamental aims of the funding are to enable the organisations to make a positive contribution to departmental policy in the field of special needs provision, and to build the organisations' capacity to deliver the department's objectives.

Contact: Kath Jakubiak Tel: 0114 259 3477; Fax: 0114 259 3902; E-mail: kath.jakubiak@dfee.gov.uk

Schools Directorate: Curriculum Division (C H) Citizenship Team
Grants for Citizenship Education

Total grant: approximately £473,750 (2000/01)

Grants are given to various voluntary sector organisations for the development of citizenship education. In 2000/01 these organisations were:

- *The Citizenship Foundation* (£50,000–£60,000);
- *Youth Passport* (£50,000);
- *Council for Education in World Citizenship* (£30,000–£80,000);
- *Institute for Citizenship* (£50,000–£60,000);
- *Community Service Volunteers* (£60,000–£80,000);
- *Heartstone Project* (£60,000–£80,000);
- *Hansard Society* (£10,000–£20,000);
- *C'mon Everybody* (£20,000–£25,000);
- *Common Purpose* (£5,000–£10,000);
- *Schools Council UK* (£5,000–£10,000);
- *Anne Frank Educational Trust* (£10,000).

Figures represent parameters within which the team expects to fund particular organisations during the financial year 2000/01.

Applications: Organisations can apply in writing to the team, who then review projects in terms of need, appropriateness and quality.

Contact: Sarah McLean, Team Leader Tel: 020 7273 5221

Powers: Regulation 15, Education (Grant) Regulations 1990

Museums and Galleries Education Programme (C H)

Total funding: £2.5 million (for the 3 years to March 2002)

This funding was made available to support a series of demonstration projects to disseminate good practice and develop new approaches to out-of-school study support. Its two aims were:

- to improve pupils' use of the educational opportunities provided by museums and galleries;
- to encourage museums and galleries to develop their educational role and their links with schools.

Although the funding was announced as to be spread over a three-year period, the programme allocated all its funds during 1999. Support was given to 63 projects. These ranged from short two-month projects to those lasting over two years. It is possible that further funds may be allocated to a similar programme in the future but in summer 2000 no such arrangements had been made. Information about this funding is available on the website of the Campaign for Learning in Museums and Galleries, see below.

Contact: Bhavena Patel Tel: 020 7273 5174; Fax: 020 7273 5004

Website: www.clmg.org.uk

Work–Life Balance Team (C H)
Work–Life Balance Challenge Fund

Total funding: £2.5 million over two years (2000/01–2000/02)

The campaign, launched in June 2000, will run for at least two years. It promotes the development of flexible working arrangements which both enable people to balance work and the rest of their lives and benefit business.

Specific project funding has been awarded to initiatives by voluntary sector organisations from time to time. Recent examples include:

- *Parents at Work*, to support PAW's Employer of the Year Award over two years (£60,000);
- *New Ways to Work*, to support information line and consultancy service (£30,000);
- *Work-Life Research Centre*, to support the proposal to set up a Work-Life Website and to pilot and evaluate its Work-Life Benchmarking which was published by the Industrial Society (£21,600).

The Challenge Fund is a resource to help employers introduce new working arrangements which benefit the business and its employers. It is open to employers in the private, public and voluntary sectors in England

and Scotland. (There is a separate challenge fund in Wales.) Selected employers will receive free advice from specialist consultants to support them in developing and implementing work-life balance policies and practices. The objective is to identify and disseminate learning and best practice. All applicants will receive information on the progress of projects which are selected.

Essential criteria: Funds will be allocated to organisations that can best demonstrate:

- how they will benefit from support from consultants;
- a commitment to improving work-life balance;
- there will be a measurable outcome;
- they are prepared to share their learning and best practice.

Applications: Full guidance and application forms are available. The first deadline for applications was end July 2000 for projects starting in autumn.

For further details contact: Tel: 020 7273 5626; Fax: 020 7273 5314; E-mail: team.work-life-balance@dfee.gov.uk

Website: www.dfee.gov.uk/work-lifebalance

Related Agencies

Learning and Skills Council (including the former Further Education Funding Council)

Cheylesmore House
Quinton Road
Coventry CV1 2WT

Tel: 024 7686 3000
Fax: 024 7686 3112
E-mail: nick.ratcliffe@fefc.ac.uk
Website: www.dfee.gov.uk/post16

Contact: Nick Ratcliffe, Assistant Director Funding

The Learning and Skills Council (LSC) comes into being in April 2001 and takes over responsibility for all post-16 education and training in England, replacing the Further Education Funding Council (FEFC) and the Training and Enterprise Councils. It will be funded with £6 billion to provide for 6 million learners, and will have two steering committees, one for youth and one for adult learning. The LSC will work through a national headquarters and 47 local arms, known as local LSCs. Each local LSC will have a budget of over £100 million.

In addition to Further Education (FE) colleges, tertiary colleges, and so on, the FEFC/LSC funds over 250 'external institutions', a small proportion of which are relevant to this guide. Provisional funding allocations to voluntary sector organisations for the academic year 2000/01 included:

- *South East Pre-school Learning Alliance* (£587,900);
- *Cambridge Women's Resource Centre* (£125,298);
- *One Love Community Organisation*, London (£101,408);
- *Chapel Green Community Centre* (£67,444);
- *Elfrida Rathbone*, Camden (£65,637);
- *The Elfrida Society* (£45,104);
- *The Hartley Centre* – Church Army (£42,137);
- *Heeley City Farm* (£34,099).

Voluntary organisations are only eligible for funding if they are acting under the sponsorship of the local FE college. The voluntary sector agency must be able to fill an identifiable gap in provision. Funding is not related to particular courses; it is up to individual institutions to decide how best to meet the needs of their students. Funding levels depend on a number of factors, including the length of the course, the subject being studied, the mode of delivery and the characteristics of the learner. In 2000/01 the funding rate for external institutions as a whole has risen significantly; this will continue under the new Learning and Skills Council in 2001/02.

Powers: Section 6(5), Further and Higher Education Act 1992; Learning and Skills Act 2000

National Youth Agency

17–23 Albion Street
Leicester LE1 6GD

Tel: 0116 285 3700
Fax: 0116 247 1043
E-mail: nya@nya.org.uk
Website: http://www.nya.org.uk

Contact: Richard Parsons, Head of Development Services

Partners in Innovation Programme

Funding: £400,000 annually (subject to review)

The National Youth Agency (NYA) aims to advance youth work to promote young people's personal and social development, and their voice, influence and place in society. Funded primarily by the Local Government Association, the DfEE and the Home Office's Active Community Unit, it works to improve and extend youth services and youth work; to enhance and demonstrate youth participation in society; and to promote effective youth policy and provision. This funding tranche – formerly known as Youth Work Development Grants – was under review at the time of writing. In previous years, the grants have been given to local or regional voluntary groups for innovative projects in the areas of training of staff and volunteers, organisational development, partnership development, inner city work, and work with 13–19 year olds. The programme is administered by the NYA for the Local Government Association.

Applications: New guidance notes are likely to be produced in late 2000 and will be available from the NYA.

The NYA is also one of the three managing agents for the DfEE Neighbourhood Support Fund (see separate entry). It is responsible for the channelling of £3 million annually from the fund.

The Employment Service

Level 6, Caxton House (C H)
Tothill Street
London SW1H 9NA

Tel: 020 7273 3000
Fax: 020 7273 6082

Rockingham House (R H)
123 West Street
Sheffield S1 4ER

Mayfield Court (M C)
56 West Street
Sheffield S1 4EP

Website: www.employmentservice.gov.uk

The Employment Service was launched as an Executive Agency by the Department for Education and Employment in 1990 and this status was confirmed in 1996. It aims to provide a competitive, efficient and flexible labour market by helping into work unemployed people, while ensuring they understand and fulfil the conditions for receipt of the Jobseeker's Allowance.

Its main offices are at Caxton House, London and Moorfoot, Sheffield. It has nine regional directors, two of which are in Scotland and Wales.

Disability Services
National Disability Development Initiative
Total funding: £447,000 (2000/01); £470,000 (1999/2000)

This initiative, first advertised nationally in July 1997, arose from a review that recommended a more coordinated and national approach across the whole of Great Britain by the Employment Service's Disability Service. The National Disability Development Initiative (NDDI) enables new approaches to be tested and developed and for the Disability Service to promote these and put them into practice. In doing so Head Office, the Employment Service regions and external partners work together to improve the service provided to both disabled people and employers. The NDDI funds projects that focus on helping people with disabilities to identify potential suitable occupations and improve their employability. The initiative is ongoing, with no fixed duration. At the time of writing, there have been two tendering rounds under the initiative. The first round of nine projects, six of which were run by voluntary groups, began in 1997 and ended in 2000. The second round focused on developing tools for employment related assessment and has given rise to three projects, which will run for three years each. One of these is being carried out by a voluntary organisation, Rehab UK, which is developing ways of matching disabled people with job opportunities. There was no funding round for the financial year 2000/01 but the service was expecting there to be one for 2001/02, which would probably take place in late 2000 or early 2001.

Funding levels: Funding can be up to 100%, depending on how closely the tender meets Employment Service criteria. Part funding is considered and there are no restrictions on sources of matching funding.

Applications: NDDI operates a competitive tendering system. NDDI Newsletters outlining information on current projects and future developments are sent out to organisations registering their interest with the NDDI Team.

Contact: Ian Gardener, Disability Services, Employment Service, Unit 19 Eagleswood Business Park, Woodlands Lane, Bradley Stoke, Bristol BS32 4EU Tel: 01454 848 575; Fax: 01454 848 585

Jobseekers' Mainstream Services Division
New Deal for 18–24 year olds (M C)
Total funding (UK-wide): £188,141,000 (2000/01); £175,407,000 (1999/2000); £403,621,000 (1998/99)

Funding to voluntary sector option: £49,034,000 (2000/01); £40,207,000 (1999/2000); £51,867,000 (1998/99)

Funding to Environmental Task Force option: £50,973,000 (2000/01); £38,360,000 (1999/2000); £113,165,000 (1998/99)

The New Deal for 18–24 year olds aims to help young people, who have been unemployed and claiming Jobseeker's Allowance for six months or more, to find work and improve their prospects of remaining in sustained employment. It begins with an initial period of up to four months individual help – the Gateway – which aims to get young people into work, or to prepare them for one of four New Deal options designed to improve their employability. The four options are:

- a subsidised job with an employer;
- full-time education or training;
- work on the Environment Task Force (ETF);
- work with the voluntary sector.

These options aim to improve the employability of young people through a combination of high quality work placements and training towards an approved qualification. Each option also aims to enable young people to move on from the option into work. The voluntary sector and ETF options are delivered by 'providers' under contract with their local Employment Service. They are funded to provide a placement, jobsearch help, advice and training up to NVQ Level 2. They range from TECs to local authorities to voluntary organisations themselves. Placements are often provided by voluntary groups subcontracted to providers. In the voluntary sector option, placements include activities from retail and administration work with charities, to more unusual things like homelessness support work or IT recycling. Work in the ETF can include restoring and renovating buildings and facilities, landscaping a local housing estate, working on a nature reserve, work to do with conserving energy and water, and setting up and running recycling schemes. The following are all organisations subcontracted to provide placements under the voluntary sector option in the South West region:

- Advice and Counselling on Drugs and Drink (admin support);
- Bristol Cyrenians (homelessness support work, admin/reception work);
- Catholic Housing Aid Society (retail, administration, electrical repair, furniture/upholstery repair);
- Wheels Project (administration, assistance with numeracy and literacy training);
- North Devon Housing Society (administration);
- Jigsaw Project, North Devon (carpentry, furniture restoration);
- Glenburn Centre, South Moldon (support work in a residential facility).

ETF projects have included:

- *BTCV Derby:* Elvaston Castle, Derby: cultivation and development of a 190-acre site in Elvaston Castle grounds with training for ETF clients to National Proficiency Test Council Federation level in Conservation and Arboriculture;
- *Groundwork Leeds:* 'The Lines', a project laying three quarters of a mile of cycle-path, providing access to the countryside for the public, with special consideration for schoolchildren and disabled people;
- *BTCV Gateshead:* various Single Regeneration Budget-funded environmental projects throughout the borough. Work includes the creation of a conservation area in Bewick Road Gardens, and land reclamation and refurbishment in the Bede Play Area on the Old Fold estate. BTCV receives funding under the New Deal for training, resources, work accommodation, transport, safety gear and so on.

Due to commercial confidentiality, the Employment Service would not release details of the amounts of money received for placements, which are provided under contract.

Applications: Organisations that wish to contribute to the delivery of the New Deal options should in the first instance contact their local Employment Service.

Contacts: Andy Tucker/ Justin McDougall Tel: 0114 259 5854;
Fax: 0114 259 6653

Website: www.newdeal.gov.uk

New Deal Innovation Fund (M C)

Total funding: £9.5 million over three years (2000/1–2002/3)

The aim of this fund is to test out ideas and activities to improve the New Deal service for 18–24 year-olds and over 25s. The hope is that the Employment Service will then take on some of the more successful ideas and apply them across the country. The fund will be allocated in three parts:

- Part I: £5 million is ringfenced for projects from the 11 inner city areas that have 'employer coalitions'. The objective is to support private and non-profit intermediaries (organisations that link employers with job seekers) using a demand-led (i.e. employer-focused) approach to help unemployed people get and keep employment.
- Part II: for projects with the same objectives as Part I, but for the rest of the country and for intermediaries in the public, private and voluntary sectors.
- Part III: for continuous improvement projects which will result in measurable increases in the quality and outcomes of the New Deal.

Applications: The first and second deadlines for expressions of interest were June and September 2000, but a programme for future bidding was due to be announced in autumn 2000.

Contact: Alasdaire Duerden Tel: 0114 259 5847; E-mail: alasdaire.duerden@employment.gov.uk

Progress Initiative (R H)

Total funding: £600,000 (2000/01–2001/02)

This one-off initiative is testing out a variety of approaches to find ways of helping ex-drug users who have come through rehabilitation get into employment, and is partly funded by the confiscated profits of drug dealers. One English voluntary organisation is receiving funding to run a project under the initiative:

– *Kaleidoscope*, Kingston-upon-Thames, for 'Surfshack', a project to set up a website design company run by recovering and recent heavy drug users, with a high work-based learning content.

The Employment Service would not release details of the amount paid, as it was 'commercial in-confidence'.

Contact: Win Hawkins Tel: 0114 259 5528

New Deal for Lone Parents Innovation Team (M)

New Deal for Lone Parents (NDLP), covering England, Scotland and Wales, is a programme designed specifically to help lone parents who want to work. It is available to lone parents in receipt of Income Support and is operated through Job Centres.

NDLP Innovation Fund

Total funding: £3 million (2000/01–2001/02)

The object of the Innovation Fund is to improve performance in the NDLP in certain specific areas. Private, voluntary and public sector organisations were invited to bid to meet one or more of the stated objectives through innovative approaches and ideas. The deadline for the receipt of application forms was July 2000.

Contact: Liz Williams, Employment Service, NDLP Innovation Team, Level 10, Moorfoot, Sheffield S1 4PQ Tel: 0114 259 3979; Fax: 0114 259 4652; E-mail: liz.williams@employment.gov.uk

Website: www.newdeal.gov.uk/english/lone_parents/innovation/

Jobseekers' Disability Services Division 6 (R H)
New Deal for Disabled People

Total funding: £60 million (2003/04); £60 million (2002/03); £50 million (2001/02); £30 million (2000/01)

New Deal for Disabled People (NDDP) is intended to help the 2.5 million people in England, Scotland and Wales who have a disability or long term illness and are entitled to incapacity benefits, to find work, if it is appropriate for them. Following a two-year pilot, in July 2000 the Chancellor announced the extension of NDDP to cover the whole of the UK (except Northern Ireland).

NDDP will be delivered through 'Job Brokers', who will prepare disabled people for work and help them find and retain jobs. The intention is that clients will choose from a range of Job Brokers in their area. The Employment Service is keen to encourage a wide range of organisations from the private, voluntary/non-profit and public sectors to bid to become Job Brokers. At the time of writing invitations to tender were about to be issued (end of November 2000). The closing date for receipt of tenders was 9 February 2001, and delivery was scheduled to commence in July 2001.

Contact: Jon Evens Tel: 020 7211 4187; Fax: 020 7211 4718;
E-mail: jon.evens@dfee.gov.uk

Website: www.dfee.gov.uk/nddp/

Department of Environment, Transport and the Regions

Ashdown House **(A H)**
123 Victoria Street
London SW1E 6DE

Eland House **(E H)**
Bressenden Place
London SW1E 5DU

Great Minster House **(G M H)**
76 Marsham Street
London SW1P 4DR

Tel: 020 7944 3000 (general line)

Website: www.detr.gov.uk

Contents
(Grant-in-aid in italics)

Related Agencies

Related Funding

See **Regional Section** for: Single Regeneration Budget; New Deal for Communities; Local Strategic Partnerships; Neighbourhood Renewal Fund; Centre for Neighbourhood Renewal

See **Appendix 1** for: Landfill Tax Credit Scheme and ENTRUST

Environmental and Energy Awareness Division
Environmental Action Fund (A H, 6/G9)

Grant total: £4,212,000 in 143 grants (2000/01)

Regional: £2,225,000 in 99 grants

National: £1,986,000 in 44 grants

The Environmental Action Fund is a matched funding scheme that helps English voluntary groups to advance the government's environmental policies, supporting work that does not qualify for grant under other programmes.

The fund's one priority criterion for 2001/02 is to promote sustainable living, which it defines as 'living in ways that achieve economic growth while protecting and, where possible, enhancing, the environment, making prudent use of natural resources and making sure that these benefits are available as widely as possible'. Funding activity for 2001/02 may be targeted within communities such as on the basis of age, ethnicity, gender, region, faith, locality or occupation, and can concern any aspect of sustainable development. Sustainable living, says the department, can be promoted through activities such as educating people in how they can live more sustainable lives; more efficient use of resources; encouraging waste minimisation, materials re-use and recycling; stimulating sustainable consumption; and promoting lifestyles that safeguard biodiversity.

Assessment criteria are that:

- the proposal has well defined and achievable objectives and performance measures;
- the organisation will develop its own longer term capacity by carrying out the work;
- the proposal could not find adequate funding other than through the EAF;
- the organisation is likely to obtain all its matching funding;
- the proposal is innovative (either wholly or in the region) and does not duplicate the work of other bodies;
- the proposal represents good value for money.

Types of funding:

- regional grants from £10,000 to £75,000 a year for regional and local groups;
- national grants from £10,000 upwards per year for national groups.

Grants are normally given for two or three financial years – subject to annual renewal – although single-year grants are also given.

New grants for the financial year 2000/01 included the following regional grants:

- *Manchester Environmental Resource Centre,* for the 'Eco Show': workshops and an exhibition showing people in Manchester how to apply sustainable development to their own lives (£33,700);
- *Elephant Jobs,* for an office furniture, fittings and equipment recycling scheme benefiting voluntary and community groups in south east London (£26,108, 1st of 3);
- *BTCV,* for the promotion of health through environmental activity, led by health professionals, in Southwater (£21,057, 1st of 3);
- *Environ,* for 'Energy 2000': a schools project, sustainability-themed events and a festival in Leicester (£12,000);
- *Learning through Landscapes,* for 'Greening Grounds for North Yorkshire': the development of school grounds for educational purposes (£10,000, 1st of 3).

National grants:

- *Tree Council,* for support for core promotional work on the economic, social and environmental importance of trees (£30,000, 1st of 3);
- *Black Environmental Network,* for its Core Development 2000 project: core funding for work to involve members of ethnic communities in sustainable development (£24,777, 1st of 2);
- *Soil Association,* for the promotion of community-supported farms through a survey, action manual and events (£19,403, 1st of 2);
- *Foundation for Local Food Initiatives,* for the development of an accessible and comprehensive database of local food initiatives (£15,900, 1st of 3);
- *Cyclists' Touring Club,* for the Right to Ride Network: training for volunteers from CTC and other environmental groups in cycling law, transport plans, planning procedures and taking part in the planing process (£10,300, 1st of 2).

Exclusions and conditions: Grant must be matched 100% from non-Exchequer sources, up to half of which can be in kind, including voluntary labour. Other possible sources include lottery money, Landfill Tax credits, private and charitable sector contributions, and income from goods and services, but not funds from local, central or European government. Funding cannot be used for the purchase of land or the construction of buildings. A group may apply for no more than three regional grants in any one region, plus up to three national grants. Multiple applications must be ranked in order of importance. If a project does not fall fully within one Government Office area, it counts as a national project.

Applications: Funding applications are usually invited each summer for schemes starting the following April; application details are posted on the website. Government Offices for the Regions are responsible for shortlisting applications for regional grants in their areas. Applications are then examined by independent assessors before consideration by ministers. National grants are considered by policy divisions within the DETR, and then by ministers. Criteria, priorities, exclusions and conditions may vary in future rounds.

Free publications are available to support projects: a six-monthly newsletter, *Activate*; a listing of 'Sources of Grant for Environmental Projects'; an annual report of grants made. The fund was being reviewed in 2000 and the results should be known in spring 2001.

Contact: Victoria Akeredolu, Environmental Action Manager
Tel: 020 7944 6654; Fax: 020 7944 6659

Website: www.environment.detr.gov.uk/eaf/index.htm

Powers: Section 153, Environmental Protection Act, 1990

Environmental Protection International Division
Darwin Initiative for the Survival of Species (A H 4/A2)

Grant total: £3 million (2000/01, also in 1999/2000)

The Darwin Initiative was set up after the Rio Earth Summit in 1992 to assist 'countries rich in biodiversity but poor in resources'. The funding helps UK biodiversity institutions carry out research and/or training with a partner in a developing country, thereby helping them to meet their obligations under the Biodiversity Convention.

Five principal areas of project work are targeted:

- institutional capacity building;
- training;
- research;
- work to implement the Biodiversity Convention of 1992;
- environmental education and awareness.

Each project is under the direction of a UK educational or scientific institution which includes many universities and other organisations. In 1999/2000 a total of 20 projects were assisted (out of 116 applications). Most were in South East Asia, Eastern Europe, Africa and Central and South America.

Examples of organisations receiving support were:

- *World Conservation Monitoring Centre:* to promote the conservation and sustainable use of medicinal plants in Ghana (£120,000);

- *CABI Bioscience:* to enable people in the Turks and Caicos Islands to develop a biodiversity management plan and initiate a sustainable programme of development based on eco-tourism (£124,000);
- *University of Edinburgh:* to develop conservation methodologies appropriate to cultural systems in the cloud forest of El Rincon, Mexico (£252,000);
- *University of Sheffield:* to study the effects of introduced species on Gough Island, Tristan da Cunha (£236,000);
- *Just World Partners:* to reduce pollution of coral reefs in Fiji (£97,000).

Although grants may be up to 100%, encouragement is given for matching funding. Grants are typically around £40,000 each year for three years.

Applications: Full details and application forms are available from the above address. Applications are usually requested in September and close in late November for projects commencing the following April.

Contact: Sylvia Smith, Assistant/Financial Adviser Tel: 020 7944 6204; Fax: 020 7944 6239; E-mail: sylvia_smith@detr.gsi.gov.uk

Website: www.environment.detr.gov.uk

Environment Consumers and Business Division: Citizen and Education Branch (A H 6/G9)
Environmental Campaigns Ltd (Encams)

Grant total: £3,763,000 (2000/01 and 1999/2000) – of which £1,260,000 is conditional on matching funding from the private sector and non-grant income.

Encams was set up in January 1998 as a parent organisation encompassing the activities of both the Tidy Britain Group (TBG) and Going for Green (GfG), both of which continue as charitable companies. Encams' head office is based in Wigan, and they also have nine regional offices throughout England. The single grant to Encams replaces the grants previously paid to TBG and GfG separately until 1998.

The funding of the TBG, based in Wigan, is a longstanding arrangement over more than three decades. GfG, based in Manchester, was set up in 1996 as a government awareness campaign for environment action at a local level, and is now Britain's largest environmental awareness campaign. Alan Woods was appointed as Chief Executive of all three bodies from 1 April 2000.

Contact: Ray Shrimpton, Sponsorship Manager Tel: 020 7944 6695; Fax: 020 7944 6559; E-mail: ray_shrimpton@detr.gsi.gov.uk

Powers: Section 153, Environmental Protection Act 1990

Regeneration Division 1
Voluntary Sector Branch: Special Grants Programme (E H Zone 4/H10)

Grant total: £2 million (2001/02); £1.44 million (2000/01); £1.4 million (1999/00)

The Special Grants Programme (SGP) supports voluntary organisations for national work in England relevant to the department's regeneration and housing policy interests. The programme's administrative rules are as follows.

- While work of national application can be supported, this may incorporate local pilot projects.
- Grants are available for project, strategic or development funding, and are mainly intended to help voluntary organisations with revenue costs, such as staff salaries and office running costs. Project and development grants are usually offered for three years, renewable annually, but may be offered for shorter periods.
- Project and development costs are limited to a maximum of 50% of costs and usually tapered in future years to reduce the percentage of the costs met by grant.
- Balancing income must come either from non-public sources, e.g. private sector funding, subscriptions, donations, fees, or from the National Lottery. Strategic funding grants are not subject to these limits but the department's expectation is that they would represent only a relatively small proportion of total expenditure.

SPG Regeneration Programme

The regeneration element provides support to establish or develop national voluntary organisations whose main activities complement the department's regeneration policy interests, which for 2001/02 are:

- improving the effectiveness and efficiency of voluntary organisations involved in regeneration;
- developing, promoting and improving the level and effectiveness of community involvement in regeneration;
- fostering and developing long-term partnerships between the voluntary, private and public sectors and the local community to achieve sustainable regeneration;
- encouraging the involvement of volunteers;
- securing better urban design;
- promoting good practice in urban management and in the creation, improvement, use and management of urban spaces, including parks and other green spaces, child play areas, and squares.

In 2000/01 grants under the regeneration heading of the SGP included the following continuing work:

- *Human City Institute,* to further local regeneration by piloting an interactive IT network among the socially disadvantaged in nine disadvantaged areas of Birmingham, Bradford and Swindon, and to develop a national model (£112,000);
- *Create Charitable Trust Ltd,* to develop units nationally that provide training and work experience for disadvantaged people in repairing and refurbishing household appliances (£60,000);
- *National Council for Housing and Planning,* to establish a positive planning practice unit to develop and assist community regeneration in social housing through publications, seminars and training (£57,000);
- *Action with Communities in Rural England,* to build network capacity in the regional voluntary sector to increase the participation of rural organisations in regeneration activities (£23,700);
- *New Economics Foundation/Church Urban Fund,* to train communities to participate in regeneration through a series of workshops (£7,500).

New programmes:

- *Citylife Ltd,* to assist in the creation and growth of community-supported organisations and community enterprises in some of the poorest wards in England (£60,000);
- *The Architecture Foundation,* to evaluate the roadshow project under which, in collaboration with a team of architects, local people and schoolchildren take the lead in developing public space sites in their boroughs (£53,900);
- *Community-owned Retailing,* to help community groups to create accessible, high quality grocery outlets (£50,000);
- *National Council of Hindu Temples,* to enable Hindu communities to be effective partners in regeneration schemes (£10,125).

SPG Housing Programme
The department's housing policy interests for 2001/02 include:

- sustaining a healthy private rented sector;
- developing policies on access to and management of social housing;
- tackling crime and anti-social behaviour in residential areas;
- meeting housing needs, particularly for homeless households and people with special needs;
- the provision and management of Gypsy sites;
- encouraging the involvement of volunteers in the housing area;
- encouraging the wider provision of social housing in rural areas;
- securing better urban design.

In 2000/01 SGP housing grants included the following continuing work:

- *Habitat for Humanity,* to establish a national office for the British branch of Habitat for Humanity International, a charity that sets up and supports local groups to build houses and provide interest-free mortgages for low-income households in housing need (£216,000);
- *Women's Aid Federation of England,* to develop training opportunities, resources and facilities for local refuge projects and service providers in the field of domestic violence (£48,786);
- *Federation of Black Housing Organisations,* to involve ethnic minority communities in regeneration schemes by increasing awareness, knowledge and skills (£45,000);
- *Walter Segal Self-Build Trust,* to develop and expand the work of the trust by providing a development worker dedicated to emerging groups in the North and Midlands (£24,150).

New work:

- *Key Potential UK,* to develop a coherent training pathway to encourage and facilitate partnerships between all professions working towards regeneration and social inclusion. This initiative follows the Social Exclusion Unit's identification of five sets of skills and knowledge needed to successfully implement a national strategy for neighbourhood renewal (£79,300).
- *SITRA,* to raise statutory awareness of, and assist in forging working relationships around, the implications of the 'Supporting People' reforms (£33,118).

Exclusions: As funding of last resort, SGP grant is not available for work which is eligible for support under any other government grant programme, or which could proceed without SGP support or be carried out to an adequate standard without this funding. Grant is not available for party-political or religious activities. Non-religious activities carried out by faith groups are eligible for SGP support.

Applications: These are sought during the summer with a deadline at the end of September.

Contact: Stacey Field, Tel: 020 7944 3726; Fax: 020 7944 3719
E-mail: stacey_field@detr.gsi.gov.uk

Website: www.regeneration.detr.gov.uk/grants/vol/index/htm

Urban Environmental Regeneration Branch (E H 4/H9)

Groundwork

Grant-in-aid: £7.5 million (2000/01)

An annual grant is made to Groundwork UK and its network of 42 autonomous trusts throughout England. This grant covers the core costs of Groundwork UK, a contribution to the core costs of the trusts, and funding towards specific projects in England.

Contact: Francesca Seymour Tel: 020 7944 3722; Fax: 020 7944 3729
E-mail: Francesca_Seymour@detr.gsi.gov.uk

Homelessness, Health and Housing Management Division: Tenant Participation Branch

Section 16 Tenant Empowerment Grants (E H 1/J6)

Grant total: £5,975,000 (2000/01); £4,155,000 (1999/2000); £3,619,000 (1998/99)

The government wants council tenants to have a say in how their homes are managed and to have a choice as to the extent and nature of their involvement. 'Tenant Participation Compacts' were introduced in April 2000 to that end. The compacts are produced by tenants and councils working together and set out how tenants will be involved in decisions. Tenants can take over all or part of the management of their homes under the statutory Right to Manage Regulations.

Section 16 Tenant Empowerment Grant is provided by the department to support and promote the development of greater tenant participation in the management of public sector housing. The grant programme supports the following.

Tenant Participation Helpline and Information Bank

The Tenant Participation Advisory Service (TPAS) receives Section 16 grant to provide information to tenants on all aspects of tenant participation. Tenants can write to TPAS or call free on 0500 844111.

Options Studies

These studies help tenants, working closely with the council, to look at their estate and consider options for greater involvement in the management of their homes. Local councils are then asked to sign up to an Action Plan to implement the chosen option. The range of options available to tenants is looked at as part of the study. These could include estate agreements, local committees, tenant panels and tenant management. Tenants choose an independent advice agency from the department's approved list to carry out the study and to apply for grant.

Tenant Management Organisations (TMOs)

There are various stages tenants' groups must go through if they decide they would like to take over the management of their estate. A short pre-feasibility study is followed by a feasibility study, both of which are paid for by the department. If tenants then decide, via a ballot, to go ahead with the decision to set up a TMO, an approved agency then carries out a development study to prepare the group for taking over management. The costs of developing a TMO are split 75%/25% between the department and the council.

Tenant Training

There a number of local courses on which tenants can learn or develop skills, for example in dealing with outside agencies, negotiating local agreements, or setting up local initiatives. Councils often run courses themselves or advise on the best ones for tenants to take. There are also national courses for which the department pays part of the cost. These come under two headings.

- The National Tenant Training Programme is a collection of short training courses held across the country. It is run through two organisations, TPAS and the Priority Estates Project (PEP), both of whom are supported via Section 16 grant. The courses are for established groups as well as those just getting started.
- The National Tenant Resource Centre (NTRC), based at Trafford Hall near Chester, manages a programme of residential courses under the 'Capacity Building Training Programme'. These courses are linked to a small grants programme, also administered by the NTRC, to help tenants attending courses to carry out small projects on their estates.

All courses involve a fee, but the department pays a subsidy to cut the costs, so that levels are often nominal. Information about how to access the courses is available from PEP, TPAS and NTRC (addresses below).

Innovation into Action Programme

This programme, run by the Chartered Institute of Housing (CIH), aims to stimulate the development of good practice in tenant involvement in housing management across England. It funds projects put forward by tenants' groups and other organisations that identify, develop and promote radical or new ways of involving tenants in the management of their estates.

The programme is open to tenants' groups, councils or other interested organisations. Partnerships are strongly encouraged and must always closely involve tenants locally. Bidders are asked to show what financial contribution the partnership can make to the overall costs of the project. Potential applicants should get in touch with the CIH for details.

The figures for total funding at the top of this entry refer to the department's funding to the three national training agencies, the approved independent agencies who carry out development studies, and the CIH.

Contacts:

DETR: Katie Haime/Julian Matthews Tel: 020 7944 3484/3488; Fax: 020 7944 3489; E-mail: tp@detr.gsi.gov.uk

TPAS, Brunswick House, Broad Street, Salford, M6 5BZ Tel: 0161 745 7904

PEP, 2 Albert Mews, Albert Road, London, N4 3RD Tel: 020 7281 3178

National Tenants Resource Centre, Trafford Hall, Ince Lane, Wimbolds Trafford, Chester CH2 4JP Tel: 01244 300 246

Chartered Institute of Housing, Tenant Participation Manager, 9 White Lion Street, London, N1 9XJ Tel: 020 7837 4280

Powers: Section 16, Housing and Planning Act 1986

Housing Care and Support Division
Supporting People Team (E H 1/F5)

The Supporting People programme is the government's attempt to put housing support services to vulnerable people on a more secure and integrated footing. It will be introduced in April 2003. The main aims are to:

- focus provision on local need;
- improve the range and quality of services;
- integrate support with wider local strategies, particularly those in health, housing, social services, neighbourhood renewal and community safety;
- monitor and inspect quality and effectiveness;
- introduce effective decision-making and administration.

For the purposes of the programme, vulnerable people include:

- older people;
- people with mental health problems, learning difficulties and physical disabilities;
- rough sleepers;
- ex-offenders;
- people with drug or alcohol problems;
- victims of domestic violence;
- people with chronic illness;
- young people leaving care.

Any provision detailed in this book for these groups may therefore come under Supporting People from 2003. Transfers are proposed from the following existing expenditure mentioned in this book: the Housing Corporation's Supported Housing Management Grant and relevant elements of the Resettlement Programme; Home Office Probation Accommodation Grants; and Home Improvement Agency Grants.

However, Supporting People will not be the sole source of funding for support services: the introductory guide states that 'Social Services authorities may have parallel programmes which in many cases will be making similar provision, e.g. through grant to or contracts with voluntary agencies'.

Supporting People will be run by local authorities, who will administer a special grant from the DETR dedicated to support services. The new grant will replace several smaller grants.

Contact: Helpline 020 7944 2556; Hidya Mustafa
E-mail: supporting_people@detr.gsi.gov.uk

Website: www.supporting_people.detr.gov.uk

Rough Sleepers Unit (A H)

Total direct grants from unit: £30,584,000 (2000/01); £24,918,000 (1999/2000) of which £20,398,000 (82%) went to the voluntary sector

The Rough Sleepers Unit represents the government's new 'joined-up' approach to tackling rough sleeping in England. Located within the DETR, it is staffed by officers from the DETR, the Department of Social Security, the Department of Health, the Housing Corporation, the NHS Executive, local government and the voluntary sector. The unit has a three-year lifespan (1999–2002) and is charged with delivering the government's target of reducing rough sleeping by two thirds by 2002. It is now administering almost all streams of funding to do with homelessness, including the Homelessness Action Programme and 'Section 180' funding. In London, funds previously coming under the Department of Health's

Homeless Mentally Ill Initiative and Drug and Alcohol Specific Grant are also administered by the unit. Outside London they continue to come under the Department of Health. The Department of Social Security's Section 30 Resettlement Grants are now administered by the Housing Corporation on behalf of the Rough Sleepers Unit for London only (see separate entry). Outside London, the unit directly funds eight local authorities under Section 30 as the Housing Corporation has no powers to do so.

The unit has a budget of £160 million for work in London – including capital and revenue funds administered by the Housing Corporation – and £34 million for work outside London, spread over its lifetime. Almost all the budget had been allocated by autumn 2000.

Voluntary sector organisations are seen as crucial partners in delivering the strategy on rough sleeping. The voluntary sector is involved in most of the key areas on which the unit is focusing, as set out in the strategy document 'Coming in from the Cold'. Some parts of the strategy apply only to London, because of the high concentration of rough sleeping in the capital. Other elements are being applied nationally. The various components in delivering the strategy include the following.

Contact and Assessment Teams
Funding: £1.3 million

These form part of the unit's more hands-on approach in the capital and in other major cities. Agencies running teams in the capital are: Thames Reach (Central (South and West) and Central), and St Mungo's (Central (North)). Both agencies share responsibility for an area of Soho.

Day Centres
Funded in central London to support the CATs and to contribute to the delivery of the strategy in their area. Funded day centres in central London are: The Passage, The London Connection, the North Lambeth Day Centre (St Mungo's), the West London Day Centre (West London Mission), St Martin's in the Fields, New Horizon, the Cardinal Hume Centre and St Giles Trust.

Day Centre-based Contact and Assessment Teams
Funding: £900,000

These have the same responsibility for streetwork and housing options as the central CATs, but for the areas around the centre of London. St. Botolph's, Bridge/Novas Ouvertures, Riverpoint and St Mungo's are funded to run these teams.

Providing Beds

The unit has funded 23 projects to provide additional bedspaces in London. In addition, the old Winter Shelter Programme in London has been replaced with a year-round rolling shelter programme. The shelter programme is managed by St Mungo's.

Tenancy Sustainment Teams

Helping rough sleepers in London and other major cities moving into settled accommodation to deal with the move to independent living. The four organisations running these teams in six areas of the capital are Look Ahead, Thames Reach, St Mungo's and New Islington and Hackney. The same approach is also being adopted in most other towns and cities with high concentrations of rough sleepers.

Drugs and Alcohol Specific Grant

All the Department of Health's Drug and Alcohol Specific Grant in 2000/01(£1,780,000) was reserved for projects with rough sleepers (see also separate entry). Funds for London are being administered by the unit for the unit's duration. The unit, in conjunction with the UK Anti-Drug Coordination Unit, is also funding an extra £1 million of services for drug users in London, with the funds coming from the Seized Assets Fund. The unit also funds the Homelessness and Drugs Unit of Drugscope.

Special Innovation Fund
Funding: £4 million (2000/01–2001/02)

This fund has two aims: to help people who have slept rough to rebuild their lives, and to prevent rough sleeping from occurring in the first place. Projects in the former category assist homeless people to move into work, education or training.

Grants included:

- *The Big Issue Foundation,* to set up activity centres in Norwich and London to help rough sleepers move into training, employment and occupation (£200,000);
- *Aspire,* to expand their Bristol-based scheme, which provides employment, training and support through a catalogue company, to other areas (£99,000);
- *The 700 Club,* for the Emma House Project, Darlington: a terraced house providing accommodation, employment advice, training and practical life skills for single homeless people (£10,000).

Grants to voluntary organisations for prevention schemes have included:

- *English Churches Housing Group,* Catterick Garrison Project: a project

working with ex-service personnel leaving Catterick barracks (£156,000);
- *Alone in London:* family mediation and returning home (£130,000);
- *Benjamin Foundation,* North Norfolk: rent deposit and housing support service for young people (£50,000).

Figures given for the Special Innovation Fund are not annual figures but represent offers made to the organisations concerned and are the maximum that will be paid up until 31 March 2002. All the money has been allocated for the fund.

Homelessness Action Programme
Funding: £34 million (1999/2000–2001/02)

This programme provides grant support to tackle and prevent rough sleeping outside London. The programme now concentrates on the 33 areas outside London with the worst homelessness problems. Projects range from advice and resettlement services, workshops renovating furniture for sale, rent deposit schemes and a national housing advice and consultancy service to Citizens Advice Bureaux.

As of autumn 2000, most grant aid for all programmes had already been allocated for the period up to mid-2002. After this point, the unit is unlikely to continue in its present form.

Contacts:

Outside London: Alastair McDonald Tel: 020 7944 3677

London: Irena Sawyer Tel: 020 7944 3443;
E-mail: irena_sawyer@detr.gsi.gov.uk

General enquiries: 020 7944 3600

Website: www.housing.detr.gov.uk/information/rough

Powers: Section 180, Housing Act 1996. Those with bearing on mental health and substance abuse may be made under Section 7E of Local Authority Social Services Act 1970.

Planning, Roads and Local Transport Directorate: Mobility Unit (G M H Zone 1/11)
Mobility for Disabled and Elderly
Grant total: £140,000 (2000/01); £140,000 (1999/2000)

The Unit supports two organisations that promote the mobility of disabled and elderly people.

- *The Community Transport Association,* for information/advice service on voluntary and community transport and training for operators of such transport schemes (£70,000);
- *Mobility Choice,* to promote personal mobility of disabled and elderly people, including Mobility Roadshows (£70,000).

The Unit does not invite bids for grants.

Contact: Ann Frye, Head of Mobility Unit Tel: 020 7944 4460; Fax: 020 7944 6102; E-mail: Ann_Frye@detr.gsi.gov.uk

Website: www.mobility-unit.detr.gov.uk

Powers: Section 17 of the Ministry of Transport Act 1919

Road Safety Division 3 (G M H Zone 2/14)
Royal Society for the Prevention of Accidents (RoSPA)
Grant-in-aid: £261,250 reviewed every three years

Road Safety Small Grants Budget
Funding: around £145,000 annually

Grant funding must support the government's road safety strategy and casualty reduction targets for 2010, as set out in 'Tomorrow's roads – safer for everyone', published in March 2000. The targets are:

- to reduce deaths and serious injuries by 10% – and by 50 % for children
- to reduce slight injuries by 10%.

Applications for grant will therefore need to promote casualty reduction and reflect the priorities of the Road Safety Strategy. These include:

- novice driver safety;
- child safety, particularly that of child pedestrians;
- drivers' attitude to speed;
- improving safety of vulnerable road users (pedestrians, cyclists, motorcyclists and horse riders);
- fleet driver safety;
- driver impairment.

These priorities are not exclusive. The department will also consider projects which tackle problem areas which they consider to be of a lower priority.

The level of grants ranged from the £13,000 to AIRSO to produce its road safety video to £500 given to ADDAPT. Grants are usually in the area of

£10,000, although larger grants are sometimes given and spread over more than one year.

Grants in 1999/2000 included:

- *Association of Industrial Road Safety Officers* (AIRSO) blue light awareness video;
- *Brake's Road Safety Week*;
- *Child Accident Prevention Trust's Child Safety Week*;
- *Bicycle Helmet Initiative Trust*;
- *Transport Vocational Group* for development of road safety NVQs;
- *Institute of Highways Transportation* for rural road safety management guidelines;
- *European Transport Safety Council* for conferences, lectures and newsletters;
- *British Horse Society* for riding and road safety test outline dates list and guidelines;
- *Brake's* tiredness leaflet print costs;
- *Association of Drink/Drive Approved Providers of Training* (ADDAPT) towards start-up costs.

Applications: There are at present no time limits for applying for grants, but as these grants become more widely known budget restraints may mean that opening and closing dates are introduced.

Contact: John Doyle Tel: 020 7944 2026; Fax: 020 7890 2029
E-mail: john_doyle@detr.gsi.gov.uk

Powers: Section 40 Road Traffic Act 1988

Related Agencies

Housing Corporation

149 Tottenham Court Road
London W1P 0BN

Tel: 020 7393 2145
Fax: 020 7393 2111
Website: www.housingcorp.gov.uk

Grant total: £674 million (capital), £142.4 million (revenue) (2000/01); £643 million (capital), £149 million (revenue) (1999/2000)

The Housing Corporation is a non-departmental public body funded by the Department of Environment, Transport and the Regions. It regulates and funds registered social landlords (RSLs), the non-profit bodies run by voluntary committees, most of which are housing associations. The corporation maintains a register of over 2,200 RSLs which are the major providers of new subsidised housing in England. It provides the following grant schemes and also commissions research as necessary.

Social Housing Grant (SHG)

Grant total: £674 million (2000/01); £643 million (1999/2000)

These capital grants fund new schemes to build, renovate and repair homes. They are only open to registered social landlords.

Supported Housing Management Grant (SHMG)

Grant total: £137 million (2000/01); £140 million (1999/2000)

This revenue grant supports the higher management and service costs of schemes for residents with support needs. From 2003 it is likely to be transferred to the DETR's Supporting People programme (see separate entry).

Innovation and Good Practice (IGP) Grants

Grant total: £5.4 million (2000/01); £9 million (1999/2000)

These revenue grants support innovation, good practice and promotion. They aim to test new approaches for the benefit of all RSLs. Proposals that can demonstrate that their findings could improve the service to tenants other than the ones they represent are particularly likely to receive support. Proposals should meet at least one of the current themes outlined in the corporation's information materials.

Current themes are:

- sustainability – covering communities; tenancies and management; buildings;
- effectiveness of RSLs – covering accountability, participation and development;
- housing strategy development – covering regeneration and partnerships; identifying and meeting needs, especially of black and minority ethnic people; new methods and approaches;
- regional initiatives – covering local priorities and partnerships.

Information: The corporation has an excellent publications service providing many useful advice booklets. In the special series about Innovation and Good Practice *Grants Advice 2* includes detailed case studies of exemplary projects and a full list of grant-aided schemes.

Applications: National projects should approach the Investment Division at The Housing Corporation's Headquarters. Regional or local projects should apply to the relevant regional office. Forms and guidance notes are available from Headquarters, or regional offices.

Housing Corporation Regional Offices

London region: Waverley House, 7–12 Noel Street, London W1V 4BA
Tel: 020 7292 4400; Fax: 020 7292 4401

South East region: Leon House, High Street, Croydon, Surrey CR9 1UH
Tel: 020 8253 1400; Fax: 020 8253 1444

South West region: Beaufort House, 51 New North Road, Exeter, Devon
EX4 4EP
Tel: 01392 428200; Fax: 01392 428201

East region: Attenborough House, 109/119 Charles Street, Leicester
LE1 1FQ
Tel: 0116 242 4800; Fax: 0116 242 4801

West Midlands region: Norwich Union House, Waterloo Road,
Wolverhampton WV1 4BP
Tel: 01902 795000; Fax: 01902 795001

North East region: St Paul's House, 24 Park Square South, Leeds LS1 2ND
Tel: 0113 233 7100; Fax: 0113 233 7101

North West region: Elizabeth House, 16 St Peter's Square, Manchester
M2 3DF
Tel: 0161 242 2000; Fax: 0161 242 2001

Merseyside region: Colonial Chambers, 3–11 Temple Street, Liverpool
L2 5RH
Tel: 0151 242 1200; Fax: 0151 242 1201

Powers: The Corporation was created under the Housing Act 1964. Its powers have changed as a result of various housing acts, the latest being the Housing Act 1996.

Resettlement of Single and Homeless People

Grant total: £9 million (£3.6 million capital and £5.4 million revenue) (2000/01)

The above figure is the Resettlement Section's element of grants made under Section 30 of the Jobseekers Act 1995. A further £9.2 million of Section 30 grants has been transferred to the Rough Sleepers Unit (see separate entry) for projects in London, to the DETR for grants paid to local authority/Housing Corporation schemes, and to the devolved executives of Scotland and Wales.

The grants, both capital and revenue, are made mainly to voluntary organisations providing supported accommodation to single homeless people. Projects must involve an active resettlement programme. Funding is given for up to the amount needed to make a project 'break even'. There are no lower or upper limits to grant levels, and grants can vary widely depending on local conditions.

The Resettlement Section transferred from the DSS to the Housing Corporation on 1 October 1999 and continues to administer Section 30 capital and revenue to projects in England, outside of London. All Section 30 grants within England, including London but excluding those paid to local authority projects, are progressively being converted to the Housing Corporation's Supported Housing Management Grant (SHMG). The conversion will be completed by 31 March 2001. Furthermore, it has been suggested that 'relevant elements' of the programme may be transferred to the Supporting People programme from 2003 (see separate entry).

Examples of revenue grants from 2000/01 are:

- *Bridge Housing Association* (£609,900);
- *Hull Resettlement Project* (£346,800);
- *Single Homeless Project* (£273,700);
- *Peasholme Centre* (£164,400);
- *Chester Aid to the Homeless* (£113,700);
- *Petrus* (£85,800);
- *Bury Young People's Housing Link* (£55,600);
- *Women in Supported Housing* (£33,900);
- *Trinity Centre* (£11,000);
- *Leeds Housing Concern* (£2,400).

The following organisations received capital funding:

- *Bristol Churches Housing Association*;
- *English Churches Housing Group*;
- the *Guinness Trust*;
- the *Peabody Trust*;
- *St Mungo's*.

All funds under this grant have been committed to the organisations currently receiving them and applications are therefore not invited.

Contact: Paul Noakes Tel: 020 7393 2254; Fax: 020 7393 2279; E-mail: Paul.Noakes@housingcorp.gsx.gov.uk

Powers: Section 30 of the Jobseekers Act 1995

Home Improvement Agencies

Foundations
Collective Enterprises Ltd
Bleaklow House
Howard Town Mills
Glossop
Derbyshire SK13 8HT

Tel: 01457 891 909
Fax: 01457 869 361

E-mail: foundations@cel.co.uk
Website: www.cel.co.uk/foundations

Contact: Ian Agnew, Director

Grant total: £6.5 million for each of the three years 1999/2000–2001/02

There are over 200 Home Improvement Agencies (HIAs) helping mainly older and disabled people with repairs, improvement and adaptation of their homes. They are usually small schemes, staffed by three or four people, operating on a district-wide basis. HIAs are managed by a variety of organisations, often housing associations but also local authorities and voluntary organisations. Grants are channelled through local authorities which are responsible for assessing the need for HIA services in their area and for bidding on their behalf. Foundations is the national coordinator of HIAs.

Financial criteria: In the period 1999/2002, the DETR is operating a matched funding scheme for HIAs. They will match the local authority contribution to HIA running costs up to a maximum of £60,000. Funds are fully committed until April 2002.

In the financial year 2002/3 there will be a single year's funding, after which funding for HIAs will be transferred to the Supporting People programme (see separate entry).

Applications: Prospective applicants for funding should approach their local housing authority. Further information can also be obtained from Foundations – see above address.

Powers: Sections 169(6), (7) and (8) of Local Government and Housing Act 1989

Housing Action Trusts (HATs)

Liverpool
Tel: 0151 227 1099

Castle Vale (Birmingham)
Tel: 0121 776 6784

Unity in Community (successor to North Hull HAT)
Tel: 01482 852292

Tower Hamlets
Tel: 020 8983 4698

Waltham Forest
Tel: 020 8539 5533

Stonebridge (Brent)
Tel: 020 8961 0278

HATs were set up under the 1988 Housing Act to take over and regenerate former local authority inner city housing estates. They take a holistic approach to improving the social, economic and environmental conditions in their areas as well as providing new and refurbished housing. HATs encourage community participation and are run by boards that include residents. Between 1991 and 1994 six HATs were set up. North Hull HAT completed its work in 1999, Waltham Forest HAT is due to do so in 2002 and the other four around 2005.

In pursuit of their aims HATs, and in some cases their partner Community Development Trusts, can give grants to individuals, organisations and community groups (including charities) for activities that contribute to their objectives.

Details are available direct from the HATs.

Further information: The Regeneration Division 1E, Zone 4/J10, DETR, Eland House, Bressenden Place, London SW1E 5DU Tel: 020 7944 3714; Fax: 020 7944 3709; E-mail: HATs@detr.gsi.gov.uk

Website (with links to HATs): www.regeneration.detr.gov.uk/policies/hat/index.htm

English Nature

Northminster House
Peterborough PE1 1UA

Tel: National office switchboard: 01733 455000
Enquiry Service Tel: 01733 455101
Fax: 01733 455103

E-mail: enquiries@english-nature.org.uk
Website: www.english-nature.org.uk

Contact: Roseanne Sparshot, Grants Officer Tel: 01733 455185

	1998/99	1999/2000	2000/01 (approx.)
Grant-aid:	£1,616,000	£1,720,000	£1,806,000
National schemes:	£1,327,000	£1,482,000	£1,556,100
Local projects:	£289,000	£238,000	£249,900

English Nature (EN) is the government-funded body set up to promote the conservation of England's wildlife and natural features. It aims to ensure that at least the present amount of wildlife is passed on to future generations, and that England's natural features are sustainably managed. EN advises government and other bodies, implements European and other international agreements, notifies outstanding areas as Sites of Special Scientific Interest (SSSIs) or, additionally, as National Nature Reserves (NNRs) and Marine Nature Reserves (MNRs). It works closely with public, private and charitable landowners and occupiers in various forms of co-operative and partnership arrangements for improved land management and wildlife enhancement. The organisation also runs an extensive research programme and a popular public enquiry service.

EN offers grants to organisations and individuals to help them conserve biodiversity. Grants are available for:

- new projects to safeguard, manage and enhance sites and species of nature conservation importance and their enjoyment by the public;
- projects enabling local communities to participate more fully in conservation programmes;
- proposals designed to encourage the development of wildlife management within natural areas of the countryside;
- innovative projects demonstrating new initiatives that are likely to have a wider relevance and further the practice of nature conservation;
- imaginative proposals for integrating nature conservation with other interests and even with potentially competing activities.

Grants for wildlife projects must contribute to Biodiversity Action Plans. EN also has a number of special grant schemes aimed at particular ends. Current schemes at the time of writing (June 2000) were as follows.

Biodiversity Grants Scheme

For research and practical projects aimed at halting losses and decline in species and protecting threatened habitats.

Voluntary Marine Initiative Grants

For the establishment and development of Voluntary Marine Nature Reserves, and for projects safeguarding and interpreting the marine environment.

Local Nature Reserves Grants Scheme

For work on Local Nature Reserves that have been formally declared by the Local Authority.

Reserves Enhancement Scheme

For the comprehensive management of Sites of Special Scientific Interest by County Wildlife Trusts.

Section 35 National Nature Reserve Capital Grants Scheme

For the capital costs of projects improving the management of a reserve. These grants are only available to Approved Bodies under Section 35 (1) (c) of the Wildlife and Countryside Act 1981, where these Approved Bodies are not eligible for the Reserves Enhancement Scheme mentioned above.

EN Local Schemes

EN Local Teams have funds for conservation action concentrating effort on enriching local biodiversity and Natural Areas.

College-English Nature Links

For students carrying out fieldwork on protected sites such as National Nature Reserves.

EN Volunteer Action Grants

To reimburse volunteers' travel expenses, thereby enabling voluntary organisations to put more volunteers into the field. These grants are offered up to a maximum of £1,000 per year and applications should be made to Local Teams.

Funding levels: Grant cannot exceed 50% of the total costs of a project. If projects have received Exchequer funding from other sources, the combined total cannot go over 50%. Applicants must therefore be able to demonstrate that they have sufficient funds to meet the balance. In exceptional circumstances EN will cost volunteer hours as part of its grant, but this is not the normal rule. The minimum grant is £250; there is no maximum.

Exclusions: National Nature Reserves, except those declared under Section 35 of the Wildlife and Countryside Act 1981; buildings; projects outside Great Britain; compensation payments; expeditions; student projects, except those eligible under the College-English Nature Grant Schemes mentioned above. Grants are also not normally available for ongoing office and administration costs, surveys, research, data collection, books or periodicals.

Applications: Can be submitted at any time, but must be received at least three months before a project is due to start. For projects outside special schemes, applications should be sent to Local Teams. National or specific scheme applications should be sent to the appropriate team at EN's National Office. Applications need to be submitted on an EN application form. Potential applicants are strongly urged to talk over a project with a member of EN staff before completing the form.

Contact: Enquiry service, Tel: 01733 455101 (this is for national grants; for local grants, approach relevant local teams).

English Nature Local Area Teams

Bedfordshire, Cambridgeshire and Northamptonshire: (Peterborough) Tel: 01733 405850; Fax: 01733 394093

Cumbria: (Kendal) Tel: 01539 792800; Fax: 01539 792830

Devon: (Okehampton) Tel: 01837 55045; Fax: 01837 55046

Cornwall & Isles of Scilly: (Truro) Tel: 01872 262550; Fax: 01872 262551

Dorset: (Wareham) Tel: 01929 556688; Fax: 01929 554752

East Midlands – Lincolnshire, Leicestershire, Nottinghamshire: (Grantham) Tel: 01476 568431; Fax: 01476 570927

Essex, Hertfordshire and London: (Colchester) Tel: 01206 796666

London: Tel: 020 7831 6922; Fax: 020 7404 3369

Hampshire and the Isle of Wight: (Lyndhurst) Tel: 01703 283944; Fax: 01703 283834

Gloucestershire, Herefordshire and Worcestershire (listed as 'Three Counties'): (Eastnor) Tel: 01531 638500; Fax: 01531 638501

Humber to Pennines: (Wakefield) Tel: 01924 387010; Fax: 01924 201507

Kent: (Wye) Tel: 01233 812525; Fax: 01233 812520

Norfolk: (Norwich) Tel: 01603 620558; Fax: 01603 762552

North and East Yorkshire: (York) Tel: 01904 435500; Fax: 01904 435520
(Leyburn) Tel: 01969 23447; Fax: 01969 24190

North West: (Wigan) Tel: 01942 820342; Fax: 01942 820364

Northumbria: (Stocksfield) Tel: 01661 845500

Peak District and Derbyshire: (Bakewell) Tel: 01629 815095;
Fax: 01629 815091

Somerset and Avon: (Taunton) Tel: 01823 283211; Fax: 01823 272978

Suffolk: (Bury St Edmunds) Tel: 01284 762218; Fax: 01284 764318

Surrey and Sussex: (Lewes) Tel: 01273 476595; Fax: 01273 483063

Thames and Chilterns: (Crookham Common) Tel: 01635 268881;
Fax: 01635 268940

West Midlands: (Shrewsbury) Tel: 01743 709611; Fax: 01743 709303

Wiltshire: (Devizes) Tel: 01380 726344; Fax: 01380 721411

Powers: Section 134, Environment Protection Act 1991

Forestry Commission

Country Services
Grants and Licences
231 Corstorphine Road
Edinburgh EH12 7AT

Tel: 0131 334 0303
Fax: 0131 314 6148

Website: www.forestry.gov.uk

Contact: Gordon Inglis, Grants and Licences Division

Grants to private woodland owners UK-wide: £42.7 million (2000/01);
£39.5 million (1999/2000); £41 million (1998/99)

The Forestry Commission is the government agency responsible for
forestry in Britain. The commission sets standards for the whole of the
forestry industry, both private and public, ensures compliance with plant
health and tree felling regulations and also administers grant schemes to
help private landowners, known as the Woodland Grant Scheme (WGS).

The Woodland Grant Scheme

The Woodland Grant Scheme aims:

- to encourage people to create new woodlands and forests to increase the production of wood, to improve the landscape, to provide new habitats for wildlife and to offer opportunities for recreation and sport;
- to encourage good management of forests and woodlands, including their well-timed regeneration, particularly looking after the needs of ancient and semi-natural woodlands;
- to provide jobs and improve the economy of rural areas and other areas with few other sources of economic activity;
- to provide a use for land instead of agriculture.

All woodlands and forests can be considered for grants under the WGS, except those which are too small or too narrow. Normally the woodland must be a quarter of a hectare in area and at least 15 metres wide, but smaller woods may be eligible if the aims of the scheme are met.

These aims are pursued by a range of grants under three main categories: New Woodlands; Existing Woodlands and Challenge Funds.

New Woodlands

- Planting Grants encourage the creation of new woodland and are paid as part of a contract in which the applicant agrees to look after the woodlands and do the approved work to reasonable satisfaction. Additional grants are also available in priority areas and these are: *Better Land Contribution* for the planting on arable or improved grassland; *Community Woodland Contribution* where access is given to local people; *Community Forest Premium* for new planting in specific areas over a limited period of time. Check for details with local office.
- Short Rotation Coppice grants for poplars and willows.
- Farm Woodland Premium Scheme (FWPS) encourages the creation of new woodlands for certain types of farm land to enhance the environment and as a productive alternative land use. The Forestry Commission is responsible for administering the scheme (though payments are made from the Agriculture Departments).

Existing Woodlands

- Woodland Improvement Grants assist projects that provide public recreation in woodlands, improve undermanaged woods, and enhance woodland biodiversity.
- Natural Regeneration Grants may be made as an alternative to planting.

- Restocking Grants towards the cost of replanting an existing wood.
- Annual Management Grants towards the cost of work to safeguard or enhance the special environmental value of a wood, improve woods which are below current environmental standards, or create, maintain or enhance public access.
- The previous Livestock Exclusion Annual Premium is under review at the time of writing.

Forest Expansion Challenge Funds

Intended to encourage the planting of new woodlands in specific areas of the country. Each year, applicants are asked to 'bid' for the amount of money they require to carry out the planting. The bids are judged on a competitive basis. Contact local offices for details of locations.

Applications: Detailed guidance about these schemes, financial rates and application forms are given in the pack available from the above address or from the Woodlands Officer in local Forestry Commission offices. Check your telephone directory or ring the English national office in Cambridge (Tel: 01223 314546; Fax: 01223 460699) for the contact you need in your local conservancy.

National Forest Company

Enterprise Glade
Bath Lane
Moira
Swadlincote
Derbyshire DE12 6BD

Tel: 01283 551211
Fax: 01283 552844

E-mail: nationalforest@cwcom.net
Website: www.nationalforest.org.

Contact: Hugh Williams

Grant total: £2,750,000 (2000/01)

The National Forest, devised by the erstwhile Countryside Commission and announced in 1990, links the ancient forests of Needwood and Charnwood and spans three counties in the English Midlands – Derbyshire, Leicestershire and Staffordshire. Its mostly rural landscape of mixed farmland was one of the least wooded areas of the country, but its wooded area has grown from 6% to 11.2% during the lifetime of the National Forest. The area suffers from economic decline and dereliction from mining and clay working. Its principal towns are Burton upon Trent (brewing), Coalville and Swadlincote (mining) and Ashby de la Zouch (historic). The National Forest Company was set up in 1995 to create this new forest. It aims to:

- promote nature conservation and cultural heritage;
- assist provision for sport, recreation and tourism;
- encourage agricultural and rural enterprise;
- stimulate economic regeneration;
- encourage community and business participation.

Central to its work are its partnerships with local authorities, farmers, landowners, companies, local communities and people all over Britain. Whilst the company receives grant-aid from government, this is 'pump priming' finance and covers a proportion of the project's total costs. It has its own specialists to generate further funds and investment opportunities, and together with other partners has made ambitious bids to the Heritage Lottery Board and the Millennium Commission.

The National Forest Tender Scheme

Grant total: £2.1 million (2000/01)

The Tender Scheme was launched in 1995 jointly with the Forestry Commission, for rapid conversion of farm and derelict land to forest. Up until April 2000, a total of 1320 hectares had been converted to woodland through this scheme. In Round 5 (1999/2000), 17 out of 25 bids were successful. Most of these were from local farmers planting new woods and providing access for walkers and horseriders.

Land Acquisition Fund

Grant total: £200,000 (2000/01)

The company has funds to buy land itself or to assist others in acquiring it, as part of its work to develop a wide range of partners in its work. Grant aid is usually made for up to 50% of a property's value, or 75% in exceptions.

NFC Development Programme Fund

Grant total: £150,000 (2000/01)

This fund allows for strategic site management, new access agreements, and supports community and arts projects within the National Forest Areas. Around 30 local projects are supported each year including parish-based wildlife surveys, heritage and art projects and specific features at forest sites. Both BTCV and Leicestershire and Rutland Trust for Nature Conservation have received support under this fund.

National Forest Locational Premium

Grant total: £300,000 (2000/01)

This is a special cash grant made available by the Forestry Commission for broadleaf tree planting in the National Forest area. Grants are up to £2,500 per hectare and can be added to payments from the standard Forestry Commission Woodland Grant Scheme (see entry on Forest Authority). The scheme has been extended up to September 2002.

Major Forest-Related Bids

The company acts as a catalyst giving advice and assistance for national and European Union funding.

Land for Sale or Purchase

The National Forest Company holds a database of all interested parties looking to buy or sell land in the National Forest area.

Countryside Agency

John Dower House
Crescent Place
Cheltenham
Glos GL50 3RA

Tel: 01242 521 381
Fax: 01242 584 270

E-mail: info/hs@countryside.gov.uk
Website: www.countryside.gov.uk

Grant total: £24,513,000 (1999/2000)

Breakdown: Local authorities/public bodies: £13,400,000; Private persons/non-public bodies: £6,601,000; Transport: £3,079,000 (provisional); Capital: £1,433,000 (provisional)

The new Countryside Agency came into being in April 1999 when the Countryside Commission and the Rural Development Commission (RDC) were merged. Some of the RDC's work passed to the regional development agencies – see separate entry.

The stated aims of the Countryside Agency are:
- to conserve and enhance the countryside;
- to promote social equity and economic opportunity for the people who live there;
- to help everyone, wherever they live, to enjoy the countryside.

The agency works with local authorities, parish councils, rural community councils, businesses, farmers, landowners, voluntary groups and individuals to achieve these aims. Grant aid is an important part of its strategy. As the agency's remit is very broad, most grant aid is directed towards projects that support identified priorities. Regional offices have their own more specific priorities within the agency's corporate national objectives, so it is best to contact them directly.

In the financial year 1999/2000, the agency allocated just over half of its grant (54%) to programmes with local authorities and public bodies. Twenty-six per cent (£6.6 million) was paid to 'private persons and non-public bodies', including voluntary organisations. The remainder (£4.5 million) was via special transport and capital schemes.

The agency has a number of strategic priorities, which are delivered through eight major work programmes:

- **Rural Assurance:** influencing the quality of rural life and increasing awareness of the rural dimension to deliver a better quality countryside environment.
- **Countryside Capital:** making the most of natural assets in order to enhance the qualities of the countryside for people today and in the future.
- **Wider Welcome:** opening up more of the countryside by establishing areas where visitors can enjoy the countryside with confidence, in particular on foot, horse or cycle, while also benefiting rural businesses.
- **Market Towns:** vitalising rural service centres for the wider countryside so they provide convenient access to the services surrounding rural communities.
- **Countryside on your Doorstep:** creating attractive, accessible green space close to home.
- **Finest Countryside:** securing the quality of our best landscapes.
- **Vital Villages:** equipping communities to shape their futures by empowering them to identify and act to meet local needs.
- **Local Heritage Initiative:** helping people to care for their landscapes, landmarks and traditions (see separate entry).

Grants are available in some, but not all of these programmes. Larger grants are often targeted specifically at existing local management group(s) and partnerships (such as to National Park Authorities, or to local authorities) and provide for the implementation of plans by these bodies over longer periods.

However, following the publication of the Rural White Paper in November 2000, the agency's new priorities include support for villages and parishes to plan and fund their services through a Community Service Fund of £15 million (available over the next four years). This will include training and support for parish clerks and councillors.

There are also transport funds totalling £36 million (available over the next four years). The Rural Transport Fund gives grants of up to 50% for transport initiatives, services and facilities in rural England, and up to 75% towards setting up partnerships to develop action plans for improvements to local transport. A Parish Transport Fund is aimed at providing small-scale local transport solutions, especially where these support local community plans (see previous paragraph). The Parish Council will be the recipient of the grant, to fund local providers as required.

Level of grant. Grants are normally between 20% and 50% of the eligible cost of a project. Only in exceptional circumstances will a grant exceed 50% (75% in the case of the Rural Transport Partnership). If a project has secured funding from other Exchequer sources, the combined grant cannot exceed 50%.

Examples of voluntary organisations receiving grants in 1999/2000 included:

- *BTCV East Midlands*, for project work (£53,230);
- *Kirkby Community Minibus* (£25,700);
- *National Trust*, to acquire sporting rights at Allen Banks, Northumberland (£20,000);
- *Sherbourne Youth/Community Centre* (£9,680);
- *North Pennines Heritage Trust*, for Nenthead Mines Heritage Centre (£9,100);
- *Voluntary Action Cumbria*, for landscaping in Eden Village (£3,500).

Applications: There is no fixed deadline for applying for grants, although most grant-aided projects work on a financial year basis. Discussions on projects usually begin in September as the agency's priorities for the next year are worked up; final details are usually requested in January. Some schemes have a prescribed application form, but others require a written statement. In all cases, preliminary enquiries should be made to the nearest regional office.

Countryside Agency Regional Offices

North East
4th Floor, Warwick House, Grantham Road, Newcastle upon Tyne
NE2 1QF
Tel: 0191 232 8252; Fax: 0191 222 0185

Yarm Road Industrial Estate, Morton Road, Darlington DL1 4PT
Tel: 01325 361368; Fax: 01325 361433

North West
7th Floor, Bridgewater House, Whitworth Street, Manchester M1 6LT
Tel: 0161 237 1061; Fax: 0161 237 1062

Haweswater Road, Penrith, Cumbria CA11 7EH
Tel: 01768 865752; Fax: 01768 890414

Yorkshire and The Humber
2nd Floor, Victoria Wharf, No. 4 The Embankment, Sovereign Street,
Leeds LS1 4BA
Tel: 0113 246 9222; Fax: 0113 246 0353

West Midlands
1st Floor, Vincent House, Tindal Bridge, 92–93 Edward Street,
Birmingham B1 2RA
Tel: 0121 233 9399; Fax: 0121 233 9286

Strickland House, The Lawns, Park Street, Wellington, Telford TF1 3BX
Tel: 01952 247161; Fax: 01952 248700

East Midlands
18 Market Place, Bingham, Nottinghamshire NG13 8AP
Tel: 01949 876200; Fax: 01949 876222

East of England
Ortana House, 110 Hills Road, Cambridge CB2 1LQ
Tel: 01223 354463; Fax: 01223 313850

South West
Bridge House, Sion Place, Clifton Down, Bristol BS8 4AS
Tel: 0117 973 9966; Fax: 0117 923 8086

2nd Floor, 11–15 Dix's Field, Exeter EX1 1QA
Tel: 01392 477150; Fax: 01392 477151

South East & London
Dacre House, 19 Dacre Street, London SW1H 0DH
Tel: 020 7340 2900; Fax: 020 7340 2911

Sterling House, 7 Ashford Road, Maidstone ME14 5BJ
Tel: 01622 765222; Fax: 01622 662102

Local Heritage Initiative

Countryside Agency
John Dower House
Crescent Place
Cheltenham
Glos GL50 3RA

Tel: 01242 521381
Fax: 01242 584270

Website: www.lhi.org.uk

Contact: Julie Millin

Funding: £12 million over three years (2000/01–2002/03)

Funding comes from the Heritage Lottery Fund (£8 million over the first three years), the Nationwide Building Society (over £1 million) and the Countryside Agency (£3 million).

The Local Heritage Initiative is a national grant scheme devised by the Countryside Agency and administered by it on behalf of the Heritage Lottery Fund. It is intended to help local groups to investigate, explain and care for their local landmarks, landscape, traditions and culture. It was launched in February 2000 and is planned to run for 10 years. The scope of LHI is very wide and includes many categories of local heritage.

- Archaeological heritage: enquiries into, and interpretation of, locally important visible features, for example, hill forts, burial mounds, moats, field systems, ridge and furrow, standing stones and ancient village sites.
- Built heritage: locally distinctive built heritage elements and small features, like field barns, pumps, wells, gates and walls, bridges, railings, milestones, architectural details, cobbles, memorials, village greens or traditional signs.
- Customs and traditions: historic and cultural associations with the land and activities of local people, for example stories, poems, songs, dialect, recipes, traditions and famous people. Also heritage features relating to how people lived, worked, played, such as place names, field names, parish boundaries, open spaces, viewpoints, and local rights of way.
- Industrial heritage: physical features related to locally important industries, such as chimneys, lime kilns, packhorse trails, wagonways, canals, quarries, mineral pits, spoil heaps, mills, mines, smithies and coopers.
- Natural heritage: locally characteristic landscape features and wildlife habitats, such as hedgerows, copses, pollards, orchards, small heathland areas, hay meadows, water meadows, reedbeds, ponds, streams and springs.

Some pilot projects have been carried out under the initiative and give an idea of the kind of project that will win funding. These include:

- partnership between Tow Law Town Council, local people, Groundwork and various experts to restore a set of 19th century beehive coking ovens;
- project to develop an action plan for the landscape and ecological management of the village green at Maulds Meaburn, Cumbria;
- investigation carried out by students and teachers at Woodlands Community School, Southampton, in conjunction with the local history society, into the heritage of the former Harefields Estate on which their school and homes are situated;

– project coordinated by the Sedbergh and District History Society in the Yorkshire Dales to survey the Howgill landscape, involving the Cumbria Wildlife Trust, Sedbergh Primary School and members of the local community.

Eligibility: The LHI is designed for rural or suburban areas of England. This includes most areas except the centres of large towns and cities.

New or existing community or voluntary groups can apply for funding. They do not have to be a registered charity but they must have a formal constitution and an open bank or building society account. Groups that are not locally based must be able to show that their project began at the community level and that it has support from local people. Grant aid is available for costs associated with:

- an investigation of local heritage, leading to an explanation and presentation of information discovered;
- material and labour for a programme of community-led action, e.g. conservation or restoration of heritage assets;
- work to help public access, enjoyment and appreciation of heritage assets;
- specialist advisers to help with the project;
- charges such as archive costs;
- activities to involve the wider community, especially young people;
- production of information;
- essential equipment to make projects efficient and effective (max 50% of costs);
- training for volunteers;
- provision for long-term care of the project and assets;
- legal advice and volunteer insurance costs specifically associated with LHI projects.

The LHI anticipates that projects will last between one and two years.

Funding levels: Standard grants are between £3,000 and £15,000, paid in arrears, to cover 60% of project costs. The remaining 40% may be made up from cash, in-kind donations, volunteer labour, or a mixture of these.

Groups are encouraged to apply for more complex projects, e.g. those involving investigation, explanation and action, in two or three phases. In exceptional circumstances it may be possible to offer a higher rate of grant aid, or advance payments. However, the maximum amount any one group or project may apply for is £25,000.

The Nationwide Building Society is offering additional payments of up to £5,000 for projects that may have difficulty raising matching funding or want to go further than is possible with standard levels of funding. The additional payments are intended for projects that would otherwise not go ahead. Awards will be made four times per year and are available through the LHI application process.

Exclusions: Individuals and profit-making organisations; work carried out prior to receiving and accepting any offer of grant; expert advice or management skills by the applicant or group members (although this can count as in-kind contributions); items that only benefit an individual; core funding; routine maintenance or one-off repair projects.

Applications: A detailed form must be completed. Applications are assessed by a regional Countryside Agency project officer; final decisions are made by the Heritage Lottery Fund. Decisions are expected within three months.

Walking the Way to Health (see also Countryside Agency)

John Dower House
Crescent Place
Cheltenham
Glos GL50 3RA

Tel: 01242 521381
WHI hotline: 01242 533258

E-mail: peter.ashcroft@countryside.gov.uk
Website: www.whi.org.uk

Contact: Peter Ashcroft, Project Manager

Overall cost: £11.6 million over five years (comprising: New Opportunities Fund – £6.4 million; Countryside Agency and British Heart Foundation – £1.2 million each; Local scheme partners – £2.4 million; National sponsorship – £0.4 million)

This five-year programme aims to set up and support 200 community based schemes targeted at disadvantaged areas in town and country across England. Each local scheme will provide programmes of short led walks, self-help information to encourage independent walking, opportunities for volunteering and connections to services and support networks concerning better health. Priorities include all Health Action Zones, local authority districts within the 25% most disadvantaged as defined by the Index of Local Deprivation, and all Rural Development Areas.

The Countryside Agency will provide grants and technical support to help local groups set up schemes. Each local scheme will operate within a local partnership of local health authorities, local councils, businesses, landowners, communities and the voluntary sector. Tailor-made training will be provided locally to give volunteers and professionals the skills and knowledge to make their own scheme successful. Five field teams will provide coverage across England.

Applications: Each application will pass through two stages of selection. Grants are offered to local groups to cover a percentage of their costs varying between 50% to 90%. The balance for each scheme will be raised locally. The first applications were sought in September 2000.

ACRE – Action with Communities in Rural England

Somerford Court
Somerford Road
Cirencester
Gloucestershire GL7 1TW

Tel: 01285 653477
Fax: 01285 654537

E-mail: acre@acre.org.uk
Website: http://www.acreciro.demon.co.uk

Contact: Jane Rowell

Grant-in-aid to ACRE: £38,500 (2000/01)
Transitional funding from the Countryside Agency

ACRE is a national charity aiming to alleviate rural disadvantage in England, with a vision of strong, articulate rural communities in which poverty and social exclusion are addressed. ACRE is also a national association of Rural Community Councils (RCCs) and shares with them the commitment to improve the quality of life of local communities.

Village Halls Loan Fund

Fund total: £700,000 (2000/01)

ACRE administers a loan programme for the Countryside Agency towards capital improvements, such as extension or rebuilding costs. The building must be open to use by all members of the community. Loans do not usually exceed £20,000. At least 10% of the total cost, or £1 per head of the population, whichever is the less, must come from local funds. Interest is laid down by the Treasury under the 'broadly commercial' rate. Loans are repaid over periods of up to eight years.

Exclusions: Loans cannot be offered to parish councils or towards work on buildings owned or run by individual organisations e.g. church halls, Women's Institute halls, etc.

Applications: Guidance notes and applications forms are available from ACRE. Applications can be processed within three weeks.

Department of Health

The departmental addresses occurring in this guide are:

Richmond House **(R H)**
79 Whitehall
London SW1A 2NS

Tel: 020 7210 3000
Fax: 020 7210 5523

Wellington House **(W H)**
133–155 Waterloo Road
London SE1 8UG

Tel: 020 7972 200

Quarry House **(Q H)**
Quarry Hill
Leeds LS2 7UE

Tel: 0113 254 5000

Website: www.doh.gov.uk

Contents

(Grant-in-aid in italics)

Related Funding
See **Regional Section** for: Health Action Zones

Health care, disability and the welfare of those people suffering from particular physical and mental problems have long been at the core of the work of the voluntary sector. The following outline is provided to help readers identify and target areas of potential interest. In 1998 the department had two main sections with most relevance to the voluntary sector – the Social Care Group and the Public Health Division. Both are based at Wellington House.

The **Social Care Group** covers social work and the social service aspects of the services for the department. It is comprised of the following branches.

- Branch SC1/2 – General social services policy and Personal and Social Services training (Section 64 grants);
- Branch SC3 – Children's services;
- Branch SC4 – Children's residential care, secure accommodation and juvenile justice;
- Branch SC5 – Community care, elderly social care;
- Branch SC6 – Disabilities, mental illness, deprivation issues.

The **Public Health Division** comprises the following.

- PH 1 Health strategy, health monitoring, health education, health inequalities;
- PH 2 Health people and communities;
- PH 3 Alcohol Policy, smoking policy;
- PH 4 Birth control, family planning, sexual health, fertility, genetics, etc.

The National Health Executive (NHE) refers separately through the Permanent Secretary to the Secretary of State for Health. The voluntary sector will have many varieties of working relationships with the regional offices of the NHE, the Health Authorities, the NHS Trusts and the proposed Primary Care Groups of GPs, but these relationships are outside the scope of this guide.

Social Care Group 2
Grants to National Voluntary Organisations Section 64 (W H, Room 609)

Total grant-aid: £21,000,000 (2000/01); £21,000,000 (1999/2000)

The Department of Health's main funding support is the Section 64 General Scheme. Under the scheme, grants are awarded to national voluntary organisations working in the health and personal social services for projects that are innovative and of national significance and that further the department's policy objectives. The types of grant offered are as follows.

Social Care: National Project Grants

Such grants must further the department's policy objectives by testing an innovative idea or by helping to develop a particular pattern of service of national significance. Arrangements for monitoring, evaluation and dissemination must be agreed before a grant is given. A grant is normally limited to a maximum of about half the total project costs. The source/s of funding for the balance of the costs must be clearly shown before a grant is approved. Such grants are given for a maximum of three years, plus another year for evaluation and dissemination. No extension to these periods is allowed. Project grants may include an element of core costs when these are not already funded from another source.

Project grants in financial year 2000/01 included:

- *National Schizophrenia Fellowship* (£260,000 in seven grants);
- *DIAL UK* (£120,000);
- *Refuge* (£80,000);
- *Young Minds Trust* (£70,000);
- *British Allergy Foundation* (£54,000);
- *Revolving Doors Agency* (£40,000);
- *United Response* (£35,000);
- *Policy Research Institute on Ageing and Ethnicity* (£30,000);
- *Vietnamese Mental Health Services* (£19,000);
- *Progress Educational Trust* (£13,000);
- *Galactosaemia Support Group* (£7,000).

Social Care: Core Grants

Although the department primarily concentrates on project funding, it recognises that core funding may also be necessary for work which fits in strategically with the department's objectives. Core grants therefore may be available to help with the central administration costs of national organisations which demonstrate clearly defined objectives. Since the department does not want organisations to be over-reliant on government funding, applicants are expected to demonstrate that other sources of funding have also been explored. Grants are usually for three years at a fixed cash level, tapered downwards over the grant period.

New and continuing core grants in 2000/01 included:

- *Drugscope* (£460,000);
- *Alcohol Concern* (£380,000);
- *The Macfarlane Trust* (£192,600);
- *British Council of Disabled People* (two grants of £40,000 and £147,000);
- *Carers National Association* (£184,000);
- *British Agencies for Adoption and Fostering* (£160,000);
- *National AIDS Trust* (£150,000);
- *Forum for Mobility Centres* (£100,000);

– *Centre for Policy on Ageing* (£60,000);
– *Resource and Service Development Centre* (£47,500);
– *Big Brothers and Sisters of the UK* (£30,000);
– *After Adoption* (£25,000);
– *Children's Rights Alliance for England* (£15,000);
– *In Touch Trust* (£4,000).

There are two other types of grant administered under the Section 64 scheme but these are only available in 'very exceptional circumstances'. These are given below.

Section 64: Local Project Grants

Local and health authorities also have powers to make grants to voluntary organisations. Local projects should therefore first seek funding from these sources, although Section 64 project grants may be made exceptionally as follows:

- pump-priming to meet exceptionally high initial costs over a limited period (where local or health authorities are unable to meet these);
- where a project spans a number of local or health authorities which are unable or unwilling to provide the necessary finance;
- where an innovative local experiment has potential national significance and the local or health authority is unable or unwilling to meet the cost;
- where the department on its own initiative wishes to test certain proposals for client care.

As with national projects arrangements for monitoring, evaluation and dissemination must be agreed before a grant is given. Local project grants may be given for up to three years, plus one further year for evaluation.

Section 64: Capital Grants

Grants for land, building or movable assets are a low priority for the scheme and are awarded only rarely. Applicants must demonstrate that they cannot achieve their objectives by other means and within their own resources. The purpose of the capital grant must rank very high amongst the department's policy objectives. Small movable assets (up to £5,000) such as office equipment may be considered as part of a core or project grant application and need not be separately requested.

In 2000/01 a total of 579 grants of all four kinds were given to some 373 different organisations. Of these 209 were 'new grants' in a rolling programme, i.e. the first year of a round of core funding or of a specific project.

Individual grants ranged from £5,000 to £460,000 per year, with the largest generally being core grants. However, the average grant is between £30,000–40,000 per year. Core grants are often given in conjunction with other grants, for instance:

- *HAS 2000* (£100,000 core plus £168,000 project);
- *British Institute of Learning Disabilities* (£35,000 core plus £42,000 project);
- *Child Accident Prevention Trust* (£40,000 core plus £80,000 in two projects).

Exclusions: Funding is not given for research projects, or to voluntary organisations serving a particular profession or sphere of employment. Only one core grant may be applied for.

Applications: Guidance notes and application forms are available from summer each year. The deadline for completed application forms is during September/October for grants starting the following April. Notification of the outcome of the application can be expected around February/March.

Organisations should have or be in the process of producing an equal opportunities policy. In 2000/01, as part of its commitment to reducing inequalities in health, the department was particularly keen to receive applications from black and minority ethnic organisations and applications promoting black and minority ethnic health and social care interests. Applications for initiatives that promote volunteering or involve volunteers were also welcome.

For each funding round, the department produces a detailed list of priorities. The list is available on request or from the Section 64 webpage (address below).

Contact: Irene Adjei-Badu, Tel: 020 7972 4394; E-mail: irene.adjei-badu@doh.gsi.gov.uk

Website: www.doh.gov.uk/sect64/grants.htm

Powers: Section 64, Health Services and Public Health Act 1968

Opportunities for Volunteering Scheme

Grant total: £6.6 million (2002/03); £6.6 million (2001/02); £6.6 million (2000/01)

The Opportunities for Volunteering scheme makes grants to voluntary organisations to increase opportunities for people, particularly the unemployed, to volunteer in health and social care. Although overall responsibility for the scheme lies with the Department of Health, the

General Fund of the programme is administered by the Consortium on Opportunities for Volunteering (COV). In addition 16 specialist charities (see below under 'Specialist Agencies') act as agents for applications within their own areas, and each have their own cycle of grant applications.

Grants are only given for new projects. Upper funding limits and time-lengths vary according to which agent is approached, although over the scheme as a whole, upper limits are £35,000 and 36 months. Grants can be used for: salaries (all posts must be concerned with work that supports the involvement of volunteers); volunteers' out-of-pocket expenses; overheads and running costs. Capital grants are limited to £20,000, of which up to £7,000 can be put towards the cost of a vehicle and up to £11,000 can be used to renovate or refurbish premises.

Grants can only be given to voluntary organisations and groups for activities of local significance. The scheme is not intended to develop opportunities for volunteering as a substitute for paid employment; jobs should not be put at risk. Whilst a project must be designed to involve primarily unemployed volunteers, it is not a requirement that all volunteers must be unemployed. The voluntary work should help people who need particular support, e.g. elderly people, isolated young mothers, children in trouble, disabled people.

Most work supported is outside the scope of services provided by health authorities and trusts, or local authority social services departments.

Exclusions: Activities closely related to other government departments; applications from statutory bodies and individuals; schemes to set up volunteer bureaux; core activities of an organisation; organisations with an annual turnover of more than £100,000 at the time of applying – this limit does not apply to the member bodies of sponsoring organisations such as Councils for Voluntary Service, Rural Community Councils, Racial Equality Councils and Volunteer Bureaux, or organisations in which a project may be based; building work, except access arrangements for disabled people; projects for people over 55 – these projects should approach Age Concern England; work previously funded by the consortium or funded by one of the specialist agencies.

Contact: Allison Noterman, Policy Manager Tel: 020 7972 4093;
Fax: 020 7972 4307

General Fund

Total grant: £2 million (2001/02 and again in 2002/03)

The General Fund of the scheme is run by the Consortium on Opportunities for Volunteering. The consortium, now established as an independent charitable company, comprised in 2000: Action for Communities in Rural England (ACRE); British Association of Settlements and Social Action Centres (BASSAC); Churches Together in England; Community Matters; National Alliance of Women's Organisations; National Association of Councils of Voluntary Service; National Association of Volunteer Bureaux; National Coalition for Black Volunteering; National Centre for Volunteering; RADAR Royal Association for Disability and Rehabilitation; Evelyn Oldfield Unit. Co-opted members include: Mencap; Cripplegate Foundation.

The General Fund is aimed at local projects that are not related to the areas covered by any of the specialist agencies listed below. It supports a broad range of projects but targets a proportion of grants to projects involving women, disabled people, black and minority ethnic communities, people living in rural areas and asylum seekers and refugees. The maximum grant for the 2001/03 round is £35,000. For 1998/2001 the majority of grants tended to be between £20,000 and £30,000.

Examples of projects supported during the 1998/2001 funding programme included:

– *Furniture Restoration and Sale Project*, Huddersfield (£30,000);
– *Kids and Us Volunteer Group*, Newcastle (£27,932);
– *Step Ahead Clubhouse*, East London (£24,920);
– *Black Drug Initiative – Peer Education*, Nottingham (£22,600);
– *Salford Women's Support Service* (£21,961);
– *Bridgegate Fenland Volunteering Project*, Peterborough (£19,969);
– *Self Advocacy*, Brierfield (£16,963);
– *T.W.I.G.S.*, Swindon (£10,348);
– *Doncaster Home Start* (£2,899).

Applications: The closing date for applications for the 2001/03 funding programme was September 2000. Contact the consortium early in 2002 for information about the next funding cycle.

Contact: Tina Jenkins, Programme Manager, Consortium on Opportunities for Volunteering, 4th Floor, 35/37 William Road, London NW1 3ER Tel: 020 7387 1673; Fax: 020 7387 1686

Specialist Agencies
Total grant: £13.8 million (2000/01–2002/03)

Each of the 16 agencies listed below administers a funding programme specifically directed at the work of its own members, associates, linked projects, etc. Each has its own definition of the type of work it aims to support agreed with the Department of Health, and its own administrative arrangements. Interested readers should contact the head office of each organisation to find out more details about its funding criteria and the timing of its funding cycles and application closing dates. Figures in brackets shown below refer to the total grant fund administered by the organisation concerned for the period 2000/03.

Age Concern, England (£3 million)
Grants Unit, Astral House, 1268 London Road, London SW16 4ER
Tel: 020 8765 7740; Fax: 020 8679 9154
Contact: Michael Mitchell

Barnardos (£630,000)
Tanner's Lane, Barkingside, Ilford, Essex IG6 1QG
Tel: 020 8550 8822
Contact: Maggie Kelly

British Association of Settlements and Social Action Centres (BASSAC) (£670,000)
Winchester House, 11 Cranmer Road, London SW9 6EJ
Tel: 020 7735 1075; Fax: 020 7735 0840
Contact: John Langenheim

Churches Together in England (£810,000)
101 Queen Victoria Street, London EC4V 4EN
Tel: 020 7332 8233; Fax: 020 7332 8234
Contact: Pauline Main

The Children's Society (£610,000)
Edward Rudolf House, Margery Street, London WC1X 0JL
Tel: 020 7841 4400; Fax: 020 7837 0211
Contact: Lynne Tallon

Community Service Volunteers (CVS) (£800,000)
237 Pentonville Road, London N1 9NJ
Tel: 020 7278 6601; Fax: 020 7713 0560
Contact: John Potter/Delphine Garr

Crisis (£360,000)
1st Floor, Challenger House, 42 Adler Street, London E1 1EE
Tel: 020 7655 8346; Fax: 020 7247 1525
Contact: Julian Jacobs

MENCAP (£940,000)
Optimum House, Clippers Quay, Salford Quays, Manchester M5 2XP
Tel: 0161 888 1200
Contact: John Oliver

MIND (National Association for Mental Health) (£1,380,000)
The Grants Unit, Granta House, 15–19 Broadway, Stratford E15 4BQ
Tel: 020 8215 2206; Fax: 020 8519 1725
Contact: Barry Watts

NACRO (National Association for the Care and Resettlement of Offenders) (£790,000)
169 Clapham Road, London SW9 0PU
Tel: 020 7582 6500; Fax: 020 7840 6440

National Association of Hospital and Community Friends (£1,350,000)
2nd Floor, Fairfax House, Causton Road, Colchester, Essex CO1 1RJ
Tel: 01206 761 227; Fax: 01206 560 244
Contact: Mike Conway

Pre-School Learning Alliance (£430,000)
69 Kings Cross Road, London WC1X 9LL
Tel: 020 7833 0991; Fax: 020 7837 4942
Contact: Jane Armstrong

RADAR (£820,000)
12 City Forum, 250 City Road, London EC1V 8AF
Tel: 020 7250 3222; Fax: 020 7250 0212
Contact: Vivien Fallows

Royal National Institute for the Blind (RNIB) (£430,000)
Voluntary Agencies Link Unit, 224 Great Portland Street, London W1N 6AA
Tel: 020 7388 1266; Fax: 020 7388 3160
Contact: Andy Winders

Scope (£360,000)
Olympus House, Britannia Road, Patchway, Bristol BS5 0TX
Tel: 0117 906 6333; Fax: 0117 906 6320
Contact: Andrew Cooper

United Kingdom Council on Deafness (UKCOD) (£360,000)
OFV Grants, 59 Banner Street, London EC1Y 8PX
Tel: 020 7689 2080; Fax: 020 7689 2082; Textphone: 020 7689 2081
Contact: Nicholas Callow

An application may be made to one agent only. In most cases funds are allocated on an annual basis.

Website: www.doh.gov.uk/volunteering/

Social Work Training, Education and Research (W H, Room 620)

Grant total: budgeted £912,000 (2000/2001); £912,000 (1999/2000)

These grants promote good practice and management, responsiveness to users, and the effectiveness of personal and social services staff, and also contribute to change in social policies and their implementation.

- *National Institute for Social Work*, London, to support its administrative infrastructure (£430,000);
- *Ruskin College*, Oxford, to support a Diploma in Social Work course (£243,000);
- *Selly Oak Colleges*, Birmingham, to support a Diploma in Social Work course (£239,000).

Note: This funding is not open to other applications. It is specific to the bodies funded and is fully committed to this purpose.

Contact: Alan Parker Tel: 020 7972 4290; Fax: 020 7972 4292

Social Care Group 3 (W H)
Women's Aid Federation (England)

Grant-in-aid: £49,000 (1999/2000 and for 2000/01)

This funding supports the operation of a telephone helpline for the women victims of domestic violence. The Women's Aid Federation also receives core funding under the Section 64 grant programme (see separate entry).

Contact: Bruce Clark Tel: 020 7972 4507; Fax: 020 7972 4418

Social Care Group 6 (W H)
Family Fund Trust (FFT)

Grant-in-aid UK-wide: £25.36 million (2000/01); £24.18 million (1999/2000)

The FFT provides grants to families with severely disabled children under the age of 16 who are being brought up in their own home. It funds items for which grants from other sources are not available (e.g. washing machines, driving lessons and holidays). It operates UK-wide and receives funding from all four UK health departments.

The Family Fund was established in 1973 by the then Secretary of State of Social Services in the wake of the Thalidomide tragedy and it was administered by the Joseph Rowntree Foundation in York on behalf of the government. The fund became an independent trust in 1996 with a cash-limited budget.

This grant is one of the department's Centrally Financed Services. The amount of the grant is determined annually and cash-limited dependent on need.

Contact: Ben Cole, Room 229 Tel: 020 7972 4128; Fax: 020 7972 4132

International Disability Action

Grant total: £84,847 (1999/2000)

These four grants, which are annually given, are made to support international disability action, e.g. international subscriptions, UK representation at conferences:

– *Disability Awareness in Action* (£40,847);
– *Royal Association for Disability & Rehabilitation* (£26,000);
– *British Council of Disabled People* (£8,000);
– *UK Disability Forum for Europe* (£10,000).

Contact: Joe Wand Tel: 020 7972 4217; Fax: 020 7972 4132

Shared Training Programme

Grant total: £100,000 (2000/01); £150,000 (1999/2000)

The department has, over a number of years, provided support for innovative staff training projects on important issues that affect people with learning disabilities. In 2000/01 the budget is being used to support the national learning disability strategy. The programme is concentrating on four policy areas:

- self-advocacy for adults with learning disabilities from minority ethnic communities;
- transition into employment – making connections with the Connexions initiative;
- support for older carers/families;
- housing options – the legalities and practicalities of people with learning disabilities having their own properties/tenancies.

The intention was to fund one project in each of these areas. Bids were called for by 21 July 2000. Allocations within this programme are subject to contract and are for a one year period.

Contact: Clive Marriot, Room 233 Tel: 020 7972 4492; Fax: 020 7972 4132

Public Health 1: Minority Ethnic Health Section (W H, Room 541)

Minority Ethnic Groups Health/Access to Health

Grant total: £739,000 (2000/01) This is the combined total of the three grant streams detailed below.

Funding is available for voluntary organisations, Health Authorities, NHS trusts, professional bodies and educational establishments to develop materials and projects to improve health and access to health services for all black and ethnic minority groups. Funding may be given for project work, the production of videos, guidance material, booklets, leaflets, and posters, or to organise conferences, seminars etc.

Grant may cover the full cost of the project or it may be a part contribution. Grants range in size from £1,000 to £40,000. Grants may be awarded for up to three years.

Voluntary organisations can apply for funding under three separate budgets.

Improving Access to Health Services for Ethnic Minorities
Grant total: £638,000 (2000/01)

This budget has two purposes:

- to improve access to health care for black and ethnic minority groups by funding the voluntary sector and other bodies to undertake work on inequalities, health, improving access and Saving Lives: Our Healthier Nation;
- to work with the royal colleges and professional bodies to support them to undertake work on diversity.

Some organisations funded under this scheme are listed below. Figures refer to grant awarded in the financial year 2000/01, although the project may be running for a longer period.

- *Council of British Pakistanis*, to produce a training pack about Safety and Accident Prevention for Older People from black and ethnic minority groups (£41,500);
- *London Sickle Cell Trust*, to develop good practice in schools and hospitals and in the homes of children suffering from sickle cell disease, and to develop practical advice and support to be disseminated nationally (£34,000);
- *Swaminarayan Hindu Mission*, to undertake health promotion and education in relation to coronary heart disease and stroke, screening and so on, among the Hindu community (£30,000);
- *East London Chinese Community Centre*, to undertake initiatives in areas such as advocacy, health visiting and counselling, and to disseminate results nationally (£20,000);
- *Cancer Black Care*, to produce a training pack for volunteers and health promotion facilitators (£15,000).

Health Promotion Budget: Haemoglobinopathy Campaign
Grant total: £150,000 (2000/01)

This budget exists to run the Haemoglobinopathy National Awareness Campaign, and funds two organisations: The Sickle Cell Society and the UK Thallasaemia Society.

Section 64: General Grants Scheme
Grant total: £101,500 (2000/01)

The Minority Ethnic Health Section administers a part of the Section 64 scheme (see also separate entry). Organisations funded under this budget are listed below. Again, figures refer to 2000/01 allocations from grants of a longer duration.

- *Iranian Association,* to provide services to improve access to health and health services for Iranian refugees (£30,000);
- *Ravidassia Community Centre,* to cover central administrative costs (£30,000);
- *Asian Health Agency,* to provide and promote community health care and health education among Asian communities (£29,000);
- *West Indian Standing Conference,* for capacity-building work with African-Caribbean organisations working with the elderly (£12,500).

Exclusions: Research projects.

Applications: Guidelines and criteria are available on request. Organisations must have or be in the process of producing an equal opportunities policy. Applications must have a built-in component for: pre-testing ideas; positive and measurable outcomes; national dissemination; evaluation and assessment. Applications must be submitted by November for grants commencing the following financial year.

Contact: Veena Bahl Tel: 020 7972 4671; Fax: 020 7972 4690

Public Health 3: Substance Misuse Branch (W H)
The Department of Health makes a number of grants to local authorities to assist them in making payments to voluntary organisations providing care and services for people who are, have been or are likely to become dependent upon alcohol or drugs.

'New' Specific Grant for Services to Drug Misusers

Grant total: £5 million (2000/01), £2 million of which was available for new bids.

The aims of the 'new' specific grant, which came into operation in 1999, are:

- to speed up and improve access to services for substance misusers;
- to support misusers in overcoming their problems and helping them to lead healthier, crime-free lives;
- to develop a coordinated and flexible service provision.

The above figure includes money for continuing projects and for new projects beginning in 2000.

From April 2001 the new National Treatment Agency will oversee provision of treatment for drug misusers. Administrative and financial arrangements are still to be agreed, but central funding streams are likely to be affected. Similar sums of money will be available overall but the process will probably be altered. Most bids are expected to be for no more than around £40,000, and awards do not exceed 90% of the total estimated costs of a project.

Contact: Kathryn Stelfox, Drug Misuse Team Tel: 020 7972 4563

'Old' Specific Grant for Services to Drug and Alcohol Misusers

Grant total: £1,780,000 (2000/01)

In the financial year 2000/01 this fund was given over entirely to two areas:

- services for rough sleepers in areas with a significant rough sleeping problem, as identified by the Rough Sleepers Unit (see separate entry);
- the Tyne and Wear Health Action Zone Demonstration Project.

It was expected that all of the approximately £962,000 available for new projects would be required by these services, and no new bids were therefore invited.

Contact: Mary Gegbe, Alcohol Misuse Team Tel: 020 7972 4859

Applications: For both the above schemes applications are made through local authorities who set local community care priorities and evaluate applications for projects from voluntary organisations in their area on that basis. Each local authority then submits a maximum of two new applications to the department, with the agreement of the voluntary organisation(s) concerned. Awards do not exceed 70% of the total estimated cost of a programme. New awards are made for a maximum of three years to any one project, but a voluntary organisation that has received funding for three years may submit a new bid for further funds in order to expand its services in a different direction.

Note that the coming into operation of the new National Treatment Agency may alter these arrangements in future.

Powers: Section 7E of the Local Authorities Social Services Act 1970 (inserted by Section 50 of the National Health Service and Community Care Act 1990).

Black and Minority Ethnic Anti-Drug Strategy Grants

Total funding: £500,000 (2000/01)

Drug misuse prevention, treatment and education services have often been designed without regard for the needs of black and minority ethnic communities. These grants are intended to redress the balance by involving black and minority ethnic community groups in the development and consolidation of practice and delivery of the national anti-drug strategy, 'Tackling Drugs to Build a Better Britain'. Groups were invited to apply to conduct local community needs assessments, so as to inform local Drug Action Teams. The process will be led by groups themselves, but additional support, guidance and training will be provided by the Ethnicity and Health Unit at the University of Central Lancashire. Applications were invited for both large and small-scale projects in the region of £5,000 to £25,000.

At the time of writing it was thought that this programme would not continue after June 2001. The application deadline was 11 December 2000 and work was scheduled to begin in January 2001. Applications were made to and processed by the Ethnicity and Health Unit of the University of Central Lancashire.

Contact: Ethnicity and Health Unit, University of Central Lancashire, Preston PR1 2HE; Tel: 01772 892 780; Fax: 01772 892 992

Website: drugs.gov.uk/ethniccommunity.htm

Public Health 4: Sexual Health Branch (WH)
HIV/AIDS and Sexual Health Grants

Grant total to voluntary sector: £2,500,000 (2000/01); £2,100,000 (1999/2000); £2,815,000 (1998/99)

National HIV/AIDS and sexual health promotion is undertaken by the statutory and voluntary sector. It supports the Secretary of State's objective 'to reduce the incidence of avoidable illness, disease and injury of the population'.

Planned expenditure for 1999/2000 was approximately £5.255 million of which 40% (£2.1 million) funded work by the voluntary sector through contracts with the department. This supports agreed priorities for HIV/AIDS prevention and sexual health promotion.

In 1999/2000 voluntary sector funding consisted of:

- Targeted health promotion work for gay and bisexual men through the Terrence Higgins Trust (£1.1 million in 1999/2000);
- Work in support of World AIDS day via a joint contract with the National AIDS Trust and the Health Education Authority (NAT received £100,000) – the department was planning to extend this contract for another year at the time of writing;
- Fpa (formerly the Family Planning Association) for work on contraceptive education (£900,000).

Work on sexual health and HIV strategy will inform contracts from 2002. The above funding is handled in a proactive and strategic manner and is not advertised. Voluntary organisations with their own funding proposals should approach the department's Section 64 programme (see separate entry).

Contact: Kay Orton, Room 406 Tel: 020 7972 4649; Fax: 020 7972 4646; E-mail: kay.orton@doh.gsi.gov.uk

Primary Care Division (R H): Dental and Optical Services
British Fluoridation Society

Grant-in-aid: £80,000 (2000/01); £78,000 (1999/2000)

Annual grant-in-aid for public education, public opinion surveys and research.

Contact: Jerry Read, Room 325 Tel: 020 7210 5743; Fax: 020 7210 5774

NHS Executive
Child Healthcare – Training Clinicians and Other Staff (W H)

Total budget: £75,000 annually

Grant total to voluntary organisations: £32,000 (1999/2000)

This budget is not restricted to applications from voluntary bodies, although applications from them are welcomed. Funds are mainly given on the basis of a detailed proposal which either directly delivers training for staff or develops new training methods.

In 1999/2000 three voluntary organisations were supported:

- *Contact a Family,* for the publication of an information resource on support groups for rare childhood conditions (£25,000);
- *Down's Syndrome Association,* for the development of a web-based educational resource for professionals (£3,500);
- *Tuberous Sclerosis Association,* for the production and distribution of a CD-ROM containing clinical guidelines (£3,525).

Contact: Noel Durkin, Room 511 Tel: 020 7972 4152; Fax: 020 7972 4663; E-mail: ndurkin@doh.gov.uk

Related Agency

Health Development Agency (formerly Health Education Authority)

Trevelyan House
30 Great Peter Street
London SW1P 2HW

Tel: 020 7222 5300
Fax: 020 7413 8900

Website: www.hda-online.org.uk

Contact: Tim Pemberton, Corporate Affairs Manager

The Health Development Agency replaced the Health Education Authority in April 2000. Its role is to raise standards in public health, through research, standard-setting and capacity development. The HDA will not carry out any public health education; this will now be done by a new agency, Health Promotion England. The old authority occasionally funded voluntary bodies for specific programmes. However, despite HDA's website saying that 'the community organisations we support include community groups, voluntary groups, community development project teams and Community Health Councils', the agency told us this support will not be financial. Similarly, Health Promotion England does not expect to fund any outside groups.

Home Office

50 Queen Anne's Gate **(Q A G)**
London SW1H 9AT

Tel: 020 7273 4000
Fax: 020 7273 2190

Horseferry House **(H H)**
Dean Ryle Street
London SW1P 2AW

Block A Whitgift Centre **(W C)**
Wellesley Road
Croydon CR9 2BY

Voyager House **(V H)**
30–32 Wellesley Road
Croydon CR9 2AD

Clive House **(C H)**
70 Petty France
London SW1H 9HD

Website: www.homeoffice.gov.uk

Contents

(Grant-in-aid in italics)

Related Agencies

The Home Office statement of purpose is to build a safe, just and tolerant society, in which the rights and responsibilities of individuals, families and communities are properly balanced, and the protection and security of the public are maintained.

It is also responsible for the special governmental unit, the Active Community Unit, concerned with developing community involvement and participation from all sectors in society. It is particularly concerned with the voluntary and community sector nationally. This unit advises government on this sector, conducts surveys of its health and vitality and also administers grant programmes to support it.

Active Community Unit (H H, Room 223)
Active Community Grants

Total funding: £21 million (2003/04); £20 million (2002/03); £18 million (2001/02)

Note: The closing date for applications for grants payable in the financial year 2001/02 was unusually late – at the end of January 2001. In subsequent years the deadlines are expected to be in the autumn.

The Active Community Unit (ACU) funds work which helps it to achieve its aims. Applications must be focused on one of the following two objectives.

Promoting increased voluntary and community involvement by:

- creating increased and diverse opportunities for volunteering or community involvement;
- making it easier for people to get involved;
- raising awareness of the importance and potential of voluntary and community involvement.

Supporting the development of active communities by:

- developing the capacity of local voluntary and community organisations;
- strengthening partnership with government;
- promoting the diversity of people involved in voluntary and community activity.

All applicants must include a strategy which explains how they will ensure that their services will reach, and are relevant to, black and minority ethnic organisations or individuals as appropriate. The success of this strategy will be monitored by the extent to which services are taken up by black and minority ethnic communities and the strategy should include how this will be measured.

Two types of grant are available.

Strategic Grants

These help with costs i.e. the everyday running expenses of an organisation (e.g. salaries, utility bills, rent, etc.). Such a grant is considered a strategic investment in the future activities of an organisation.

Project Grants

These help meet the costs of a distinct piece of work. The project may, or may not, relate to the core business of an organisation, but in all cases it will have an easily identifiable conclusion, for example, a publication or an event. When considering the size of grant needed, applicants should not forget that they might need to buy more furniture, computers or other goods and services to enable the project to be completed. The application should show these as costs of the project.

Capital grants are not on offer through this programme.

Grant criteria for 2001/02 are as follows.

Eligibility: Before applying all applicants should read the leaflet, 'Notes for Applicants', to check the criteria for grants and their eligibility. Strategic grant applicants must be national, generalist voluntary organisations which promote one or more of the Active Community Unit's objectives. Applicants whose existing strategic funding from the Active Community Unit ends on 31 March 2001 will be given priority over other applicants for strategic grants. 'National', in this context, means an organisation operating across England or across England plus any combination of Wales, Scotland or Northern Ireland. It is unlikely that an application for similar work recently rejected by one of the ACU's counterparts in Scotland, Wales or Northern Ireland would be supported by this grant programme. Project grant applicants can be local, regional or national organisations. Projects must:

- be innovative; and
- show how they will spread and disseminate good practice; and
- fit one of this year's themes (described below); and
- be of national significance.

'Innovative' means meeting new needs or tackling existing needs in a new way and not currently replicated in the sector.

'National significance' means an approach which has the potential to be replicated in a wide range of different areas of the country.

Joint applications for project grants will be given priority.

Project Themes for 2001/02: All applications for project grants must either support the Prime Minister's Challenges to increase voluntary and community involvement by:

- employees; or
- diversifying the volunteer base of voluntary organisations;

or develop active communities by:

- supporting black and minority ethnic led organisations; or
- promoting community self-help to combat social exclusion; or
- improving services that develop the capacity of local voluntary and community organisations.

Applicants for a Project Grant must say to which of these project themes their project relates (see application form).

Size of grants: The programme aims to support a wide range of organisations. Bids under £50,000 a year are, therefore, more likely to succeed than larger bids.

Applications: The closing date for applications was 31 January 2001. Announcements of grants will be made by 31 March 2001. If an application is successful, and routine checks prove satisfactory, a formal offer of grant is made which sets out the terms and conditions and also asks for information about internal financial controls. Subject to the satisfactory outcome of these enquiries, strategic grants will be paid from April 2001 and project grants as soon as possible thereafter.

Applicants are strongly advised, particularly if applying to the ACU for the first time, to discuss their ideas with the unit before completing the application form.

Contact: Applications must be made on the ACU's application form, available at the web address below, or from the Grants and Government Funding Policy Team, Active Community Unit, Home Office, Horseferry House (Room 223), Dean Ryle Street, London SW1P 2AW
Tel: 020 7217 8565; Fax: 020 7217 8572;
E-mail: public_enquiries.acu@homeoffice.gsi.gov.uk

Website (including access to the application form):
www.homeoffice.gov.uk/acu/acu.htm

Capital Modernisation Grants

Total funding: up to £7 million (to be spent over the three financial years beginning 1 April 2001)

Grant criteria – 2001/02:
Types of work funded: All applications must be projects which fit one or more of the following Project Themes.

To modernise the infrastructure for volunteering and community involvement by:

- developing high profile, volunteer agency sites; or
- co-locating and integrating volunteer agency services with other local organisations including other voluntary and community organisations; or
- modernising delivery of services using integrated information technology.

Applicants must say on the application form to which of these themes their project relates. All applicants must include a strategy which explains how they will ensure that their services will reach, and are relevant to, black and minority ethnic organisations or individuals as appropriate. The success of this strategy will be monitored by the extent to which services are taken up by black and minority ethnic communities and the strategy should include how this will be measured.

Types of grant available: Project grants are available. The greater part of a project proposal is expected to be for capital development activity.

'Capital development activity' means: modernising delivery of services through, for example, refurbishment of premises, IT hardware and software purchases, website construction and IT training development.

Eligibility: Before taking steps to apply for a grant, please read the leaflet, 'Notes for Applicants' to check the criteria and the eligibility of an organisation to apply to this Grant Programme. Local, regional and national voluntary organisations may apply. Joint applications will be given priority over applications from organisations applying alone; as will those that demonstrate commitment from local statutory funders.

Size of grant: The programme aims to support a wide range of organisations. As a rough guide, bids between £150,000 and £250,000 are more likely to succeed than larger bids.

Applications: Applications must reach the ACU by 30 April 2001. Announcements of successful applicants will be made in July 2001. If an application is successful, and routine checks prove satisfactory, a formal offer of grant is made which sets out the terms and conditions and also asks for information about internal financial controls.

It is unlikely that these grants will be paid before August 2001.

All applicants are strongly advised, particularly those applying for the first time, to discuss their ideas with the funding team before completing the application form.

Contact: Applications must be made on the ACU's application form, available at the web address below, or from the Grants and Government

Funding Policy Team, Active Community Unit, Home Office, Horseferry House (Room 223), Dean Ryle Street, London SW1P 2AW
Tel: 020 7217 8565; Fax: 020 7217 8572;
E-mail: public_enquiries.acu@homeoffice.gsi.gov.uk

Website (including access to the application form):
www.homeoffice.gov.uk/acu/acu.htm

Community Resource Fund

Total funding: £150,000 (2000/01 and in 1999/2000)

This fund is being managed for the Active Community Unit by Community Foundation Network and the Community Development Foundation. It may be extended for a third year to 2001/02.

Thirty small multiply-disadvantaged communities around England, in each of the nine regions, are taking part in a pilot to test the effectiveness of small funds for small or emerging community groups. The areas are mostly the size of electoral wards, or smaller. Many are pockets of extreme deprivation within affluent areas. The holders of the 30 Local Funds are all community foundations experienced in local grant making. Each received £5,000 to disburse before the end of December 2000. Small grants of up to £500, a sum deliberately below the National Lottery Charities Board minimum level, have been available for the development of new grassroots projects and the development of local solutions to local issues and needs.

Applications: Decisions were taken in the summer of 2000 on the precise location of local funding for year 2. If the scheme is extended to year 3 a similar timetable will operate in 2001 (decision on precise areas by end August, grant made in December).

For full details of these areas contact: The Community Foundation Network, 2 Plough Yard, Shoreditch High Street, London EC2A 3LP
Tel: 020 7422 8611; Fax: 020 7422 8616;
E-mail: network@communityfoundations.org.uk

Family Policy Unit (H H)
Family Support Grant

Total Funding: £7 million (1999/2000–2001/02)

Annual allocations: £3 million (2001/02); £3 million (2000/01); £1 million (1999/00)

This fund is to be extended beyond the initial three-year period. In addition two grants were also made for the three-year period to:

– *National Family and Parenting Institute* (£2 million);
– *Parentline Plus* (£1 million).

Both these organisations are also eligible to bid for project work.

Funds for work by voluntary organisations concerned with family relationships and parenting support work are available under three strands. Bids are assessed against criteria set out annually in a leaflet.

- **Strand A:** (20% of funding in 2001/02) Funding for national umbrella organisations in the family and parenting support sector. Grants are made to national organisations which support the work of organisations delivering frontline services through the provision of information, advice, representation, training, publications and development services as well as the publication and dissemination of research.
- **Strand B:** (30% of funding in 2001/02) For promotion of innovation and spreading of good practice. Grants are given for work that develops existing models of practice in new ways, develops innovative work or disseminates and rolls out effective models of parenting support practice.
- **Strand C:** (50% of funding in 2001/02) In order to focus on areas of work where there are gaps in provision, ministers select a theme each year. In 1999/2000 the theme was work with fathers, boys, and young men; in 2000/2001 it was parenting of teenagers; in 2001/02 it will be 'parenting in challenging circumstances'.

Up to 100% of a project's costs is given and there are no matched funding requirements. Maximum grant size is £50,000 a year. Grants were available for up to three years in year 1 and up to two years in year 2. Percentage allocations to strands B and C vary from year to year, in the light of demand, and the quality of bids received.

The allocation of £3 million for 2000/01 was given in 42 grants, 26 of which were receiving continued funding from the previous year. 'New' grants totalling £600,000 were made to 16 organisations.

Grants included:

– *Divert Trust* [†], a trust primarily concerned with crime prevention. Its parental support programme works with parents and young people to enable them together to find solutions to family conflict (£42,364).
– *Fathers Direct* [†], to establish a national network of agencies working, or planning to work with fathers, consisting of regional conferences, a newsletter and network for professionals (£50,000).
– *National Council for One Parent Families* [†], to set up a Lone Parent Helpline and supporting referral database with NFPI and Parentline Plus (£30,000).

- *Family Rights Group*, to identify the needs of grandparents who care for their grandchildren full-time (£34,284).
- *Family Welfare Association*, to set up a mentoring programme to support parents of boys and young men involving family members and friends (£49,040).
- *Child Psychotherapy Trust*, to set up a support service to provide family organisations with psychotherapy expertise on issues concerned with bringing up children and teenagers (£15,176).
- *Disability, Pregnancy & Parenthood International*, to establish a national centre supporting disabled parents and prospective parents, including a technological link providing easy access to advice and support (£49,739).
- *Newham Bengali Community Trust*, work with Bengali parents and their teenage children through schools looking at family relationship issues including forced marriages. The project will reach parents who have physical/mental impairments or those who have experienced domestic/racial violence (£50,000).
- *Trust for the Study of Adolescence*, two grants. To produce a video and supporting materials on parenting skills using acted out scenarios and live discussion by parents to draw out key issues and learning points and to join up all projects for parents of teenagers by the grant programme (£48,957).

[†] also supported for projects in the previous year.

Applications: New guidelines for funding beginning April 2001 were available in October 2000. The closing date was not fixed at the time of writing but should be at least eight weeks after the round opens. (2000/01 round materials were published in mid-October with the closing date end December 1999.) Announcements on successful applications will be made in March 2001.

Enquiries for grant leaflet and application pack: Tel: 020 7217 8545; Fax: 020 7217 8800. These are also available on:

Website: www.homeoffice.gov.uk

Advice on FSG applications: Virginia Burton Tel: 020 7217 8108; E-mail: VirginiaEsther.Burton@homeoffice.gsi.gov.uk; Dave Dwyer Tel: 020 7217 8373; E-mail: Dave.Dwyer@homeoffice.gsi.gov.uk Natalie Ford Tel: 020 7217 8557; E-mail: Natalie.Ford@homeoffice.gsi.gov.uk

Race Equality Unit (Q A G)
Connecting Communities: Funding for Race Equality

Total funding: £12 million, (over three years 2000/01–2002/03)

Four areas of support for projects in England, Scotland and Wales:

- community networks;
- opportunity schemes;
- towards more representative services;
- positive images.

Programme 1 – community networks

Community networks at local authority level will be funded to connect communities with service providers, policy-makers and funders. They will give minority ethnic communities a collective voice locally and encourage the sharing of expertise and good practice. In England these networks will connect to the government offices (GOs), the regional development agencies (RDAs), and the minority ethnic voluntary sector regional networks funded by the Active Community Unit of the Home Office. These interconnected structures will enable local groups to have a voice in regional and national policy formation. Applicants can apply for three-year funding for salaries and running costs, and capital costs such as IT equipment.

Programme 2 – opportunity schemes

Funding is available for schemes to benefit vulnerable, disadvantaged women and men. They may be gender-based to address the often different needs of women and men.

Opportunity schemes for women: These projects will provide women-only space where marginalised, disadvantaged women of all ages can have access to appropriate education, training, employment and enterprise opportunities.

Funded projects are required to have the following objectives, against which their success will be measured:

- to help women access skilled work, whether at home or in outside employment, or progress to further training or education;
- to provide counselling, mediation and other advice and support;
- to broaden the funding base of the programme;
- to link with similar schemes for the exchange of expertise and information.

(All age groups are eligible under this grant, but supplementary schooling for girls still attending statutory education is excluded.) Funding is available for salaries and running costs including childcare, some capital costs such as IT equipment, and costs relating to the recruitment training and work of the volunteers.

Opportunity schemes for men: Projects will provide services and support to young men aged between 15 and 25 years who are alienated and disengaged from active citizenship as a result of racism and negative stereotyping. Many of the potential beneficiaries of these projects may have experienced exclusion from school, either on a temporary or permanent basis, and are either long-term unemployed or in poorly-paid, unskilled work.

Funded projects are required to have the following objectives, against which their success will be measured:

- to help beneficiaries move into training, education or employment;
- to forge links with employers in the public and private sectors;
- to unlock additional and new funding for the project;
- to link with similar schemes in other parts of the country for the exchange of information and expertise.

Funding is available for salaries and running costs, some capital costs such as IT equipment and costs relating to mentoring programmes.

Programme 3 – support towards more representative services

This funding programme is designed to help build respect and confidence between people from minority ethnic communities and Home Office service providers. It is the beginning of a long-term programme to make the Home Office service areas fully representative of the communities they serve. Projects should have innovative approaches to four objectives. Since local areas will have different needs and priorities, the focus of individual projects is expected to vary and the emphasis will also vary on each of the following objectives:

- to increase the trust and confidence between communities and Home Office Services locally;
- to encourage members of minority ethnic communities to seek employment in local Home Office service areas;
- to assist members of minority ethnic communities throughout their application;
- to assist minority ethnic staff during their initial time once employed in a Home Office service area.

Funding would support a project worker/s, together with necessary administrative and ancillary back up.

Programme 4 – positive images

The objective of this funding is to publicise and celebrate the achievements of minority ethnic communities and individuals, and the positive contribution they have made, and are making to our society.

Likely activities:

- school-based projects;
- national or local award schemes;
- essay competitions for all ages.

Activities are expected to be one-off events or short-term projects. Festivals/conferences and cultural/sporting events are not eligible.

In October 2000 a total of 75 awards made over a three-year period were announced (out of the 876 applications).

Grants were allocated regionally in England as follows:

- *East Midlands* (5 projects totalling £543,207). The largest award was made to BUILD Nottingham Mentor Programme, to establish a cross-cultural network across Nottingham's city and county areas to bring all sections of the community together to celebrate and build on diversity (£182,225).
- *Eastern* (3 projects totalling £780,276). The largest award was made to Watford Race Equality Council, to work in partnership with four Home Office service areas for a project to raise understanding and confidence (£324,250).
- *London* (14 projects totalling £1,782,512). The largest award was made to Account3 Women's Consultancy Service, for an opportunity scheme to provide a women-only environment for women who feel disadvantaged and need help in the areas of training, employment and enterprise to improve their opportunities (£223,796).
- *North East* (5 projects totalling £663,429). The largest grant was made to Darlington & Durham County REC, to build an effective network, which will empower minority ethnic communities and individuals to have a greater access to, and influence over, policy makers and service providers (£210,887).
- *North West* (10 projects totalling £1,411,558). The largest award was made to Lancashire Council of Mosques, to raise awareness and understanding of the police service as a potential employer (£237,610).
- *South East* (5 projects totalling £881,238). The largest award was made to Reading Council for Racial Equality for a partnership between Reading REC and Royal Berkshire Fire and Rescue Service, seeking to make the latter more representative of the diverse ethnic communities in the area by enhancing their recruitment and involvement in the service (£248,086).

- *South West* (5 projects totalling £931,190). The largest award was made to Bristol Racial Equality Council, to increase representation of ME communities in the Home Office service areas by arranging open days, school visits, publicity through various media and providing information (£270,000).
- *West Midlands* (10 projects totalling £1,319,384). The largest award was made to Birmingham Race Action Partnership, to create a women's network to link women's organisations in the city together to identify and address problems, build up confidence and influence policy and service provision (£311,280).
- *Yorkshire and the Humber* (8 projects totalling £1,498,211). The largest award was to Bradford and District Minority Ethnic Communities Police Liaison Committee for a series of initiatives designed to improve trust and confidence between West Yorkshire Police and minority ethnic communities (£273,986).

Smaller grants were made to:
- *The Soft Touch Community Arts Co-op* in the East Midlands to celebrate its arts achievements (£12,307);
- *VOIS* for a borough-wide inter schools competition to debate racism and design a blueprint for a society of diverse communities (£68,735);
- *Toxteth Educational Trust*, to develop awareness, understanding and appreciation of different cultures in schoolchildren (£44,693);
- *Portsmouth Foyer*, for education, training and employment opportunities for disadvantaged Bengali women, as well as career advice and guidance (£97,290).

Applications: Full details about these four programmes should be obtained. The policy paper, application form and guidance notes are also available on the Home Office website (see address below, select 'Constitutional & Community Issues' then 'Race Equality'). The first deadline was at end July 2000, with results announced end September. Be sure to check for future deadlines.

Contact: The Communities Funding Team will be happy to help with enquiries:

Richard Brett Tel: 020 7273 3772;
E-mail: RichardJ.Brett@homeoffice.gsi.gov.uk

Also Rob Murphy Tel: 020 7273 3402; Peter Smyly Tel: 020 7273 2964; Bernice Alexander Tel: 020 7273 3548; Kathy Badhams Tel: 020 7273 3587; Henna Yazdani Tel: 020 7273 2417; Kimberley Bingham Tel: 020 7273 2719; Alex Fordyce Tel: 020 7273 4220; Fax: 020 7273 3771;
Head of Unit: Sara Marshall

Website: www.homeoffice.gov.uk

Immigration and Nationality Directorate: National Asylum Support Service

Refugee Integration and Voluntary Sector Coordination (V H)

Grant total: £16,904,000 (2000/01)

Grants are made to voluntary organisations to support the development of refugee self-help community groups, and to promote networking between refugee groups and other local agencies to improve their access to statutory services, and so contribute to their successful settlement in the UK.

By July 2000/01 seven national and regional refugee councils received grants ranging from £35,000 to £1,374,000 totalling £2,099,000. They were:

– *Refugee Council* (£1,374,000);
– *Refugee Action* (£550,000);
– *Scottish Refugee Council* (£35,000);
– *Welsh Refugee Council* (£35,000);
– *Midlands Refugee Council* (£35,000);
– *Northern Refugee Centre* (£35,000);
– *North of England Refugee Services* (£35,000).

A further grant was made to the Refugee Council Panel of Advisers for Unaccompanied Minors, to enable it to provide support for unaccompanied asylum seeking children (£805,000). These grants were under review and may be revised upwards later in the financial year.

The National Asylum Support Service (NASS)

This service was established in April 2000 within the Home Office with responsibility for providing support to destitute asylum seekers in the form of accommodation and vouchers while their asylum applications are considered. NASS provides additional funding by way of grant (£14 million in 2000/01) to the following key voluntary organisations to provide a reception service to newly arrived migrants and to develop a network of One Stop Services within the dispersal regions.

One Stop Services and Reception Services:

- **Refugee Council** – London North East, Yorkshire, Eastern Region and West Midlands;
- **Refugee Action** – North West, East Midlands, South Central and South West;
- **Migrant Helpline** – Kent and Sussex;
- **Welsh Refugee Council** – Wales;
- **Scottish Refugee Council** – Scotland.

Reception Services only:

- **Refugees Arrivals Projects** – London Airports;
- **NIACRO** – Northern Ireland.

Funding is given to those groups which are working with a national or regional remit. Emerging groups receiving this funding need first to be recognised by the National Refugee Forum, facilitated by the Refugee Council, which draws together existing refugee organisations to implement a national framework for assisting refugees.

Contacts: Rachael Reynolds, Head of Section Tel: 020 8633 0068; Ian Barton Tel: 020 8633 0069; Fax: 020 8633 0079

Website: www.homeoffice.gov.uk/ind/hpg.htm

Immigration Appeals and Asylum Seekers (W C, Block A)

Grant total: £18 million (2000/01); £6.6 million (1999/2000); £5.9 million (1998/99)

Discretionary grants can be made to organisations providing free advice and assistance to people with rights of appeal. Eligible organisations must be able to provide a comprehensive and nationwide service. Two independent organisations received core-funding grant-aid in 1999/2000. They were:

- *Refugee Legal Centre*, to help asylum seekers (£3.6 million);
- *Immigration Advisory Service*, to help people with immigration rights of appeal (£3 million).

Contact: Pam Culley Tel: 020 8760 3486; Fax: 020 8760 3128; E-mail: pam.culley@homeoffice.gsi.gov.uk

Website: www.homeoffice.gov.uk/ind/hpg.htm

Powers: Section 23, Immigration Act 1971; Section 81, Immigration and Asylum Act 1999

Probation Unit (Q A G)
Probation Unit Grants

Grant total: £2.8 million (budgeted) (2000/01); £3.4 million (1999/2000); £3.23 million (1998/99)

Direct grants are made to organisations concerned with the rehabilitation of offenders or support for those on bail. Assistance is given for projects or organisations that are national or serve a national purpose. Grants are also given as 'seed money' for innovative projects which support Home Office priorities. Funding is available for 100% of costs with no set minimum or maximum grant level.

Grants in the financial year 2000/01 were:

- *NACRO*, for: programme funding; Race Unit; Easy Accessible Service Information (EASI); Resettlement Information and Advice Service (RIAS); and Race and Criminal Justice Unit (£1,234,800);
- *SOVA*, for work with volunteers on offender resettlement (£285,750);
- *Langley House Trust*, for accommodation for the integration of offenders into the community (£982,800);
- *Payback*, for promoting community punishment (£30,000);
- *Prisoners Abroad*, for the aftercare of repatriated offenders (£121,500);
- *Venture Trust*, for outdoor activities (£50,000).

Applications: Organisations need to have contacted the unit by November for grants in the following year. There is no standard form, but applications should be well-structured and include clear summaries of the purpose/s for which the grant is sought, evidence of need, precise objectives, breakdowns of proposed expenditure, time-scales and information about how the applicant would 'demonstrate progress during the work and the achievements of objectives'.

Note: Individual probation boards are expected to spend 7% of their budgets on partnerships with voluntary and private sector organisations. Contact should be made direct with the local probation services.

Contacts: Michael Dewey, general partnership grants Tel: 020 7273 3278; Marcus Smart, Education, training and employment of offenders Tel: 020 7273 2874

Powers: Section 20 (1) (d) Probation Service Act 1993.

Voluntary-Managed Approved Hostels

Total grant: £3,823,000 (1999/2000)

In April 2000 there were 100 approved hostels (7 bail and 93 probation/bail). The majority are managed by probation services and 13 by voluntary organisations. Approved hostels are intended as a base from which residents take full advantage of community facilities for work, education, training, treatment and recreation. Funding comes from three different sources: 80% of the net running costs from Home Office revenue grant; the remaining 20% from the relevant local authority plus a contribution from the residents towards their accommodation costs. In 2003 this funding is likely to be transferred to the DETR's Supporting People programme (see separate entry). In 1999/2000 the grants to the 13 voluntary-managed hostels ranged between £271,800 and £346,400.

Contact: John Russell Tel: 020 7273 2786; Fax: 020 7273 3944

Powers: Sections 20(2)(b & c) Probation Service Act 1993

Justice and Victims Unit (Q A G)

Justice and Victims Unit (JVU) grant-in-aid in 1999/2000 was given to two organisations and represented about 80% of their total income.

Victim Support

Grant-in-aid: £17.5 million in 1999/2000 rising to £18.3 million in 2000/2001

An annual grant is made to Victim Support which provides practical help and emotional support to victims of crime and support for victims/witnesses in the Crown Court. About 10% goes towards the costs of the national office while the major part supports the work of local victim support groups.

SAMM (Support After Murder and Manslaughter)

Grant total: £100,000 in 1999/2000 and also in 2000/2001

An annual grant is also made to SAMM, a self-help organisation that provides support to the families and friends of homicide victims.

Contact: Richard Thew Tel: 020 7273 3368; Fax: 020 7273 2967

NACRO Mental Health Unit

Grant-in-aid: £196,054 (2000/01); £190,344 (1999/2000); £184,800 (1998/99)

The Mental Health Unit of NACRO (National Association for the Care and Resettlement of Offenders) has been funded since 1990, initially for a three-year pilot project, then for a rolling programme of work to promote effective local inter-agency arrangements for dealing with mentally disordered offenders. Funding of a further three-year programme of work has been agreed from 1998/99 which includes:

- project development work with local groups;
- providing training and advisory services, and guidance production of good practice.

Two other organisations also receive a non-statutory grant:

- *The Southside Partnership*, an organisation based at Brixton Prison that encourages 'befriending links' with prisoners with mental health and other needs (£25,000 in 1999/2000 and 2000/01);
- *The Revolving Doors Agency*, London, a similar organisation based in police stations and courts (£10,000 a year for three years from 2000/01).

Contact: Helen McKinnon Tel: 020 7273 3233; Fax: 020 7209 4130

Crime Reduction Unit (C H)
Reducing Burglary Initiative
Total funding to voluntary sector: £573,000 (2000/01)

The RBI is part of the Crime Reduction Programme, the government's three-year (1999/2000–2001/02) crusade against crime. The initiative works through local anti-burglary partnerships, generally led by the police with the involvement of local authorities. Crime Concern and NACRO each receive £286,500 per year for the duration of the initiative to act as an 'advice resource' for the partnerships.

Contact: Chris Downe Tel: 020 7271 8245

Crime Concern
Grant-in-aid: £750,000 annually (1999/2002)

Crime Concern, an independent crime prevention charitable company set up in 1988 and based in Swindon and London, receives core-funding on a three year basis from the Home Office. It is required to submit to the Home Office for a further three years' funding for the period 2002/2005.

Contact: Roger Pearson Tel: 020 7271 8642; Fax: 020 7271 8202

Action Against Drugs Unit
Drugs Prevention Advisory Service (H H)

The function of the Drugs Prevention Advisory Service (DPAS) is to strengthen society's resistance to drugs by supporting the delivery of the government's anti-drugs strategy through work at local, regional and national level. There are nine DPAS teams based in Government Offices for the Regions covering the whole of England. DPAS provides information, advice and support to local Drug Action Teams (DATs) – the bodies charged with local implementation of the national strategy – to encourage good practice in tackling drug misuse based on available and emerging evidence. DPAS fosters links with other government initiatives such as Crime and Disorder partnerships, Health Action Zones, New Deal for Communities, Connexions and other initiatives aimed at tackling social exclusion.

Demonstration Project Research Programme
Grant total: £1.9 million (2000/01)

DPAS is developing this programme in collaboration with DATs and other area-based partnerships, which may include voluntary sector organisations. This programme is designed to further knowledge about effective practice in a number of work areas. Grant funding for the programme is disbursed via the partnership organisations or their member agencies. Grant funding for work outside this programme is unlikely to be available. However, voluntary sector bodies that have robust proposals for evaluated work that will develop the national drugs strategy evidence base are welcome to make contact in case funding does become available.

Contact: General Enquiry line: 020 7217 8631;
E-mail: Public_Enquiry.dpas@homeoffice.gsi.gov.uk

Website: www.dpas.gov.uk

Corporate Management Unit (QAG): Research Development Statistics (RDS)
RDS Innovative Research Challenge Fund (Q A G)

Total funding: £200,000 (2000/01); £840,000 (1999/2000)

This fund exists to promote research that contributes directly to the Home Office's aims and purposes, which are, briefly:

- crime reduction;
- maintenance of public safety and good order;
- delivery of justice;
- prevention of terrorism and other threats to national security;
- effective execution of sentences;
- helping to build a fair and prosperous society;
- regulation of entry and settlement into the UK;
- reduction in the incidence of fire and related death, injury and damage.

Bids must be original and innovative, or address an area where gaps in knowledge currently exist.

Most successful bidders have been academic institutions, although voluntary organisations involved in crime research and prevention are welcome to apply. Projects generally last for around a year.

The fund's expenditure for 1999/2000 was for 23 projects; another £200,000 was earmarked for 2000/01 for further payments and a second strand of the competition. Note that it was likely, although not certain, that the fund would move on to a regular annual basis.

Applications: Bids are invited and applications processed in two stages. A short note outlining the project provides the basis for a shortlist. Those selected are then asked to draw up more detailed and properly costed proposals. The intention is that the fund will run on an annual basis with deadlines falling around the end of March each year.

Contact: Mark Greenhorn Tel: 020 7273 3067;
E-mail: mark.greenhorn@homeoffice.gsi.gov.uk

Related Agencies

H M Prison Service

Prison Service Headquarters
Cleland House (C H)
Page Street
London SW1P 4LN

Tel: 020 7317 3000
Fax: 020 7217 6635

Abell House (A H)
John Islip Street
London SW1P 4LH

Tel/Fax: see above

The Prison Service, an Executive Agency in the Home Office, is responsible for prison services in England and Wales. The Prison Service uses the voluntary sector in a number of roles. Some voluntary groups receive direct grant-in-aid from central government funds. These are detailed in the separate entries below. In addition, there are several hundred national and local voluntary and community organisations funded by individual prisons to carry out work ranging through education, drugs counselling, black prisoner support groups, support to foreign nationals, religious provision, providing visitors' centres, healthcare, and so on. The Prison Service was unable to quantify this spending precisely but estimated it to be 'several millions'.

In 2000/01, the service was developing a strategy for partnership with the voluntary and community sector, to reflect the government's 1998 compact with the voluntary sector. The strategy was expected to be ready by April 2001.

Prisoner Administration Group (C H)
National Association of Prison Visitors

Grant-in-aid: £11,000 (2000/01)

This body receives annual grant-in-aid for administrative purposes.

Boards of Visitors

Grant-in-aid: £1.5 million per year

Each prison has a Board of Visitors made up of members of the local community. Boards of Visitors are NDPBs, but members are volunteers and number some 1,750 across the UK. Boards are provided with funds from the Prison Service's Board of Visitors Secretariat for their members' travel and administration costs.

Contact: Glyn Jones, Prisoner Administration Group Tel: 020 7217 6398; Fax: 020 7217 6462

Prisoners Abroad

Grant-in-aid: £85,000 (2000/2001 and in 1999/2000)

An annual ongoing grant contributes towards the core costs of Prisoners Abroad. This charity works with British citizens detained overseas, their families in this country, and prisoners returning here, who have served custodial sentences abroad and have then been deported after their release from prison. There is no competitive funding system as this is the sole organisation working in this field.

Contact: Graham Wilkinson Tel: 020 7217 6732; Fax: 020 7217 6462

Regimes Policy Unit (A H)
NACRO Prisons Link Unit

Grant-in-aid: £226,000 (1999/2000 and in 1998/99)

NACRO Prisons Link Unit provides information and training on setting up and running housing and employment advice services for prisoners. All establishments are expected to have a pool of officers trained by the Prisons Link Unit. It has been fully funded since 1988 by the Prison Service.

NACRO Core Strategic Funding

Grant-in-aid: £175,000 (1999/2000 and in 1998/99)

Prison Service strategic funding for NACRO enables NACRO to contribute to the development and implementation of Prison Service policy. A work programme is agreed annually.

Contact: Elizabeth Barnard Tel: 020 7217 5086; Fax: 020 7217 5865

Voluntary Work by Offenders Pre-Release Scheme: Community Service Volunteers

Grant-in-aid: £150,000 (1999/2000); £150,000 (1998/99); £200,000 (1997/98)

This long-standing grant from the Young Offenders Group helps CSV to place offenders on a volunteer scheme for a period prior to their release.

Contact: Ron le Marechal Tel: 020 7127 5123; Fax: 020 7127 5227

Youth Justice Board for England and Wales

11 Carteret Street
London SW1H 9DL

Tel: 020 7271 3058
General enquiries: 020 7271 3010
Fax: 020 7271 3020

E-mail: yjb@gtnet.gov.uk
Website: www.youth-justice-board.gov.uk

Contact: Tom Burnham, Grants Manager

The Youth Justice Board (YJB) for England and Wales is a NDPB that exists to ensure the reform of the youth justice system. Its aims and objectives are:

- tackling delays in the youth justice system;
- confronting young people with the consequences of their offending;
- intervening to reduce the risk of re-offending;
- appropriate punishment;
- encouraging reparation to victims;
- reinforcing the responsibilities of parenting.

Development Fund

Total funding: £35,000,000 (2000/01); £30,000,000 (1999/2000)

The YJB administers a fund aimed at encouraging the development of innovation and good practice in fulfilling the statutory aim of the youth justice system, i.e. to prevent offending by young people. There were five rounds of grant awards for proposed projects in England and Wales. Rounds 1 and 3 were for bail supervision and support schemes; Round 2 was for 'intervention schemes'; Round 4 was mostly for IT, and Round 5 was for training, research and development. Bail supervision schemes are run exclusively by local authorities, but voluntary organisations are involved in all other areas. Of the 540 grants funded by the Development Fund, voluntary groups have set up and run around 80, and are involved as partners in a further 80.

The majority of voluntary sector involvement is in intervention projects, of which there are 263, at a cost of £35 million over three years (1999/2002). Intervention projects fall into the following categories:

- alcohol, drug and substance misuse;
- cognitive behaviour;
- education, training and employment;
- mentoring;
- parenting;
- prevention;
- restorative justice;
- the Youth Inclusion Programme, a £13 million initiative working with the 50 worst young offenders in each of the country's 47 worst crime 'hot spots'.

An example of each type of intervention scheme is listed below. The figure for YJB funding covers three years. The projects receive local partnership funding in addition to this sum.

- Alcohol, drug and substance misuse: *Tardis Youth Project* and *Lifeline West Yorkshire*, for contacting young people in their own environment and working with them on issues relating to their drug abuse (£224,250).
- Cognitive behaviour: *Barnardos North West*, for working with young people in Merseyside with abusive sexual behaviour patterns (£155,954).
- Education, training and employment: *INCLUDE*, for the Bridge Course, a course of work experience, education, vocational training, basic skills enhancement and personal and social development for at-risk 14–16 year-olds in County Durham (£148,501).
- Mentoring: *Waltham Forest YMCA*, for providing mentoring to young people aged 10–21 and already involved in the youth and criminal justice system (£136,719).
- Parenting: *Fostering New Links*, for providing support to the parents of 20 young people accommodated by Fostering New Links, a care service for traumatised young people aged 11–18 who are in the care of the local authority (£43,088).

— Prevention: *The Children's Society*, Bristol, for 'Right Track', a support service for black children and young people aged 10–17 who are involved in the criminal justice system, aimed at redressing the over-representation of black young people in the criminal justice system (£82,016).
— Restorative justice: *AMENDS*, for making available victim–offender mediation to young people engaged in the youth justice system in Enfield and Haringey (£283,000).
— Youth inclusion Programme: *Crime Concern*, for 'Youth Works Plus': projects in Southwark, Southampton, Hull, Cardiff, Wolverhampton, Birmingham, and London working with young people to promote their social inclusion. Methods include preventative, diversionary, remedial and community work, and skills development (£945,000 in total; £135,000 for each scheme).

In addition to these intervention projects, the YJB is funding the Children's Society with a grant of £1.8 million to widen the Remand Review project, aimed at avoiding the unnecessary use of custodial remands for young people.

Applications: All allocations of funding were made at the beginning of the 1999/2002 three-year cycle. When the cycle is finished, local funding sources will be used to sustain successful schemes. If the YJB is able to make further grants during 2001 and beyond, it will advertise the opportunity on its website (see address above) and will contact potential applicants direct, according to the type of funding available.

Alcohol Education and Research Council

Room 520
Clive House
Petty France
London SW1H 9HD

Tel: 020 7271 8379/8337
Fax: 020 7217 8877

E-mail: len.hay@aerc-sec.demon.co.uk
Website: www.aerc.org.uk

Contact: Leonard Hay

Grant total: £366,571 (1998/99)

The council, founded in 1981, administers the Alcohol Education and Research Fund, set up as a charitable foundation (number 284748) with assets from the former licensing compensation authorities. The fund finances projects within the UK concerned with education and research and for novel forms of help to those with drinking problems, including offenders. The fund may also be used to aid other charitable organisations having similar purposes. The council aims:

- to generate and disseminate research-based evidence to inform and influence policy and practice;
- to support appropriate innovative educational initiatives;
- through its studentship scheme, to contribute towards the formation of the next generation of academic researchers and to assist workers in the treatment field to provide a better service for their clients by enabling them to obtain appropriate qualifications.

The council's 15 members are appointed by the Home Secretary from a variety of professional and business backgrounds.

In 1998/99 the fund had assets of over £12.5 million with a gross income of over £532,300 from which grants of £366,571 were paid. The kinds of work it seeks to support include the following:

- researching socio-economic, culture and media influences on drinking;
- promoting public health and responsible drinking;
- understanding early drinking patterns among high-risk groups and providing advice and prevention projects;
- public education and effective cooperation between statutory and voluntary bodies.

Grants made in 1998/99 ranged from £10,000 to £32,728 and included:

– *Alcohol Concern* (£32,728);
– *Medical Council on Alcoholism* (£21,000).

The council will not normally fund bio-medical research projects or contribute to the running costs of organisations.

Applications: The council meets quarterly to consider applications and reports from grant holders. Applications are first assessed by independent assessors. All projects are expected to include proposals for monitoring progress, final evaluation and dissemination. Full details of the scheme, including application forms and a complete list of current grants, are contained in the council's website.

Commission for Racial Equality

Elliot House
10/12 Allington Street
London SW1E 5EH

Tel: 020 7828 7022
Fax: 020 7630 7605

Website: www.cre.gov.uk

Contact: Ken Grainger

Total funding to Racial Equality Councils: £5,109,000 (2000/01) of which grant-in-aid: £4,520,000; special funding: £589,000

The commission, which receives grant-in-aid from the Home Office, provides financial support to 96 Racial Equality Councils (RECs) around the UK, all of which are set up as registered charities. Grant-in-aid covers the employment costs of racial equality officers; special funding is for specific work in various areas. Funding is matched by contributions from local authorities for project and administrative costs.

Powers: Section 44 of the Race Relations Act

Lord Chancellor's Department

Lord Chancellor's Department
Selbourne House
54/60 Victoria Street
London SW1E 6QW

Tel: 020 7210 8500

Contents

(Grant-in-aid in italics)

Marriage and Relationship Support Branch
Funding for Marriage Relationship Support

Total grant: £3,643,205 (2000/01); £3,180,962 (1999/2000)

The government initiative to develop a new strategic approach to marriage support services is being led by the Lord Chancellor's Department, which is providing an extra £3 million spread over three years, 2000/01–2002/03. This will bring total funding to £5 million in 2002/03. Grant-in-aid is being provided to a number of voluntary organisations who provide the bulk of specialised marriage support.

The following bodies were funded in 2000/01:

– *Relate* (£2,284,585);
– *Tavistock Marital Studies Institute* (£484,361);
– *One Plus One* (£304,130);
– *Catholic Marriage Care* (£299,016);
– *London Marriage Guidance Council* (£100,000);
– *Jewish Marriage Council* (£48,313);
– *Family Welfare Association* (£62,800);
– *Parentline Plus* (£60,000).

Contact: Rukhsana Hussain, Room 516 Tel: 020 7210 1252; E-mail: rhussain@lcdhq.gsi.gov.uk

Related Agencies

Legal Services Commission (formerly the Legal Aid Board)

Planning and Partnership Development
85 Gray's Inn Road
London WC1X 8YX

Tel: 020 7759 1000
Fax: 020 7759 0548

Website: www.legalservices.gov.uk

The Legal Services Commission (LSC) is an executive non-departmental public body created under the Access to Justice Act 1999. It replaced the former Legal Aid Board in April 2000.

The Community Legal Service

This service was launched in April 2000 as part of the government's drive to increase justice for ordinary people. The CLS aims to ensure that everyone can get information and help about their legal rights and understand how to enforce them in the right place and at the right time.

The Community Legal Service Fund (CLS Fund)

The CLS Fund, which replaces the civil legal aid scheme, exists to help those people who meet certain eligibility rules and who cannot afford to pay for legal services. Financial contributions may be necessary in some circumstances. Organisations may be CLS partners but not be in receipt of funding from the CLS Fund. Such organisations may offer some or all of their services free. Others may charge. Fund supports legal services working under Legal Help contracts (broadly equivalent to the old green form scheme). By April 2001 only contracted suppliers will be funded by the LSC to deliver legal services at all levels including representation at court and in judicial reviews. Funding of non-profit organisations by way of contract is explained below.

Community Legal Service Partnerships (CLSP)

Community Legal Service Partnerships bring together those who fund legal and advice services (such as the Legal Services Commission, the local authority, local and national charities) with those who supply these services (both solicitors in private practice and non-profit advice agencies). Partnerships can also involve groups who represent the interests of users of legal and advice services, such as community groups. The job of partnerships is to assess the local need for legal services. They must also work together to ensure that the right kind of services are available to meet priority needs.

The CLSPs agree strategic plans which inform the funder members of the partnership in making their funding decisions, including the Legal Services Commission via their Regional Legal Services Committees. To ensure that the public has access to legal help and advice which is quality assured and of the right kind and at the right level, the CLS brings together organisations offering legal and advice services in local Referral Networks. These networks include solicitors, Citizens' Advice Bureaux, Law Centres, local authority services (including libraries), community centres, and a host of other organisations. The networks are organised and supported by the Community Legal Service Partnerships and members sign up to a Referral Protocol.

At the time of the launch of the CLS in April 2000, over 70 partnerships had been formed, covering more than a third of the population. The aim is to cover at least 90% of the population of England and Wales with a CLSP by March 2002. Outlines of two examples, as at spring 2000, follow.

Setting up a CLS partnership in Gloucestershire: The Gloucestershire Community Legal Service Partnership was set up in June 1999 as an 'Associate Pioneer' to explore ways of establishing the CLS and developing best practice for partnership-working. It was initially decided to focus on the Gloucester City Council areas, with the intention of bringing in the other five district councils and forming a county-wide partnership the following year. The approach was to build the partnership slowly, with the maximum consultation. For example, representatives of the voluntary sector met with the Advice Services Alliance, the national body representing non-profit advice centres, to discuss the CLS from their perspective before deciding to join the partnership. Terms of reference for the partnership were then drawn up for an initial CLSP membership of the Legal Services Commission for Gloucester City Council, Gloucestershire County Council, two solicitors from the Law Society, four representatives from the advice centres network, and a representative from the local Race Equality Council.

One of its first tasks was to survey and report on suppliers of advice within the partnership's boundaries. The mapping of need for legal services presented some difficulties because Gloucester City had already been defined as having 'high priority' need in all areas of social welfare law, based on the Commission's predictive needs model. As a result, it was decided to investigate contracting an independent researcher to look further at needs.

A 'Referrals Working Party' was set up to plan a directory of advice providers and draft a referrals protocol, and a training seminar was run for all the country's voluntary advice agencies, with a particular focus on the Quality Mark, the standard which now has to be achieved before getting a contract.

Following the initial work, the Legal Services Commission Regional Planning & Partnership consultant (based in the Bristol office) began approaching other district councils with a view to widening the partnership, meeting with various officers and giving a verbal briefing to a meeting of all the county chief executives.

Northumberland CLS Partnership and the 'Action Against Poverty' area initiative: There are two distinct parts to Northumberland: most of the county, particularly the north and west, is characterised by small isolated rural communities, while the south east is dominated by a number of urban communities previously dependent on coal mining and related industries. The Northumberland CLS Partnership was also set up as an 'Associate Pioneer'. Advice providers and funders groups have met regularly, a local needs analysis has been completed and a mapping exercise is underway. The advice providers group has agreed a referral protocol and a local directory of advice provision has been produced to support this development.

The funders group has been set up as a subgroup of the Northumberland Strategic Partnership, a body established with the purpose of overseeing and co-ordinating regeneration activities in the county. One initiative was the 'Action against Poverty' proposal, drawn up by a partnership of the Northumberland Health Action Zone, Northumberland County Council, the Distance Debt Unit (a Methods of Delivery pilot) and the Legal Services Commission. 'Action against Poverty' aims to provide support and advice for vulnerable individuals suffering health problems that may be linked to debt. Improving access to advice will be achieved by locating debt advisers within primary care settings throughout Northumberland. This will raise awareness of debt issues and advice provision amongst health and social care practitioners and enable them to refer individuals in need to debt advice. Ultimately, it is hoped that the projects will enable people to overcome the barriers to social inclusion created by debt and associated health problems. Funding for the project has been sought from the Northumberland HAZ, the National Lottery Charities Board and CLS. 'Action Against Poverty' was expected to be underway in September 2000.

Funding of Non-Profit Organisations by Contracts

Total funding in contracts: £226 million (2000/01) of which approximately £27.4 million in 340 contracts to non-profit organisations

Since April 2000, the Legal Services Commission has had responsibility for running two schemes – the civil scheme for funding civil cases as part of the CLS, and a separate scheme for funding criminal cases.

The commission is moving towards a fully contracted civil scheme whereby only those suppliers of legal services who have a contract with the commission will be able to receive money from the CLS Fund. In order to be awarded a contract, amongst other things, providers of legal services must demonstrate that they meet (or are working towards meeting) the standards set out in the CLS Quality Mark accreditation scheme.

The first step towards contracting has already been taken. From 1 January 2000 only those organisations with a contract with the commission have been able to give initial legal help (broadly equivalent to the old green form/Claim 10 scheme) in civil matters. This is extended for family and immigration cases (and for certain categories of Personal Injury which remain within the scope of the scheme) where contracts must be held to provide all levels of service to be funded from the CLS Fund (i.e. legal help through to full representation). The civil contracting scheme will be extended to cover all levels of service for all types of cases from 1 April 2001. Contracts with non-profit organisations are most typically in areas of social welfare law such as Debt, Employment, Housing, Immigration and Welfare Benefits. Most contracts are for one or two categories only, but some organisations, in particular law centres, cover a wider range.

Funding of Law Centres

Grant total: approximately £967,500 (2000/01)

Nine law centres (all but three in London) and the Law Centres Federation have received grants for the years 2000/01. These grants are separate from any other public funding claimed, either under a general civil contact or on a case by case basis. The grants range from £38,000 to £169,000 and include:

– *Law Centres Federation* (£69,000);
– *Tower Hamlets Law Centre* (£169,000);
– *Cardiff Law Centre* (£106,000);
– *Saltley & Nechells Law Centre* (£90,000).

In addition to this, all the law centres have been awarded a civil contract.

Contacts:
Non-profit contracts: Nishma Malde, Civil Contracting Team
Tel: 020 7404 5202

Law Centres/Advice Services Alliance: Barbara Holburn, Secretariat
Tel: 020 7759 1135

CLSPs: Regional Planning & Partnership teams in LSC's 12 regional offices in – London, Reading, Birmingham, Brighton, Bristol, Cambridge, Cardiff, Leeds, Liverpool, Manchester, Newcastle upon Tyne, Nottingham.

For further information about the CLS, CLSPs and local legal services:

Website: www.justask.org.uk

For further information about the LSC and the CLS Fund:

Website: www.legalservices.gov.uk

Powers: Access to Justice Act 1999

Department of Social Security

Adelphi
1–11 John Adam Street
London WC2N 6HT

Tel: 020 7962 8000
Website: www.dss.gov.uk

The department has a series of addresses with leading offices close to Parliament at:

Richmond House
79 Whitehall
London SW1A 2NS

The Adelphi address above is the one where funding relevant to this guide has been identified.

Contents

(Grant-in-aid in italics)

Disability and Carer Benefits
Increasing the Independence of Disabled People

Grant-in-aid: £139.2 million (2000/01)

Annual grants are made to the following organisations only for their work UK wide. Bids are not invited. Grants in 2000/01 are as follows.

Independent Living Funds (ILFs)

ILFs are designed to enable people to live independently in the community who would otherwise be unable to do so (£131.3 million for the UK excluding Northern Ireland).

Contact: Geraldine Darcy Tel: 020 7962 8869

Powers: Disability Grants Act 1993

Motability

A grant of £5.7 million was made to the Mobility Equipment Fund which funds the cost of vehicle adaptations, plus a £2.2 million grant for administration.

Contact: Julie Guthrie Tel: 020 7962 8788

Powers: Disability Grants Act 1993

BLESMA (Ex Servicemen's Limbless Association)

An annual allocation of £15,000 is made for administrative costs and grants to purchase specialist adaptations.

Contact: Colin Pike Tel: 020 7962 8062

Powers: Section 64 of the Health Services and Public Health Act 1968 and Section 5 of the National Health Service Act 1977

Department of Trade and Industry

1 Victoria Street **(V St)**
London SW1H OET

Tel: 020 7215 5000
Fax: 020 7222 2629

Level 2
St Mary's House **(M)**
c/o Moorfoot
Sheffield S1 4PQ

Website: www.dti.gov.uk

Contents

(Grant-in-aid in italics)

Consumer Affairs Directorate (V St)

Branch 1 grant total: £180,000 (2000/01); £170,000 (1999/2000)

Royal Society for the Prevention of Accidents (RoSPA)

RoSPA receives the entire Branch 1 grant above to fund Home and Safety Officers in England and Wales through its Home and Leisure Safety Division.

Contact: Jan Krefta Tel: 020 7215 6723; Fax: 0207 215 0357

Branch 3 grant total: about £33,000,000 (2000/01); £23,345,000 (1999/2000)

The Consumer Affairs Directorate sponsors bodies which represent the UK consumers' interests and promote consumer safety and is responsible for ensuring that they operate according to the terms and conditions of their funding.

Branch 3 (see total above) is responsible for funding official consumer bodies and also for ensuring that these bodies represent consumers effectively. It regularly funds nine organisations: the national consumer councils, the national industry consumer councils for gas, telecommunications and the Post Office and the two national CABx. The Post Office Users' Councils and the Gas Consumer Council were due to be replaced by new consumer councils with wider remits towards the end of 2000. Funding for 1999/2000 shows the major part of funding allocated to the National Association of Citizens' Advice Bureaux and Citizens' Advice Scotland (see below). In 2000/01, 55% of the Branch 3 figure above was due to be allocated to these two bodies.

National Association of Citizens' Advice Bureaux

Funding: £14,416,000

Citizens' Advice Scotland

Funding: £1,690,000

Contact: Robert Draper Tel: 020 7215 0317; Fax: 020 7222 6260

Powers: Section 20 of the 1980 Competition Act

Partnership at Work Fund (V St)

Total funding: £5 million over four years (1999/2000–2002/03)

This fund is concerned with:

- developing joint approaches to solving business problems;
- implementing change through the consultation and involvement of employees;
- emphasising shared culture and shared learning;
- helping to improve the balance between work and home;
- recognising the rights and responsibilities of both management and employees.

Partnership at Work is about developing better employment relations within the workplace, but is not about developing wider relationships between organisations.

The fund aims to make more organisations aware of the benefits of partnership by supporting projects to spread best partnership practice more widely. Support can be provided for up to 50% of the eligible costs of individual projects, up to a maximum of £50,000 per project. The remainder of the costs must be met from non-public sector sources. Projects to be supported generally come into four categories:

- projects that implement a culture change programme to introduce partnership within an individual workplace or across a particular sector;
- projects that foster partnership by addressing business issues facing the organisation, such as low productivity or high staff turnover;
- projects that address work/life balance issues and adopt a partnership approach towards the introduction of flexible working patterns and family-friendly policies in the workplace (see also separate entry on DfEE's Work-Life Balance Fund for funds available for consultancy on work-life balance issues);
- local, regional or national level dissemination projects that spread best practice in partnership.

Eligibility: Companies, business intermediaries including employer federations, trade unions and other employee representatives, trade associations, Business Links, Training and Enterprise Councils, public sector bodies and charities are all eligible to apply. Bids can come from an individual workplace submitting a project between the employer (or their representatives) and employees (or their representatives); a trade union working with the employer/employees; or a Business Link or TEC working with a business or organisation.

There is no set number or combination of partners. Eligible costs include personnel costs; overheads and office equipment; specialist advice or consultancy; development of training activity; dissemination costs; promotion and publicity material; and travel and subsistence. Capital costs, time spent by staff attending training, and costs for employing temporary staff to replace employees involved in project activities, are not eligible.

There were 35 successful bidders in the first round of the Partnership at Work Fund, announced in March 2000. Examples of some of the successful projects are given below.

– *The NCVO* is aiming to build partnership in the workplace within the voluntary sector with a project designed to help voluntary organisations overcome barriers to adopting partnership and new legislation. They are developing a range of tools in collaboration with unions to enable voluntary sectors to change employment relations culture.
– *The Family Welfare Association* is developing Heath and Safety issues with Unison in order to consolidate working relationships. It will share any resources that are produced with other voluntary organisations.
– *The Daycare Trust* with the Maternity Alliance and New Ways to Work is developing a programme of training and consultancy to promote a partnership approach to identifying policies and practice to support employees and employers in balancing priorities at work and home.

Applications: Government support is being made available in a series of calls over four years, although projects may continue after that date without public funding.

Contact: the Partnership Fund Helpline on 020 7215 6252; E-mail: partnership@dti.gsi.gov.uk

Website: www.dti.gov.uk/partnershipfund.

Social Inclusion Unit: Small Business Service (M)
Phoenix Fund

This £30 million fund, announced in November 1999, is intended to help boost entrepreneurship in deprived areas. It will provide support, advice and access to finance in areas where these resources are normally lacking. It has four elements as follows.

Mentoring
Total funding: £3 million over three years (2000/01, 2001/02, 2002/03)

The DTI has set up a pilot network of business mentors, the Business Volunteer Mentors Association (BVMA), modelled on the US Service

Corps of Retired Executives. The organisation is being developed and piloted by the National Federation of Enterprise Agencies (NFEA) and operates independently of government. The aim is to train 1,000 retired and volunteer business people to give advice and support to new enterprises in areas of high unemployment. The NFEA is a network of independent non-profit local enterprise agencies.

Contact: Alan Bretherton, National Federation of Enterprise Agencies Tel/fax: 01234 354 055; E-mail: alan.bretherton@nfea.demon.co.uk

Challenge Fund

Total funding: £12 million over three years (2000/01, 2001/02, 2002/03)

This fund will help finance Community Finance Initiatives (CFIs), which are generally local non-profit organisations who lend small amounts of money to businesses that have been turned down by the banks. They can take diverse forms, from community loan funds and micro-credit initiatives to social funds, credit unions and so on. Around £3 million is being made available in the first bidding round.

Eligibility: To be eligible a CFI must promote the social inclusion of disadvantaged groups through encouraging entrepreneurship by providing finance to start-up or existing businesses and/or social enterprises. It must be a non-profit organisation and be able to demonstrate the necessity of Phoenix Fund support. Support from the fund does not exclude other forms of government funding.

The CFI must be a provider of finance of last resort and it is expected that it will be receiving a commercial rate of return from its customers.

Applications: Invited each year and closing dates will be announced at least three months in advance.

Contact: Andrew Moore, Small Business Service Tel: 0114 259 7422; Fax: 0114 259 7316; E-mail: andrew.moore@sbs.gsi.gov.uk

Development Fund

Total funding: £12.6 million over three years (2000/01, 2001/02, 2002/03)

The Development Fund is designed to encourage innovative ideas to promote and support enterprise in disadvantaged areas and in groups currently under-represented in terms of business ownership. Its purpose is to encourage experimentation, the evaluation of new ideas and the identification and spread of best practice. The fund is looking to support a limited number of high quality projects to help inform this process. The following list gives an indication of the sort of proposals that might be considered:

- outreach workers to encourage and develop business opportunities in hard-to-reach communities;
- supporting business incubators;
- promoting networking opportunities amongst businesses;
- funding individual 'enterprise champion' posts in local areas;
- building the capacity of local communities to encourage enterprise through professional training and development;
- encouraging the use of new technologies to improve business efficiency;
- local enterprise award schemes;
- support for social and community enterprises.

Eligibility: Organisations bidding for funds must demonstrate that their proposals: target specific areas or groups which are either disadvantaged or under-represented; are innovative; contribute to the development of best practice; support commercially viable businesses, or businesses with the potential to be viable; include measurable outcomes that encourage enterprise; and contain an effective strategy for disseminating best practice.

Organisations bidding for support may help either start-ups (enterprises in either their pre-trading or very early trading stage), or existing enterprises, but both must be small or medium-sized. Assisted businesses could be social enterprises or businesses with a purely economic purpose. Funding can be used to lever in other government or EU support.

Applications: Applicants may seek funding for a single year or for staged projects running over the three-year period of the fund. The application deadline for the first round of the fund was 31 October 2000; second and third rounds will be announced via the SBS website in early and late 2001.

Contact: Maria Kenyon, Small Business Service Tel: 0114 259 7453; Fax: 0114 259 7330; E-mail: maria.kenyon@sbs.gsi.gov.uk

Loan guarantees
To encourage commercial and charitable lending to CFIs.

Website: www.businessadviceonline.org/press/phoenix.asp

Related Agency

Business Links

Tel: Business Link Signpost Number 0845 756 7765
Websites: www.businesslink.co.uk
www.businessadviceonline.org

A national network of 45 Business Link advice centres provides help for all sizes of business, whether starting up or looking to expand. It provides business advice and puts enquirers in touch with the sources of funding support within a specific area. These vary, with different combinations of organisations and different funding opportunities from area to area. Some Business Link offices may themselves have funding to support particular kinds of initiative.

Regional Section

Area-based Initiatives, Central Government Initiatives and Funding

This section (including area-based and other initiatives) offers information to assist organisations in dealing with the effects of regionalisation and contacting the voluntary sector networks which have developed to address this challenge.

In addition it includes special government initiatives to tackle different kinds of social exclusion and deprivation. Many are based in selected areas throughout England and most involve 'partnership' working with the full range of agencies, public, private and voluntary, which have an interest in combating these problems. Voluntary and community groups new to such partnerships are strongly advised to read the article *Making Partnerships Work*, which is reprinted on pages 27–40 of this guide.

Also included are central government department funding schemes directed at local voluntary and community groups within selected locations, and the funding programmes of the metropolitan associations.

Contents

Related Funding
See **Department for Education and Employment:** Learning and Skills
Council

See **Department of Trade and Industry:** Business Links

Regional Development Agencies (RDAs)

A Regional Coordination Unit (see separate entry) coordinates the government regional initiatives and is responsible for the staff in the nine regional offices.

Regional Development Agencies (RDAs) were formally launched in eight English regions in April 1999. The ninth, in London, was set up in July 2000 following the establishment of the Greater London Authority (GLA). They aim to coordinate regional economic development and regeneration, enable the English regions to improve their relative competitiveness and reduce the imbalances that exists within and between regions. They have five core areas of statutory responsibility:

- economic development and regeneration;
- competitiveness, business support and investment;
- skills;
- employment;
- sustainable development.

Their specific functions are:

- formulating a regional strategy in relation to their purposes;
- regional regeneration;
- taking forward the government's competitiveness agenda in the regions;
- taking the lead on regional inward investment;
- developing a regional Skills Action Plan to ensure that skills training matches the needs of the labour market;
- a leading role on European funding.

RDA boundaries: They have the same boundaries as the Government Offices for the Regions.

Composition of boards, appointment of chairs and board members: The boards of the RDAs are business-led, with other board members reflecting regional interests, such as the voluntary sector, rural areas, and tourism, and will include four local authority members out of a total of 13.

Regional Chambers or Assemblies: The terms 'Chamber' and 'Assembly' tend to be used interchangeably and refer to either of two different forms of regional association in the non-London regions. This can cause confusion! They are either:

- designated by government – these bring together elected representatives from local authorities (70%) and other regional partners, including the voluntary sector (30%). Each RDA is required to have regard to the regional viewpoint of this association in preparation of its economic development strategy, consult it on its corporate plan, and be open to scrutiny by it. Their powers are indirect and imprecise and their role seems to be advisory and precautionary. No funding has been made available for these associations which depend on support from their member organisations and sectors (see separate entry for full address list of these regional chambers); or

- organised by local authorities – these are groupings of local authorities which have developed in some regions and which are also known either as chambers or assemblies. Some of them work together with the designated associations.

The Greater London Authority (GLA) and the London Development Agency

The situation in Greater London has been more complicated and extended. Here a whole new strategic body of government and democratic system has been developed. Since May 2000 the Greater London Authority has been led by an elected Mayor and Assembly. It coordinates and funds many basic services – the London Development Agency, Transport for London, the Metropolitan Police Authority, London Fire and the Emergency Planning Services. The GLA has also absorbed the London Planning Advisory Committee, the London Ecology Unit and the London Research Centre.

The London Development Agency is responsible for the economic and regeneration strategy for London as with other RDAs but with no specific mention of responsibility for environmental sustainablity (there are particular arrangements with the Mayor and the Assembly for this in London).

Website: www.London-decides.detr.gov.uk

Regional Economic Strategies (RES)

All RDAs have been required to produce a strategy, the fundamental purpose of these is to 'improve economic performance and enhance the region's competitiveness'. The guidance from the DETR made it clear that the strategy should give an integrated and sustainable approach to regional economic issues and address the underlying problems of unemployment, skills shortages, inequalities, social exclusion and physical decay. The RDAs are also expected to identify 'key partners' to help in the delivery of their action plans and the DETR guidance made it clear that these partners were expected to include the voluntary sector. A report by the National Council for Voluntary Organisations, *Regionalism: a commentary on relationships*, published in June 2000, points to the key areas where voluntary and community organisations should promote an understanding of the contribution they can make:

- 'as a major economic player (charities provide the equivalent of more than 350,000 full time jobs and are worth almost £5 billion to the UK economy);
- increasing skills (through the provision of volunteering opportunities and as a provider of training);
- supporting social inclusion (by providing services for or giving a voice to people from deprived or vulnerable communities, or by providing support to communities or individuals to enable them to take action themselves;
- promoting understanding of and mechanisms to increase sustainability (in particular, voluntary organisations in the environmental sector are good at ensuring that environmental concerns are taken into account when developing economic strategy);
- by sharing the local knowledge they have.'

Regional networks of voluntary and community organisations have been formed to address these new challenges (see separate listing).

RDA Contact Details for agencies/offfices are available:

Website: www.local-regions.detr.gov.uk/rda/info

(The information below is as at end January 2000.)

One NorthEast
Great North House, Sandyford Road, Newcastle upon Tyne NE1 8ND
Tel: 0191 261 2000; Fax: 0191 232 9069
E-mail: Enquiries-greatnorthhouse@onenortheast.co.uk
Website: www.onenortheast.co.uk

North West Development Agency
PO Box 37, Kings Court, Scotland Road, Warrington WA1 2FR
Tel: 01925 400 100; Fax: 01925 400 400
E-mail: information@nwda.co.uk

Lancaster House, Mercury Court, Tithebarn Street, Liverpool L2 2QP
Tel: 0151 236 3663; Fax: 0151 236 3731
Website: www.nwda.co.uk

Yorkshire Forward
Victoria House, 2 Victoria Place, Leeds, LS11 5AE
Tel: 0113 394 9600; Fax: 0113 243 1088
E-mail: skills@yorkshire-forward.com
Website: www.yorkshire-forward.com

ADVANTAGE (West Midlands)
2 Priestley Wharf, Holt Street, Aston Science Park, Birmingham B7 4BZ
Tel: 0121 380 3500; Fax: 0121 380 3501

E-mail: messages@advantagewm.co.uk
Website: www.advantage-westmidlands.co.uk

east midlands development agency,
Apex Court, City Link, Nottingham, NG2 4LA
Tel: 0115 988 8300; Fax: 0115 853 3666
E-mail: info@emda.org.uk
Website : www.emda.org.uk

East of England Development Agency
Compass House, Chivers Way, Histon, Cambridge CB4 9ZR
Tel: 01223 713 900; Fax: 01223 713 940
E-mail: knowledge@eeda.org.uk
Website: www.eeda.org.uk

South West of England Regional Development Agency
Sterling House, Dix's Field, Exeter EX1 1QA
Tel: 01392 214 747; Fax: 01392 214 848
Website: www.southwestengland.co.uk

SEEDA
Cross Lanes, Guildford, GU1 1YA
Tel: 01483 484 226; Fax: 01483 484 247
E-mail: info@seeda.co.uk
Website: www.seeda.co.uk

London Development Agency
Romney House, 28 Marsham Street, London SW1 3PY
Tel: 020 7983 4800; Fax: 020 7983 4801
Website: www.london.gov.uk

Regional Chambers/Assemblies

Regional Chambers/Assemblies	Regional Development Agency
East Midlands Regional Assembly	East Midlands Development Agency
East of England Regional Assembly	East of England Development Agency
North West Regional Assembly	North West Development Agency
North East Regional Assembly	One North East
South West Regional Chamber	South West of England Regional Development Agency
South East England Regional Assembly	South East England Development Agency
West Midlands Regional Chamber	Advantage West Midlands
Regional Chamber for Yorkshire and Humberside	Yorkshire Forward

Addresses for Regional Chambers/Assemblies

East Midlands Regional Chamber
Chair: Councillor Robert Jones
Derby City Council, The Council House, Corporation Street, Derby
DE1 2FS
Tel: 01332 258449

East of England Regional Assembly
Chair: Councillor John Kent
East of England Local Government Conference, Flempton House,
Flempton, Bury St Edmunds, Suffolk IP28 6EG
Tel: 01284 728 151; Fax: 01284 728 144

North East Regional Assembly
Chair: Councillor Mike Davey
North of England Assembly, Guildhall, Quayside, Newcastle upon Tyne
NE1 3A
Tel: 0191 261 7388

North West Regional Chamber
Chair: Councillor Derek Bateman
Leader of the Assembly: Councillor Frank McKenna Co-op Business
Centre, 4th Floor, 1 Dorning Street, Wigan WN1 1HR
Tel: 01942 737912

South East England Regional Assembly
Chair: Councillor David Shakespere
South East England Regional Assembly, Bridge House, 1 Walnut Tree
Close, Guildford, Surrey GU1 4GA
Tel: 01483 882310; E-mail: secretariat@southeast-ra.gov.uk

South West Regional Chamber
Chair: Councillor Chester Long
Exeter City Council, Civic Centre, Paris Street, Exeter EX1 1JN
Tel: 01823 355509

West Midlands Regional Chamber
Chair: Councillor Colin Beardwood
West Midlands Local Government Association, Lombard House,
145 Great George Street, Birmingham B3 3LS
Tel: 0121 678 1010

Regional Chamber for Yorkshire and Humberside
Chair: Councillor David Ashton
Leader of the Assembly: Peter Box
County Hall, Bond Street, Wakefield, West Yorkshire WF1 2QW
Tel: 01924 306985; Fax: 01924 306767

Regional Coordination Unit

Riverwalk House
157–161 Millbank
London SW1P 4RR

Tel: 020 7217 3595
Fax: 020 7217 3590
Website: www.go-region.gov.uk

In the action plan, *Reaching Out: The Role of Central Government at Regional and Local Level*, published in autumn 2000, the Regional Co-ordination Unit (RCU) identified four key areas where government needs to take a new approach to developing and implementing regional policy.

- Better coordination of area-based initiatives. Policies and programmes aimed at specific areas have made a real difference, particularly in deprived neighbourhoods. But many of them overlap and make competing demands on local partners. By linking up initiatives and simplifying their management structures, it should be possible to make them more effective.
- Government Offices need to be involved more directly in policy making. Too many policies are developed in the centre without reference to experience and expertise at regional and local level. Government Offices (GOs) have a valuable regional perspective to bring to policy making. They should have more opportunity to get involved and contribute.
- Government Offices need to be the key representatives of Government in the regions. GOs have historically served three Whitehall departments – DTI, DfEE and DETR – with only limited involvement from other departments. Many other departments have their own regional structures. This is confusing. Government at regional level needs to be rationalised and simplified.
- RCU as a unified head office for the Government Offices. The unit will work as the single reference point for managing the GOs and setting their objectives; and a simple way for the GOs to get their views across in Whitehall. (Each of the GOs' three parent departments has managed its contribution separately.)

The action plan, *Reaching Out: The Role of Central Government at Regional and Local Level*, can be accessed via:

Website: www.government-offices.gov.uk

Government Offices for the Regions

Government Office for the East of England
Heron House, 49–53 Goldington Road, Bedford MK40 3LL
Tel: 01234 796332; Fax: 01234 276252

Victory House, Vision Park, Histon, Cambridge CB4 4ZR
Tel: 01223 346700; Fax: 01223 202020

Building A DTI, Westbrook Centre, Milton Road, Cambridge CB4 1Y
Tel: 01223 346700; Fax: 01223 346701

Website: www.go-east.gov.uk

Government Office for the East Midlands
The Belgrave Centre, Stanley Place, Talbot Street, Nottingham NG1 5GG
Tel: 0115 971 9971: Fax: 0115 971 2404
Website: go-em.gov.uk

Government Office for London
Riverwalk House, 157–161 Millbank, London SW1P 4RR
Tel: 020 7217 3456; Fax: 020 7217 3450
Website: www.go-london.gov.uk

Government Office for the North East (GONE)
Wellbar House, Gallowgate, Newcastle upon Tyne NE1 4TD
Tel: 0191 202 3300; Fax: 0191 202 3744
Website: www.go-ne.gov.uk

Government Office for the North West
Sunley Tower, Piccadilly Plaza, Manchester M1 4BE
Tel: 0161 952 4000; Fax: 0161 952 4099

Washington House, New Bailey Street, Manchester M3 5ER
Tel: 0161 952 4000; Fax: 0161 952 4169

Lancaster House, Mercury Court, Tithebarn Street, Liverpool L2 2QP
Tel: 0151 236 3663; Fax: 0151 236 3731

Website: www.go-nw.gov.uk

Government Office for the South East
Bridge House, 1 Walnut Tree Close, Guildford, Surrey GU1 4GA
Tel: 01483 882255; Fax: 01483 882259
Website: www.go-se.gov.uk

Government Office for the South West
The Pithay, Bristol, BS1 2PB
Tel: 0117 900 1700; Fax: 0117 900 1900

Mast House, Shepherds Wharf, 24 Sutton Road, Plymouth PL4 OHJ
Tel: 01752 635000: Tel: 01752 227647

Prosper House, Cardrew Industrial Estate, Redruth, Cornwall TR15 ITH
01209 312622; Fax: 01209 312628
Website: gosw.gov.uk/gosw

Government Office for the West Midlands
77 Paradise Circus, Queensway, Birmingham B1 2DT
Tel: 0121 212 5050; Fax: 0121 212 1010
Website: www.go-wm.gov.uk

Government Office for the Yorkshire and the Humber
City House, New Station Lane, Leeds LS1 4US
Tel: 0113 280 0600; Fax: 0113 283 6394
Website: www.goyh.gov.uk

Voluntary Sector Regional Networks

These networks are developing to address and mirror the new Regional
Development Agencies and Regional Chambers. At the time of compiling
this guide some under-represented and overlapping areas were apparent.
Changes will inevitably occur.

The Regional Voluntary Sector Networks Forum has been created to help
the sharing of information and experiences within different RDA areas
and to provide a nationwide voice. The individual regional networks are
listed below. The networks were still in early stages of development at the
time of writing and changes are therefore likely to occur.

The National Council for Voluntary Organisations (NCVO) provides
information and support to voluntary organisations working within the
regional agenda on its website (see below). The NCVO also has a 'Regions
Network' which you can join via the website.

Website: www.voluntaryorganisations-regions.org.uk

East Midlands Voluntary Sector Forum
Engage East Midlands, 7 Mansfield Road, Nottingham NG1 3FB
Tel: 0115 934 8471; Fax: 0115 934 8440;
E-Mail: emvsf@hotmail.com
Contact: Wynne Garrett

Eastern
COVER, Centre 4A, Gonville Place, Cambridge CB1 1LY
Tel: 01223 471 682; Fax: 01223 471 683;
E-mail: andrew.cogan@cover-east.org.uk
Contact: Andrew Cogan

London Region
Third Sector Alliance, c/o London Voluntary Service Council,
356 Holloway Road, London N7 6PA
Tel: 020 7700 8124; Fax: 020 7700 8108; E-mail: 3sa@lvsc.org.uk
Contact: Dinah Cox

North East
Voluntary Organisations Network North East (VONNE), 9th Floor Cale
Cross House, 156 Pilgrim Street, Newcastle upon Tyne NE1 6SU,
Tel: 0191 233 2000; Fax: 0191 222 1998; E-mail: vonne@vonne.co.uk;
Website: www.vonne.co.uk
Director: Ray Cowell

North West
Voluntary Sector North West, c/o Greater Manchester Centre for
Voluntary Organisations, St Thomas Centre, Ardwick Green North,
Manchester M12 6FZ
Tel: 0161 273 7451; Fax: 0161 273 8296; Website: www.netc.org.uk
Chief Executive: Gil Chimon

South East
RAISE, Berkeley House, Cross Lanes, Guildford GU11UN
Tel: 01483 500 770; Fax: 01483 574 439;
E-mail: rob@raise-networks.org.uk
Chief Executive: Rob Woolley

South West Forum
c/o Community Council of Devon, County Hall, Topsham Road, Exeter
EX2 4QB
Tel: 01392 382822; Fax: 01392 382258;
E-mail: admin@southwestforum.org.uk
Chief Executive: Stephen Woolett

West Midlands
Regional Action West Midlands, 4th Floor, Daimler House, Paradise
Circus, Queensway, Birmingham B1 2BJ
Tel: 0121 616 4720; Fax: 0121 616 4728; E-mail: rawm@rawm.co.uk
Chief Executive: Chris Bonnard

Yorkshire & the Humber
Yorkshire/Humberside Regional Voluntary Sector Forum, 3rd Floor
Goodbard House, 15 Infirmary Street, Leeds LS1 2JS
Tel: 0113 243 8188; Fax: 0113 243 5446;
E-mail: office@yhregforum.org.uk Website: www.yhregforum.org.uk
Chief Executive: Helen Thomson

Black and Minority Ethnic Regional Networks

The Active Community Unit of the Home Office has been supporting the development of these new networks. At the time of writing it was only possible in certain cases to list the bodies which, for an interim period, are financially accountable whilst the new organisations are in the process of being established.

London

Council for Ethnic Minority Voluntary Sector Organisations (CEMVO), 9 Artillery Lane, London E1 7LP, Tel: 020 7377 8484
Contact: Krishna Sarda, Chief Executive
accountable body for

MiNet, The Leathermarket, 2.2 Lafone House, Weston Street, London SE1 3HN, Tel/fax: 020 7378 0380 E-mail: minet@ukonline.co.uk
Contacts: Wendy Irwin; Paulette Haughton

East

Cambridge Ethnic Community Forum, 99 Victoria Road, Cambridge CB4 3B7, Tel: 01223 315 877/355 034
Contacts: Bryn Hazel; Margo Moore, Network Co-ordinator

East Midlands

East Midlands Black and Minorities Voluntary Sector Forum, c/o Nottingham Community College, Carlton Road, Nottingham NG3 2NR, Tel: 0115 910 1455; Mobile: 0850 000914; Fax: 0115 9799 525
Contact: Mr Hassan Ahmed, Chair

North East

BmeCon (Black and minority ethnic Community Organisation Network), c/o VONNE, 9th Floor, Cale Cross House, 156 Pilgrim Street, Newcastle upon Tyne NE1 6SU, Tel: 0191 233 2000; Fax: 0191 22 1998;
E-mail: vonne@vonne.co.uk Website: lou.evan-wong@virgin.net
Contact: Louise Evan-Wong

North West

Black and Ethnic Minority Voluntary Forum Forward North West, c/o Progress Trust, 3rd Floor, Barclay House, 35 Whitworth Street West, Manchester M1 5NG, Tel: 0161 906 0020; Fax: 0161 952 4365
Contact: Abdul Malik Ahad, Development Officer

South East

The Asian Health Agency, 49 Queen Caroline Street, London W6 9QH, Tel: 020 8748 5769
Contact: Mr Balraj Purewal

South West
Black South West Network, Black Development Agency, Area Community
Resource Office, 5 Russell Town Avenue, Redfield, Bristol BS5 9LT,
Tel: 0117 939 6645; Fax: 0117 939 6646;
E-mail: ariafhussain@bswn.fsnet.co.uk
Contact: Ariaf Hussain, Project Manager

West Midlands
Black Regeneration Network, EMBRACE, Cheltenham House, 2nd Floor,
14 Temple Street, Birmingham B2 5BG, Tel: 0121 616 1881
Contact: Owen McFarlane, Network Co-ordinator

Yorkshire and Humberside
Details not available.

Single Regeneration Budget

Important note: 2001/02 is the last year for the Single Regeneration
Budget (SRB). Its funding will be included in the Regional Development
Agencies 'single funding pot' from 2002 and then it will cease to exist as a
separate programme.

2001/02 will be a transition period on which the DETR will be issuing
guidance at the end of 2000. Voluntary and community groups need to be
informed of their RDA's regional strategy and objectives and also be in
contact with the appropriate sub-regional offices about their priorities
and action plans. This guidance had still not been issued by mid February
2001.

Up to now SRB has emphasised the need for widespread community
involvement through local partnerships. The focus is likely to move away
from community schemes to economic development.

At the time of writing it was impossible to give information about the
arrangements for the final transition year. The following information is
retained in the expectation that some of it will still be useful.

Since 1994 the Single Regeneration Budget (SRB) has been the major
source of urban funding in England contributing millions of pounds
annually to a rolling programme. It then combined under one banner the
20 or so separate programmes which had previously been operated from
different government departments: the main financial contributor has
been the Department of Environment, Transport and the Regions, with
contributions also from the departments of Education and Employment,
Trade and Industry and the Home Office.

The budget for SRB is now administered at a regional level by the
Regional Development Agencies which coordinate the main programmes

and policies at local level and ensure that businesses, local government and voluntary agencies have just one port of call.

Website: www.regeneration.detr.gov.uk

SRB Round 6 (2000/01)

SRB provides resources, within a competitive bidding process, to support regeneration initiatives in England carried out by local partnerships. It aims to enhance the quality of life of local people in areas of need by reducing the gap between deprived and other areas, and between different groups. The types of bid supported differ from place to place according to local circumstances, but they are expected to include some or all of the following objectives:

- improve the employment prospects, education and skills of local people;
- address social exclusion and improving opportunities for the disadvantaged;
- promote sustainable regeneration, improve and protect the environment and infrastructure, including housing;
- support and promote growth in local economies and businesses;
- reduce crime and drug abuse and improve community safety.

Partnerships are expected to involve a wide range of local organisations in their management – local authorities, other public bodies, businesses, the voluntary sector and the local community. In particular partnerships are expected to demonstrate that local communities are directly involved in and supportive of schemes. This can also include capacity building programmes to enable local community groups to be strengthened in order to participate in these partnerships.

Funding is made available in response to 'bids' submitted to the relevant regional offices. Each region also produces its own specific guidance within the parameters of the general bidding guidance. Bids are expected to generate the greatest possible investment from the private sector and support from European Structural Funds as well as involving local communities and drawing on 'the talents and resources of the voluntary sector'. Funding is available for bids lasting from one to seven years, resources permitting.

From Round 5 the major part of the new money (80%) has been targeted on the areas of greatest need, while the balance of the resources tackles pockets of need elsewhere including rural areas and former coalfield areas. Resources can contribute to a comprehensive strategy concentrated on a relatively small area, e.g. a rundown town centre, one or more housing estates or a large, multifaceted development site. But small free-standing schemes, which do not link into a wider local regeneration strategy, are unlikely to be successful.

Under Rounds 1–5 over 750 schemes have been approved, worth over £4.4 billion in SRB support over their lifetime of up to seven years. It is estimated that these will attract over £8.6 billion of private sector investment and help to attract European funding. The partnerships forecast that they will create/safeguard some 790,000 jobs, complete/ improve some 296,000 homes, support over 103,000 community organisations /voluntary groups together with over 94,000 new businesses.

Support to community empowerment/capacity building

The SRB Round 5 projects are investing at least £50 million in community capacity building, with more than 3,200 initiatives being pursued. However there are significant regional variations with London and the North West accounting for a high proportion (two thirds) of these initiatives. (Source: *Neighbourhood regeneration: resourcing community involvement* by Pete Duncan and Sally Thomas published for the Joseph Rowntree Foundation by the Policy Press Tel: 0117 954 6800.)

Examples of voluntary organisation and community group involvement, Round 5: Support to region-wide network of voluntary and community groups to develop its contribution to regeneration programmes in the region.

- *Community and Voluntary Forum for the Eastern Region* (COVER) (£500,000);
- *Network for the regeneration of communities in South East England* (£300,000);
- *East Midlands* – promoting inclusive regeneration partnership programmes (£250,000);
- *West Midlands Voluntary and Community Sector Strategic Partnership* (£2 million).

Capacity building:

- *London Ethnic Minority Voluntary Sector Capacity Building Programme* by the Council for Ethnic Minority Voluntary Organisations (£2.5 million);
- *Pan London Regeneration Consortium* to involve communities in their own regeneration and to enable them to take part in SRB initiatives (£791,000), also supported in SRB 4.

General and capacity building:

- *Groundwork Macclesfield* and *Vale Royal* – the Colshaw Farm Estate is a pocket of severe deprivation in an otherwise prosperous area. The

scheme strongly features capacity building. It seeks to involve local residents in a range of initiatives including education and employment, personal/social development, business advice, safer communities, health initiatives and environmental works (£723,000).
- *Isle of Dogs Community Foundation* – 'Creating a Confident Community' programme focusing on community development, education, youth, training and employment (£3.1 million);
- *South East London Community Foundation* linked up with a local SRB programme to administer its special funding for small community groups.

Education:

- *L'Ouverture* – involvement in multimedia projects to motivate disaffected and socially-excluded young people towards education and learning (£640,000) also supported in Round 3.

It is invaluable for newcomers to identify other voluntary organisations which have projects benefiting from SRB funding to find out how they managed to achieve this. Partnerships run for several years and it is important to find partnership and regeneration agencies in your area and to find out how to become involved. For example, Arts Worldwide, which organises major festivals of culture outside the Western tradition, was mounting a Bangladeshi Festival in Tower Hamlets during June 1999. In the previous summer it had made contact with Cityside Regeneration, a local agency in the west of the borough, with which it formed a partnership. This arrangement enabled it to access SRB part funding for its projects.

In spring 2000 the Manningham Mills Community Association received a £30,000 grant from the Round 3 SRB programme in Manningham to upgrade the small corner of the South Mill then in community hands. The funds were used to prepare the space to receive a major touring exhibition from Reggio Emilia 'The Hundred Languages of Children'.

Most SRB programmes have some form of 'community chest' from which small grants are made to support community and voluntary groups within their area.

General information about regeneration programmes: Regeneration Policy Unit, DETR Regeneration Division 2, Zone 4/A6, Eland House, Bressenden Place, London SW1E 5DU

Contact: Andy Golding Tel: 020 7944 3792;
E-mail: andy_golding@detr.gsi.gov.uk

Website: www.regeneration.detr.gov.uk

Publications:

Update, a quarterly newsletter, published by the Regeneration Division about SRB, is available in print. For *Update*, contact: Carole Dawson Tel: 020 7944 3772 or consult the DETR website. Find Regenet via the heading 'Regeneration' and then 'Single Regeneration Budget'.

Involving Communities in Urban and Rural Regeneration, published by HMSO for DETR, 1997; ISBN 185 1120 483

Regeneration and Sustainable Communities by Gabriel Channon and Alison West, published by the Community Development Foundation, 2000

New Deal For Communities Race Equality Guidance; draft for consultation published by DETR, November 1999, guidance on involving black and ethnic minority groups effectively in regeneration partnerships and schemes.

Making Partnerships Work – a practical guide for the public, private, voluntary and community sectors by Andrew Wilson and Kate Charlton, published by the Joseph Rowntree Foundation.

Developing effective community involvement strategies; guidance for single regeneration budget bids: The government is giving a higher profile to building capacity within communities so that they can play a more substantial part in regeneration work. Up to 10% of Single Regeneration Budget (SRB) funding is to be available specifically to support community involvement – significantly more than has previously been available. Since 1992, the Joseph Rowntree Foundation (JRF) has been looking at what works in the regeneration of deprived neighbourhoods, with a strong focus on the role that local residents and community organisations can play. This paper was prepared at the request of the DETR to share JRF's research findings with bidders for SRB funds. Experience shows that successful involvement is more likely when partners, including the community, develop clear strategies as early as possible and are prepared to invest time and resources in building the capacity of local organisations. Available by selecting Research Summaries from the JRF website (see below), searching on reference number 169.

Contact: Tel: 01904 615905 and quote reference.

Voluntary Sector Regional Networks contact: Voluntary groups are strongly advised to approach their coordinatory bodies – the regional voluntary sector networks (see separate entry for listing) and their local council for voluntary service, for further information and assistance.

Website: www.jrf.org.uk

The Urban Forum

Set up as the voluntary sector voice on regeneration policy and has over 300 local and national community and voluntary organisations as members, with associate members from other sectors. Its activities include an information service for members, representing the sector on urban policy issues and lobbying for increased community involvement in regeneration.

Coordinator: John Routledge, 4 Dean's Court, St Paul's Courtyard, London EC4V 5AA Tel: 020 7248 3111; Fax: 020 7248 3222; E-mail: info@urbanforum.org.uk

Website: www.urbanforum.org.uk

Ask for contacts with other voluntary organisations in your region which are part of a successful bid/programme of activities. This should help strengthen your resolve if the processes seem difficult and laborious and you need greater understanding of official practices.

Also ask about any coordinatory services provided in their area to assist voluntary organisations. For example training, advice and support to organisations in the Greater London area is provided free (funded through the SRB) by the Pan London Community Regeneration Consortium, 356 Holloway Road, London N7 6PA Tel: 020 7700 8120; Fax: 020 7700 8108; E-mail: plcrc@lvsc.org.uk

Website: www.lvsc.org.uk/plcrc

Applications: Always first approach the Regional Development Agency to obtain full information and guidance about the details of the programme currently operating (see pages 233–4 for list of addresses). Ask to be put on the mailing list for information about the new programme. When a new programme starts make sure that a meeting is arranged to discuss the information and how to proceed further in forming a partnership. The RDAs have sub-regional offices so each applicant should make contact with the office nearest to their interests.

Government Offices for the Regions are still involved as consultees and comment on bids, including the extent of voluntary sector involvement.

New Deal for Communities

Funding: £774 million has been allocated to the first 17 partnerships over the next 10 years from 2000/01

New Deal for Communities tackles multiple-deprivation in the very poorest areas, taking forward the government's commitment to tackle

social exclusion in the context of the Social Exclusion Unit's report
'Bringing Britain Together; a national strategy for neighbourhood
renewal'. It targets money on the most deprived neighbourhoods to
address problems such as:

- poor job prospects;
- high levels of crime;
- educational under-achievement;
- poor health.

The schemes are led by local partnerships formed between local people,
community and voluntary organisations, public agencies, local authorities
and business. The programme is administered through Government
Offices for the Regions. The chosen neighbourhoods comprise between
1000 and 4000 households. Funding for each partnership will be for a
period of up to 10 years, and will be sufficient to secure a lasting
improvement in the quality of life of the community.

Round 1: The initial 17 pathfinder neighbourhoods and partnerships are:
Birmingham (King's Norton); Bradford (Little Horton); Bristol (Barton
Hill); Brighton (East Brighton); Hackney (Shoreditch); Hull (Preston
Road); Leicester (Braunstone); Liverpool (Kensington); Manchester
(Beswick and Openshaw); Middlesbrough (West); Newcastle (West Gate);
Newham (West Ham and Plaistow); Norwich (North Earlham and
Marlpit); Nottingham (Radford); Sandwell (Greets Green); Southwark
(Aylesbury Estate); and Tower Hamlets (Ocean Estate). These
partnerships are currently implementing their 10-year delivery plans.

Round 2: A further 22 new partnerships submitted initial proposals in
April 2000. These are: Birmingham; Brent; Coventry; Derby; Doncaster;
Hammersmith and Fulham; Haringey; Hartlepool; Islington; Knowsley;
Lambeth; Lewisham; Luton; Oldham; Plymouth; Rochdale; Salford;
Sheffield; Southampton; Sunderland; Walsall; Wolverhampton.

For further information contact: John Houghton, Regeneration
Division 4 Tel: 020 7944 3783, E-mail: john_houghton@detr.gsi.gov.uk

Website: www.regeneration.detr.gov.uk

Local Strategic Partnerships
Research by the Social Exclusion Unit, the Performance and Innovation
Unit and others shows that main services need to work together at the
local level to improve outcomes – in particular to tackle the linked
problems facing deprived neighbourhoods. Building on the new
community planning duty and the wide range of existing cross-sectoral
partnerships, service providers across the country are being encouraged to

establish Local Strategic Partnerships (LSPs). The aim is for a 'single coordinating partnership for an area [...] linking the neighbourhood to the regions, coordinating across and between partnership activity'.

The area an LSP covers will depend on local circumstances. Some of the existing partnerships with whom LSPs would be expected to build working relationships are:

- Early Years Development and Childcare Partnerships;
- Health Action Zones;
- New Deal For Communities Partnerships;
- Single Regeneration Budget Local Partnerships;
- Sure Start;
- Community Legal Service Partnerships.

More detailed guidance was set out in *Local Strategic Partnerships* (consultation document), October 2000, also available electronically from the website below.

The consultation document states: 'From the first stages of preparing to establish the partnership, special care needs to be taken to ensure resident, business, voluntary sector and community representatives are accorded equal weight in influence and decision-taking with the local authority and other statutory agencies balancing the needs and wants of the various partners; for example by introducing revolving chairing arrangements and appropriate levels of representation and accountability.'

LSPs in the most deprived areas will receive start-up funding through the New Deal for Communities. This will ensure local people and communities are empowered to play their full part in setting local priorities and determining local action to turn around their neighbourhoods. This will include funding to cover the cost of residents' and groups' participation, and to allow LSPs to use innovative approaches to involving local people, alongside funding for small 'Community Chests'.

For further information contact: James Holdaway Tel: 020 7944 3678; E-mail: james_holdaway@detr.gsi.gov.uk

Website: www.regeneration.detr.gov.uk/conindex.htm

Neighbourhood Renewal Unit

The unit will spearhead the delivery of the National Strategy for Neighbourhood Renewal. The unit will be fully operational from April 2001 and will be responsible for coordinating and monitoring the work from the many departments and agencies contributing to the National Strategy.

Neighbourhood Renewal Fund

Funding: £200 million (2001/02); £300 million (2002/03); £400 million (2003/04)

As part of the local government settlement, the new Neighbourhood Renewal Fund (NRF) will channel support to the most deprived areas. It will make a key contribution to the delivery of the National Strategy for Neighbourhood Renewal – including new targets for education, crime, employment, health and housing in deprived areas – and help to get money to where it is most needed. Authorities will work with new Local Strategic Partnerships (see above) to draw up local deprivation strategies which will spell out how the additional funding will help to renew the most deprived communities and promote closer cooperation with the police, health and other local services. A total of 88 areas were announced in October 2000 as eligible for the fund which will be distributed between 2001 and 2004.

A consultation paper in October 2000 stated: 'Continuation of support through the Neighbourhood Renewal Fund will be conditional on effective local strategic partnerships, which fully involve key local players particularly voluntary groups and local communities, being in place.'

Community Empowerment Fund
Total funding: £400,000 (over three years, 2001–4)

To be made available in each of the 88 areas eligible for the Neighbourhood Renewal Fund to collect the views of local residents and to provide training to help them participate in Local Strategic Partnerships.

Community Chests
Total funding: £50 million (over three years, 2001–4)

Funds will be channelled directly to community groups through new Community Chests, which will be established in the 88 areas eliglible for the Neighbourhood Renewal Fund.

Contact your relevant Government Regional Office for information about the location of the 88 areas and how to contact its community chest.

For further information contact: James Holdaway, Neighbourhood Renewal Implementation Unit, Regeneration Directorate, Eland House, Bressenden Place, London SW1E 5DU Tel 020 7944 3678; E-mail: james_holdaway@detr.gsi.gov.uk

Website: www.info4local.gov.uk
www.local-regions.detr.gov.uk

Early Years Development and Childcare Partnerships

Funding: £470 million for the National Childcare Strategy (1999–2003); £390 million for education of three-year-olds (1999–2002)

These partnerships take place in all 150 local authority districts in England. Members of partnerships are drawn from a range of local people and organisations with an interest in early education and childcare. These include the local authority, private and voluntary sector providers of early education and childcare, maintained schools, parents and employers.

Local partnerships aim:

- to expand good quality early education and childcare;
- to build sustainable services;
- to integrate early education and childcare.

Early Years Development Partnerships were first established in summer 1997, with responsibility for planning local early education. In autumn 1998 the partnerships took on the additional remit of childcare. Partnerships plan early education for three- and four-year-olds; and childcare for children up to 14 years of age. Partnerships are required to set out annually in their plans proposals for delivery of local early education and childcare services. Plans are submitted to the Secretary of State for approval.

Contact: Colin Stiles, Partnership Team, Childcare Unit, Department for Education and Employment, Level 2A, Caxton House, 6–12 Tothill Street, London SW1H 9NA Tel: 020 7273 5855; Fax: 020 7273 5606; E-mail: colin.stiles@dfee.gov.uk

Website: www.dfee.gov.uk/eydcp/index.htm

Sure Start Unit (C H)

Funding: £452 million over three years to March 2002, broken down into £265 million for current and £187 million for capital expenditure. A further £580 million over the three years 2001/02–2003/04 was announced in July 2000 spending review. This doubles the number of planned programmes to 500 so that Sure Start should reach a third of poor children under four in England.

The unit is interdepartmental, with staff drawn from various government departments. Sure Start aims to improve the health and well-being of families and their children before birth and up to four years, so that they are ready to thrive when they go to school. It does this by:

- setting up local Sure Start programmes to improve services for families with young children;
- spreading good practice learned from these local programmes to everyone involved in providing services for young children.

By 2002 there will be 250 Sure Start local programmes, concentrated in neighbourhoods where children's needs are most pressing. The first 60 Sure Start programmes called 'Trailblazers', were launched in January 1999, and were under way by late 1999. The experiences of these trailblazers is helping to shape the Second Wave – another 69 local programmes. A third wave of 65 programmes was launched in July 2000 and should be up and running by spring 2001. (Programmes listed below.)

The initiative targets children and parents in disadvantaged and deprived areas. Typical Sure Start catchment areas are small (about one to two miles in radius) so people can walk to the services, though rural areas will tend to be larger.

Sure Start programmes are run by partnerships representing all the key interests in the area, including the community and voluntary sectors and existing local partnerships such as the Early Years Development and Childcare partnerships and those funded by the Single Regeneration Budget.

Funding: Sure Start is funded by the interdepartmental Sure Start Unit based in the Department for Education and Employment with additional advice available from Government Offices for the Regions, NHS Executive Regional Offices and Social Care Regions. Sure Start funding is available to reshape services and fill gaps, and to provide better and more coordinated support for families. Its funding cannot be used to replace existing funding. Parents and the community are expected to be involved at every stage, to ensure that Sure Start responds to real local needs rather than simply providing what the professionals currently offer.

Sure Start's objectives are as follows:
- Improving children's social and emotional development: in particular, by supporting early bonding between parents and their children, helping families to function and by enabling the early identification and support of children with emotional and behavioural difficulties.
- Improving children's health: in particular, by supporting parents in caring for their children to promote healthy development before and after birth.
- Improving children's ability to learn: in particular, by encouraging stimulating and enjoyable play, improving language skills and

through early identification and support of children with learning difficulties.
- Strengthening families and communities: in particular, by enhancing families' opportunities for involvement in the community and improving the sensitivity of existing services to local needs.
- Increasing productivity.

Sure Start is a national strategy and all local programmes work towards these objectives. However, since the needs of young children and their families in each Sure Start area are different, what needs to be done may not be same. Each programme aims to deliver the following core services in an integrated and coherent way:

- outreach and home visiting;
- support to families and parents;
- support for good quality play, learning and childcare experiences;
- primary and community health and social care, including advice about family health and child health and development;
- support for children and parents with special needs, including help getting access to specialised services.

On the basis of these key principles local Sure Start programmes can:

- provide services not already in the area;
- add value to existing service (Sure Start money cannot be used to replace or make up for a reduction in existing services, although it can help to reshape or expand them);
- provide new facilities for delivering services, such as a new Sure Start centre to provide a 'one stop shop' for parents; an extension or refurbishment to allow existing early years and childcare facilities to cater for younger children and their families; new play areas; a new minibus or playbus;
- give parents clear information about the services available to them;
- train existing professionals, new workers and volunteers to deliver Sure Start in ways that are sensitive to local needs;
- improve joint working and coordination between existing service providers.

Sure Start Programme Districts
60 Districts in 1st round:
Barrow-in-Furness, Birmingham, Blackburn with Darwen, Blackpool, Bradford, Brent, Brighton and Hove, Bristol, Camden, Copeland, Corby, Derby, Doncaster, Enfield, Fenland, Great Yarmouth, Greenwich, Hackney, Halton, Haringey, Hastings, Kingston-upon-Hull, Kirklees, Knowsley, Lambeth, Leeds, Leicester, Liverpool, Luton, Manchester, Mansfield, Middlesborough, Newcastle, Newham, North East Lincolnshire, North Tyneside, Norwich, Nottingham, Oldham, Oxford, Penwith, Plymouth,

Redcar and Cleveland, Rotherham, Salford, Sandwell, Sedgemoor,
Sheffield, Southampton, Southwark, St Helens, Stoke-on-Trent,
Sunderland, Telford and Wrekin, Thanet, Thurrock, Tower Hamlets,
Waltham Forest, Wealden, Wolverhampton.

69 Districts in 2nd round:

Ashfield, Barking and Dagenham, Barnsley, Birmingham, Blyth Valley,
Bolsover, Bolton, Boston, Bournemouth, Bradford, Bristol, Burnley,
Calderdale, Cannock Chase, Coventry, Croydon, Derwentside, Dover,
Dudley, Ealing, Easington, Gateshead, Gloucester, Hammersmith and
Fulham, Harlow, Hartlepool, Hounslow, Hyndburn, Ipwich, Isle of Wight,
Islington, Kensington and Chelsea, Kerrier, Kingston-upon-Hull, Leeds,
Leicester, Lewisham, Lincoln, Liverpool, Manchester, Medway Towns,
Newcastle Upon Tyne, Nottingham, Nuneaton & Bedworth, Pendle,
Peterborough, Portsmouth, Preston, Reading, Redbridge, Rochdale,
Sedgefield, Sefton, Sheffield, Slough, Solihull, South Tyneside, Stockton-
on-Tees, Sunderland, Tameside, Torbay, Wakefield, Walsall, Wandsworth,
Wansbeck, Wear Valley, Westminster, Wigan, Wirral.

65 Districts in 3rd round by region:

East Midlands

Leicester, Derby, Bassetlaw, East Lindsey, Northampton, Newark and
Sherwood, Chesterfield.

London

Hackney, Tower Hamlets, Newham, Southwark, Lambeth, Haringey,
Brent, Camden, Bromley, Hillingdon, Havering.

Eastern

Kings Lynn and West Norfolk, Waveney, Tendring, Southend-on-Sea.

North East

Middlesbrough, Hartlepool, Darlington, Berwick-upon-Tweed,
Chester-le-Street.

North West

Liverpool, Manchester, Knowsley, Blackburn with Darwen, Halton
(Runcorn), Sefton, Salford, Allerdale, West Lancashire, Stockport,
Ellesmere Port and Neston, Rossendale, Warrington, Bury, Lancaster.

West Midlands

Birmingham, Sandwell, Stoke-on-Trent, Wolverhampton, Oswestry,
Herefordshire, East Staffordshire.

Yorkshire and the Humber

Leeds, Bradford, Sheffield, Kingston Upon Hull, Doncaster, Barnsley,
Rotherham, North Lincolnshire, East Riding of Yorkshire, Scarborough.

South East
Milton Keynes, Havant, Shepway.

South West
Restormel, North Devon, Swindon.

Examples of the activities supported:

- In Ore Valley, Hastings, the three Sure Start centres now provide a health and baby clinic, a children's music group, a 'get cooking' group to teach good nutrition on a budget and speech and language therapy programmes;
- In Sheffield, parents are using a 'toolkit for babies', which helps them develop their child's sound and speech development;
- In Fenland, the Sure Start bus visits the six villages – bringing play activities, a toy library, and a crêche to families in this very rural area; and parents use the project's video-conferencing and e-mail facilities to help them gain NVQ qualifications in childcare;
- In Barrow, a freephone helpline has been set up to provide health and childcare advice to local parents every evening up to 11pm;
- In Southwark, an 'art in the park' play and learning scheme works with the whole family to develop children's early communication skills through art;
- In Birmingham, young homeless mothers living in a local hostel are offered 'play and stay' sessions for their children while they receive health advice.

Sure Start is intended to be a model for providing services for children and families. Areas without programmes funded by central government are encouraged to develop the Sure Start approach and it is understood that many have done so.

For further information contact: David Jeffrey, Head of Communications and Personnel, Department for Education and Employment, Level 2, Caxton House, Tothill Street, London SW1H 9NA Tel: 020 7273 5728; Fax: 020 7273 5182; E-mail: sure.start@dfee.gov.uk

The website is comprehensive and includes useful outlines of each of the programmes and contacts within them:

Website: www.surestart.gov.uk

Health Action Zones
Funding: £120 million (2000/01); £86 million (1999/2000)

As well as supporting specific work programmes and projects, this funding is also being used to lever change within the mainstream budgets of health and local authorities.

Health Action Zones (HAZs) are long term programmes of work and cover a wide range of activities. They work at changing structures and the way things are done, as well as progressing work which tackles health and social care, lifestyles and the wider determinants of health.

Twenty-six HAZs have been established in England in areas of deprivation and poor health to tackle health inequalities and modernise services through local innovation. Although the HAZ communities vary significantly in their local characteristics, they face common problems of ill-health and disadvantage. HAZs represent areas of the country with some of the highest levels of deprivation and the poorest levels of health.

HAZs will aim to:

- develop and implement a health strategy that cuts inequalities, and delivers within their areas measurable improvements in public health and health outcomes, and quality of treatment and care;
- increase sustainability by developing contacts with other zones, by disseminating ideas more widely – and by playing a major role in joining up existing initiatives.

Target areas/population: The 26 selected zones have populations ranging from 180,000 to 1.4 million in areas of deprivation and high health need. In total, HAZs cover over 13 million people. HAZs include 34 health authorities and 73 local authorities. They range in complexity from those that comprise multiple health and local authorities and have the largest populations (such as Merseyside and Tyne and Wear), to those based on unitary local authorities but which take in only part of associated health authorities (such as Luton and Plymouth).

First wave HAZs which began in April 1998: Bradford, East London and the City, Lambeth with Southwark and Lewisham, Luton, Manchester with Salford & Trafford, North Cumbria, Northumberland, Plymouth, Sandwell, South Yorkshire Coalfields, Tyne & Wear.

Second wave HAZs which began in April 1999: Brent, Bury and Rochdale, Camden and Islington, Cornwall and the Isles of Scilly, Hull and East Riding, Leeds, Leicester City, Merseyside, North Staffordshire, Nottingham, Sheffield, Tees, Wakefield, Walsall, Wolverhampton.

There will be no third wave. HAZs will operate for seven years.

Key features: HAZs have two strategic objectives:

- identifying and addressing the public health needs of the local area, in particular trailblazing new ways of tackling health inequalities;
- modernising services by increasing their effectiveness, efficiency and responsiveness.

HAZ programmes represent a new approach to public health – linking health, regeneration, employment, education, housing and anti-poverty initiatives to respond to the needs of vulnerable groups and deprived communities.

Their plans provide for greater flexibility in service provision and should lead to the integration of these services and new approaches into mainstream activity.

Coordination and delivery: HAZs are partnerships between the NHS, local authorities, the voluntary and private sectors, and community groups. HAZs are coordinated locally by a partnership board. Performance management is via NHS Executive regional offices (working with colleagues in social care and government office regions, linking with regional development agencies as appropriate), through those health authority(ies) covered by the HAZ.

Haz Fellowships: About 20 fellowships are awarded to enable frontline staff to forward specific projects. Applications are called for annually with the deadline during autumn. Two CABx workers have received fellowships.

HAZnet

The HAZ website (see below) engages the organisations, partners and communities that make up the 26 Health Action Zones. Here you can find out what's going on in Health Action Zones – with the focus on sharing experiences and good practice.

Community Involvement Network: This part of HAZnet provides useful background information about the involvement by voluntary/community groups within the specific HAZs.

Special funding programmes for voluntary/community groups: Voluntary/community groups should always be sure to check with their local HAZ, and/or the Community Involvement Network, part of the HAZnet website, to find out whether there are any special funds set up to support voluntary and community groups within a HAZ, e.g. the HAZ covering Lambeth, Southwark and Lewisham has a Healthy Communities Fund to which £1.5 million has been allocated to be used by March 2002. It provides grants for activities to improve the well-being and health of children and young people.

Website: www.haznet.org.uk

Other Information
The Healthy Living Project

This project has launched a website to bring those people and groups developing healthy living initiatives together. The project encourages communication and information sharing between healthy living initiatives in England that are funded by the New Opportunities Fund. The site includes a database which seeks to encourage people and groups who are working on healthy living initiatives to find out about each other.

Website: www.healthyliving.org.uk/

Contact: Michael Swaffield, HAZ policy manager, NHS Executive

Quarry House, Quarry Hill, Leeds LSU 7UE Tel: 0113 254 5002, E-mail: michael.swaffield@doh.gsi.gov.uk

HAZ Project Managers: Contacts

Bradford HAZ

Elaine Appelbee, Bradford HA, New Mill, Victoria Road, Saltaire, Shipley, West Yorkshire BD18 3LD
Tel: 01274 366169; Fax: 01274 366017;
E-mail: elaine.appelbee@bradford-ha.northy.nhs.uk

Brent HAZ

Patrick Vernon, HAZ Director, Brent and Harrow Health Authority, Wembley Health & Care Centre, Wembley, Middlesex HA0 4UZ
Tel: 020 8795 6210; Fax: 020 8795 6231;
E-mail: Patrick.vernon@b-hhpd.org.uk

Bury and Rochdale HAZ

Kate Lucy, Project Manager, Bury and Rochdale Health Authority, 21 Silver Street, Bury, Lancs BL9 0EN
Tel: 0161 762 3125; Fax: 0161 762 3157;
E-mail: Kate.lucy@bury-roch-ha.nwest.nhs.uk

East London and City HAZ

Liza Cragg, Project Manager, Fifth Floor, Aneurin Bevan House, 81 Commercial Road, London E1 1RD
Tel: 020 7655 6600; E-mail: liza@elcha.co.uk

Camden and Islington HAZ

Gail Findlay, Project Manager, Camden and Islington Health Authority, 110 Hampstead Road, London NW1 2LF
Tel: 020 7853 5542; Fax: 020 7853 5549;
E-mail: Gail.findlay@cai-ha.nthames.nhs.uk

Cornwall and Isles of Scilly HAZ

Tracey Sweet, HAZ Coordinator, Cornwall and Isles of Scilly HA, John Keay House, Tregonissey Road, St Austell, Cornwall PL25 4NQ
Tel: 01726 627922; Fax: 01726 627901;
E-mail: Tracey.sweet@ho.cios-ha.swest.nhs.uk

Hull and East Riding HAZ
Simon Hunter, Health Action Now, c/o East Riding and Hull Health
Authority, Grange Park Lane, Willerby, East Yorkshire HU10 6DT
Tel: 01482 672070; Fax: 01482 672197;
E-mail: Simon.hunter@eriding-ha.northy.nhs.uk

Lambeth, Southwark and Lewisham HAZ
Kathryn MacDermott, Acting Director of Health Action Zones, Lambeth,
Southwark and Lewisham HAZ, 1 Lower Marsh, London SE1 7NT
Tel: 020 7716 7000 x7661; Fax: 020 7716 7018;
E-mail: kathryn.macdermott@ob.lslha.sthames.nhs.uk

Leeds HAZ
Adrian Booth, HAZ Project Manager, Leeds Health Authority, Blenheim
House, West One, Duncombe Street, Leeds LS1 4PL
Tel: 0113 295 2001; Fax: 0113 295 2222;
E-mail: Adrian.booth@lh.leeds-ha.northy.nhs.uk

Manchester, Salford and Trafford HAZ
Edna Robinson, Room 125, Trafford Town Hall, Talbot Road,
Old Trafford, Manchester M32 0YX
Tel: 0161 912 1271; Fax: 0161 912 1149;
E-mail: ednar@masthaz.freeserve.co.uk
Admin: Janets@masthaz.freeserve.co.uk

Merseyside HAZ
Marie Armitage, HAZ Coordinator, c/o Liverpool Health Authority,
Hamilton House, 24 Pall Mall, Liverpool L3 6AL
Tel: 0151 285 2340; Fax: 0151 285 2397;
E-mail: Marie.armitage@gww.liverpool-ha.nwest.nhs.uk

Leicester HAZ
Iain Harkness, Leicestershire Health Authority, Gwendolen Road, Leicester
LE5 4 QF
Tel: 0116 258 8693; Fax: 0116 258 8577;
E-mail: Iain.harkness@mail.leicester-ha.trent.nhs.uk;
E-mail: Janet.gibbins@mail.leicester-ha.trent.nhs.uk

Luton HAZ
Bob Nessling, Apex House, 30–34 Upper George Street, Luton, Beds
LU1 2HA
Tel: 01582 657591; Fax: 01582 657592;
E-mail: bob.nessling@beds-ha.anglox.nhs.uk

North Cumbria HAZ
Sharon Ombler-Spain, HAZ Director, Unit 7F, Lamplugh Road, Lakeland
Business Park, Cockermouth, Cumbria CA13 0QT
Tel: 01900 324134; Fax: 01900 324136;
E-mail: healthactionzone@ncha.nhs.uk

Northumberland HAZ

Sue Cornick, Merley Croft, Loansdean, Morpeth, Northumberland
NE61 2DL
Tel: 01670 394400; Fax: 01670 394501;
E-mail susan.cornick@northumberland-haz.org.uk

North Staffordshire HAZ

Judith Kurth, North Staffordshire Health Authority, Heron House, Great
Fenton Business Park, Grove Road, Stoke on Trent ST4 4LX
Tel: 01782 298055; Fax: 01782 298298;
E-mail: judy.kurth@nsha.wmids.nhs.uk

Nottingham HAZ

Pauline Davis, HAZ Lead, Nottingham Health Authority, Standard Court,
Park Row, Nottingham NG1 6GN
Tel: 0115 912 3324; Fax: 0115 912 3351;
E-mail: Pauline.davis@nottinghm-ha.trent.nhs.uk

Plymouth HAZ

Debra Lapthorne, Plymouth Health Action Zone, Public Dispensary,
18 Catherine Street, Plymouth PL1 2UN
Tel: 01752 515470; Fax: 01752 515481;
E-mail: Deb.Lapthorne@sw-devon ha.swest.nhs.uk

Sandwell HAZ

Fran Fahy, Sandwell HA, Kingston House, 438 High Street,
West Bromwich B70 9LD
Tel: 0121 500 1669; Fax: 0121 500 1667;
E-mail: fran.fahy@sandwell-ha.wmids.nhs.uk

Sheffield HAZ

Steve Pintus, Director of Sheffield Health Action Zone, Sheffield Health,
5 Old Fulwood Road, Sheffield S10 3TG
Tel: 0114 271 1311; Fax: 0114 271 1318;
E-mail: Stephen.pintus@sheffield-ha.nhs.ukSouth

Yorkshire Coalfields HAZ

Brigid Kane, Health Action Zone Coordinator, White Rose House, Ten
Pound Walk, Doncaster DN4 5DJ
Tel: 01302 320111 Ext 3203/4; Fax: 01302 730613;
E-mail: Brigid.kane@doncaster-ha.trent.nhs.uk

Tees HAZ

Jim Willson, HAZ Planning Manager, Tees Health Authority, Poole House,
Stokesley Road, Nunthorpe, Middlesbrough
Tel: 01642 304132; Fax: 01642 304023;
E-mail: jim.willson@email.tees-ha.northy.nhs.uk

Tyne and Wear HAZ
David Eltringham, Suite B, Ground Floor, Nickalls House, Metro Centre,
Gateshead, Tyne and Wear NE11 9NH
Tel: 0191 461 9200; Fax: 0191 461 9201;
E-mail: Pam.McDougall@exchange.gatesh-tr.northy.nhs.uk

Wakefield HAZ
Lee Adams, Project Manager, Wakefield HA, White Rose House, West
Parade, Wakefield, West Yorkshire WF1 1LT
Tel: 0192 421 3154; Fax: 0192 421 3004;
E-mail: Lee.adams@gw.wakeha.northy.nhs.uk

Walsall HAZ
Karen Wright, Specialist Health Promotion Manager Walsall Health
Authority, Lichfield House, 27–31 Lichfield Street, Walsall, West Midlands
WS1 1TE
Tel: 01922 720255; Fax: 01922 628843;
E-mail: WrightK@ha.walsall-ha.wmids.nhs.uk

Wolverhampton HAZ
Jo Richards, HAZ Coordinator, HAZ Office, West Park Hospital, Park
Road West, Wolverhampton, West Midlands WV1 4PW
Tel: 01902 444113; Fax: 01902 444189;
E-mail: joanna.richards@whc-tr.wmids.nhs.uk

Education Action Zones

Funding: For large zones: up to £1 million per zone per year from the
government and private sector for a period of between three and five
years.

For small zones: up to £350,000 per zone per year from the government
and private sector for a period of between three and five years.

Education Action Zones (EAZs) were established to encourage innovative
and flexible approaches to raising attainment and overcoming barriers to
learning in areas of deprivation. EAZs are partnerships of schools, local
education authorities, teachers, TECs, community groups, parents,
businesses and others. Zones typically cover between 15 and 25 schools
and are expected to work with other local partnerships and plans
including SRB and local education authority EDPs, etc.

EAZs are run by Action Forums under the leadership of a project director
for a period of three to five years. The forum sets annual action plans in
agreement with the schools in order to raise standards and to tackle issues
such as truancy, exclusions, and disaffection. Plans are approved by
government on an annual basis. All schools in the zone have a right to a

place on the forum, as does the Secretary of State's representative. Beyond this, membership is determined locally.

The first 25 EAZs started in September 1998 and January 1999. By March 2000 there were 73 large EAZs approved nationally.

In July 2000, 20 of the 25 first round zones were approved for extension from three to five years. Decisions about the remaining five zones were made in December 2000.

The 25 Round 1 zones are in:
Barnsley, Basildon, Birmingham (Aston and Nechelles), Birmingham (Kitts Green/ Shard End), Blackburn with Darwen, Brighton, Croydon, Halifax, Herefordshire, Kingston-upon-Hull, North East Lincolnshire, Lambeth, Leicester City, Middlesbrough, Newcastle-upon-Tyne, Newham, Norfolk, Nottingham, Plymouth, Salford and Trafford, Sheffield, North Somerset, Southwark, South Tyneside and Wigan.

(12 zones began in September 1998 and the remaining 13 in January 1999.)

The 48 Round 2 zones are in:
Derby North East, Great Yarmouth, Central Bristol, City of Westminster, SE England Virtual EAZ, Easington and Seaham, Peterlee, Ashington, East Cleveland, North Stockton, Sunderland, Breightmet and Tonge, Ellesmere Port, Barrow, Preston, Dingle with Granby and Toxteth, Speke Garston, East Manchester, Wythenshawe, South Bradford, Withernsea and Southern Holderness, South East Sheffield, Wakefield, Clacton and Harwich, North Gillingham, Southend, Bedford, The North East Derbyshire Coalfields, Corby, Camborne, Pool and Redruth, Gloucester, Bridgewater, Coventry, Dudley, Wednesbury, Shropshire, Stoke, Telford and Wrekin, Wolverhampton, Hackney, North Islington, Downham and Bellingham, Hastings and St Leonards, Leigh Park, Kent/Somerset Virtual EAZ, Greenwich, Oxford and Slough.

(11 began in December 1999 and the remaining 35 by September 2000.)

The first 12 small EAZs (announced in April 2000) are in:
Greenwich (2 zones), Newham, Wandsworth, Hammersmith and Fulham, Rotherham (2 zones), Sheffield, Leeds, Liverpool, Salford and Tower Hamlets.

The second 14 small EAZs (announced in September 2000) are in:
Birmingham (4 zones), Manchester (2 zones), Camden, Haringey, Southwark, Islington (2 zones), Liverpool.

Up to 16 more will begin by January 2001.

All small zones are in Excellence in Cities areas. Up to 42 further small zones are planned to be set up over the next three years.

Funding: Large EAZs receive 75% funding from the DfEE and 25% from the private sector up to a maximum of £1 million a year for three to five years. Small zones receive £250,000 guarantee baseline funds per year with up to another £50,000 available from the Department to match fund contributions the zones can raise from the private sector.

Progress in Round 1 zones: The percentage improvements as compared to 1998 figures – the early signs of improvements in attainment as indicated by the summer 1999 results – are very promising, particularly for the 12 zones which started in September 1998 and so have been running longest. For example, at Key Stage 2, there was a 6% improvement in English and 14% improvement in Maths in EAZ schools (September starters) as compared to 5% and 10% nationally. At GCSE, zone schools (September starters) saw an improvement of 4% in the number of pupils gaining 5+ A*–C grades, and 2% for 1+ A*–G, compared to 1% nationally in both cases.

Contact: Sue Dasey, Team Leader Tel: 020 7925 6366; Pamela Stenson, for information on established zones, finance, social inclusion, and support for pupils and families Tel: 020 7925 5051; Angela Overington, for information on developing small EAZs, press and publicity, teaching and learning in zones and cross team and legal issues Tel: 020 7925 6338.

Standards and Effectiveness Unit, Department for Education and Employment, Sanctuary Buildings, Great Smith Street, Westminster, London SW1P 3BT

Website: www.standards.dfee.gov.uk/eazs

Connexions

Total funding: £420 million (2001/02–2002/03)

The Connexions Strategy is a new youth support strategy for 13–19 year olds, to be phased in from 2001. It will guide and support all young people through their teenage years and in the transition to working life. There are four key themes:

- a flexible curriculum;
- high quality sixth form, FE college, and work-based learning provision;
- targeted financial support for those in learning;
- outreach, information, advice, support and guidance for young people.

Part of the fourth theme, but 'at the heart' of the strategy, is the Connexions Service, to be delivered through a network of personal advisers (PAs), linking in with specialist support services. PAs will be drawn from a range of existing public, private, voluntary and community sector organisations. The key aim is to enable all young people to participate effectively in appropriate learning, i.e. in school or FE colleges, through training providers or in a community setting. The service aims to remove any wider barriers to effective engagement in learning that young people are suffering. It will do this by providing high-quality support and guidance and by brokering access for young people to a range of more specialist services.

Connexions will be a universal service, but will give particular priority to those young people most at risk of disaffection and social exclusion. The service prospectus states that 'voluntary and community groups will have a key role to play in the provision of the service, including as part of the network of personal advisers'.

The structure for the Connexions Service includes:

- the cross-departmental Connexions Service National Unit;
- partnerships at local Learning and Skills Council area level, responsible for strategic planning and funding – there are 47 such areas in England; funding to partnerships may be via grant agreement, contractual payment or other mechanism;
- local management committees at the local authority level with responsibility for education and social services, or groupings of them, to suit local circumstances, bringing together local partners and responsible for day-to-day management of local delivery.

Committees will agree with partnerships the level of funding to be available to the local manager to deliver the service locally. The department wants voluntary and community organisations to be intimately involved in both partnerships and local management committees.

The Connexions Service will include services previously provided under New Start (see separate entry).

Applications: All Connexions Partnerships were invited to produce an outline partnership proposal by 9 June 2000. Those then assessed as being most likely to deliver an effective service from April 2001 were invited to complete more detailed plans.

The first 16 partnerships were announced in October 2000. They will begin operating in April 2001 in the following areas: Milton Keynes/ Oxfordshire/Buckinghamshire, North London, South London, Suffolk (July start), West of England, Devon/Cornwall/Scillies/Plymouth/Torbay, Black Country, Coventry/Warwickshire, Shropshire/Telford/The Wrekin, Lincolnshire/Rutland, South Yorkshire, Humber sub region, Greater Merseyside (September start), Cheshire/Warrington, Cumbria, Tyne and Wear (September start).

Contact: Connexions Service National Unit, Moorfoot, Sheffield, S1 4PQ; General enquiries: 0114 259 1104

Website: www.connexions.gov.uk

Neighbourhood Support Fund

Total funding: £60 million (1999/2000–2001/02)

This fund, launched in September 1999, will channel funds over three years to some 600 community-based projects in 40 of the most deprived local authority areas in England. The programme aims to open up opportunities of education, training and employment to the young, unemployed and disaffected. Local groups will be helped to run activities 'geared to reconnecting these young people with their communities'. The programme is aimed at 13–19 year olds in general, with 16–17 year olds specially targeted. Projects will include:

- vocational activities and key skills development:
- information technology;
- numeracy and literacy;
- job-searching.

A range of social and developmental activities will also be included such as music and video workshops, community work, art and drama.

This programme is being administered for the department by three different 'managing agents'.

- The Community Development Foundation (CDF) and the Community Education Development Centre (CEDC) in partnership are managing the major part of the funding – £42 million over three years – and are targeting voluntary and community groups;
- The National Youth Agency – managing funding of £9 million over three years – are targeting local authorities and youth services;
- The Learning Alliance, comprising CSV, NACRO, Rathbone and YMCA – are managing funding of £3.2 million over three years and identifying projects with their own affiliates.

Examples of groups supported by the Community Development Foundation, where grants range between £20,000 and £100,000 a year, include:

- *BTCV*, Sunderland, Southwick Environmental Project (£20,000 x 3);
- *Disability North*, Newcastle (£18,649 x 3);
- *Single Parent Action Network*, Bristol, for study centre (£20,000 x 3);
- *Leeds Women's Aid*, for support worker (£79,988 over 3 years);
- *Heeley City Farm*, Sheffield (£20,000 x 3);
- *Yemeni Community Association*, Sandwell (£20,000 x 3);

- *Walsall Community Radio Association* (£109,000 over 3 years);
- *Interplay Theatre Trust*, Leeds (£71,000 over 3 years);
- *Forest of Bradford*, for youth wood (£57,800 over 3 years);
- *Tile Hill South Residents Association*, Coventry, for cybercafes (£66,000 over 3 years).

For further information contact:
CDF, 60 Highbury Grove, London N5 2AG
Tel: 020 7226 5375; Fax 020 7704 0313,
Contact: Sorcha Mahony

CEDC, Woodway Park School, Wigston Road, Coventry CV2 2RH
Tel: 02476 655700; Fax: 02476 655701
Contacts: Chris Jones, John Grainger, Paul Woodcock

National Youth Agency, 17–23 Albion Street, Leicester LE1 6GD
Tel: 0116 285 3728; Fax: 0116 285 3777
Contacts: Terry Cane/Mary Mills

Learning Alliance – coordinated by Rathbone C I, Churchgate House, 56 Oxford Street, Manchester M1 6EU
Tel: 0161 236 6333

Contacts with the department: Madeleine Durie, Team Leader, Youth Inclusion Team, Connexions Unit, Lifelong Learning Directorate, Sanctuary Buildings, Great Smith Street, London SW1P 3BT
Tel: 020 7925 5260; Leroy Hoyte Tel: 020 7925 5258.

Community Champions Fund
Total funding: £3 million each year (2001/02–2003/04); £1 million (2000/01); £0.5 million (1999/2000)

This initiative started in 1999 to run for a two-year period. In February 2001 its continuation was announced over a further three years with greatly increased funding. The fund encourages people to get involved in the renewal of their communities. It makes small awards (usually between £500 and £2,000) to support individuals who have shown leadership in stimulating community activity and also to support small-scale community-inspired projects. The fund supports a wide range of projects and people. It encourages the spread of good practice. Examples of the kind of support that may be considered:

- visits to other communities, or talking to someone already doing what you aim to do;
- specific training;
- assembling a project bid;

- attending a conference to exchange ideas and good practice;
- publishing a community newsletter.

The fund is managed on behalf of the Department for Education and Employment by Government Offices for the Regions who work with voluntary sector organisations to ensure that community groups benefit.

Applications: To find out who is administering this fund in your region contact the following individuals at the Government Offices (G O) for the Regions. The full address for each office is separately listed below.

East G O
Clare Witcombe Tel: 01223 346700/01954 250268; Fax: 01223 346701;
E-mail: cwitcombe.goe@go-regions.gsi.gov.uk

East Midlands G O
Leonie Nelson Tel: 0115 934 8493; Fax: 0115 971 2557;
E-mail: lnelson.goem@go-regions.gsi.gov.uk

London G O
Peter Fiddeman Tel: 020 7217 3057/020 7217 3460;
E-mail: pfiddeman.gol@go-regions.gsi.gov.uk

North East G O
Lynne Michelson Tel: 0191 202 3663; Fax: 0191 201 3626;
E-mail: lmichelson.gone@go-regions.gsi.gov.uk

North West G O
Pauline Morgan-Williams Tel: 0161 952 4445; Fax: 0161 952 4170;
E-mail: pmorgan-williams.gonw@go-regions.gsi.gov.uk

South East G O
Jonathon Robinson Tel: 01483 88280; Fax: 01483 882409;
E-mail: jrobinson.gose@go-regions.gsi.gov.uk

South West G O
Mark Johnson Tel: 0117 900 1820; Fax: 0117 900 1920;
E-mail: mjohnson.gosw@go-regions.gsi.gov.uk

West Midlands G O
Sue Naughton, Tel: 0121 212 5184; Fax: 0121 212 5301;
E-mail: snaughton.gowm@go-regions.gsi.gov.uk

Yorkshire & the Humber G O
Carol Cooper-Smith, Tel: 0113 280 6414;
E-mail: ccooper-smith.goyh@go-regions.gsi.gov.uk

Dorothy Davies, Tel: 0113 280 5295;
E-mail: ddavies.goyh@go-regions.gsi.gov.uk

The programme is coordinated from the Department for Education and Employment's Regional Policy Division, Moorfoot, Sheffield S1 4PQ

Contact: Steven Nesbit Tel: 0114 259 4808; Jim Hewitt Tel: 0114 259 3409

Rural Development Programme

Total funding: £24,703,000 (2000/01) for RDP plus Redundant Building Grant

The Rural Development Programme (RDP) is a capital and revenue funding programme that supports social and economic projects aimed at diversifying and strengthening local economies, while also supporting measures to assist communities and disadvantaged groups. Grants are provided for a wide range of initiatives including business support, tourism, training, workspace, environmental improvements and social projects to encourage community development.

The RDP only applies within Rural Priority Areas (RPAs), designated on the basis of key indicators of social and economic problems. It is administered by the eight Regional Development Agencies (RDAs) outside London. Each RDA has its own regional development agenda that may affect RDP priorities. Furthermore, each Rural Priority Area has its own strategy, agreed upon by a local partnership, made up of local authorities, TECs and their successor bodies, Rural Community Councils, Chambers of Commerce and Business Links.

The national priorities of the RDP are likely to be affected by the Rural White Paper, expected to be published in autumn 2000. Furthermore, some RDAs are in the process of restructuring their funding programmes according to their own strategic priorities. This means that, in some cases, RDAs may still be receiving RDP funds from the DETR, while presenting a different interface to grantseekers.

Applicants can come from the private, public and voluntary sectors. A maximum of 50% of total project costs can be granted, although funding is often for the minimum necessary for a programme to go ahead. There is no maximum grant level, but projects must be within the indicative budgets set for each RPA. The following are some examples from the Co Durham, Northumberland and Peak District RPAs. Figures refer to funding over the total duration of the project, which in some cases may be a number of years:

- *Brassington Voluntary Youth Club*, for facilities and activities for young people, to encourage voluntary activity (£9,000);
- *Beth Johnson Foundation*, for two projects extending phone link services into isolated rural communities (£81,400);

- *High Peak CAB*, for information, support and assistance to GPs and other health care staff in their involvement with welfare systems on behalf of their patients (£32,000);
- *Flash Village Hall/Conference Committee*, for the creation of a conference centre in Britain's highest village (£59,500);
- *The Gallery*, Alnwick, to support disaffected young people by providing recreational facilities during evenings, weekends and school holidays; the scheme includes a full programme of training and social education to prepare participants for adulthood (£40,000);
- *The Durham Dales Centre*, Wear Valley, to commission a range of new interpretive materials displays and further attractions with the aim of increasing tourist numbers (£10,000).

The following groups received funding from the Shropshire Partnership for 1999/2000:

- *Furniture Scheme Community Workshop*, to provide training for volunteers in upgrading and recycling old donated furniture, which is then given to low income families or individuals in need (£18,800);
- *Rural Care Information Contact Network*, to develop a directory and network of services and providers in order to improve knowledge and take-up of these services (£14,100);
- *Participating in Regeneration*, to help local communities identify their needs, develop action plans and implement projects and the delivery of services (£11,300);
- *Rural Stress Network*, for a telephone helpline providing support, advice and information for those in rural areas under stress (£8,600);
- *Long Mynd Shuttle*, funding for a mini-bus providing access to the Long Mynd and reducing congestion in a small town (£4,500);
- *Oswestry Citizen's Advocacy Project*, to assist people with learning disabilities to develop self-advocacy skills, self-esteem and self-confidence (£1,400).

Applications can be received throughout the year and are made via local RDP committees. Contact should be made initially with a rural development officer from the local RDA. Contact details for the RDAs can be found in the separate entry. In addition to grants under the RDP, there is also a Redundant Building Grant available in RPAs to businesses or individuals who want to bring unused buildings back into commercial use.

The following RDP allocations were made to RDAs for 2000/01. The figures include funds for the Redundant Building Grant:

- South West RDA £7,023,000;
- SEEDA (South East RDA) £1,799,000;
- emda (East Midlands RDA) £3,381,000;

- EEDA (East of England RDA) £3,100,000;
- Advantage West Midlands £1,883,000;
- NWDA (North West RDA) £1,283,000;
- Yorkshire Forward £3,375,000;
- One North East £2,859,000.

Powers: Regional Development Agencies Act 1998

Coalfields Regeneration Trust

2 Portland Place
Spring Gardens
Doncaster
South Yorkshire DN1 3DF

Contact: Marc Cole, Finance

Tel: 01302 304 400
Fax: 01302 304 419
E-mail: info@coalfields-regen.org.uk
Website: www.coalfields-regen.org.uk

Total funding: £45,000,000 (2002/03–2004/05); £50,660,000
(1999/2000–2001/02)
Note: As the trust is a charitable organisation, it raises funds from a
variety of sources. Its income and expenditure are therefore unpredictable.
The above figures refer to funding from the DETR, the Scottish Executive
and the Welsh Assembly. The figures include grants and operational costs.

The Coalfields Regeneration Trust is a new independent grant-giving
body that forms part of the government response to recommendations
made in the Coalfields Task Force report. It is both a registered charity
and a company limited by guarantee. The trust works with partners to
promote and achieve social and economic regeneration in the coalfields
(which includes the ex-coal mining areas) of England, Scotland and
Wales.

The trust has six main priorities for support:

- resourcing communities through support for community facilities,
  community transport, welfare and debt advice and other measures;
- creating enterprising communities, through community business
  development, local business compacts and support to small new
  start-up businesses;
- improving the natural and built environment of coalfield
  communities;
- supporting innovative approaches to intermediate labour market
  and new deal initiatives;

- contributing to lifelong learning activities;
- promoting good practice (grant support will be available under this priority area to fund visits by community groups to different coalfield areas).

The trust funds a broad range of projects, including those that:

- support people in their efforts to return to work;
- provide facilities and opportunities for local people, including playgroups, meeting rooms, sports facilities, environmental projects, arts and cultural activities, feasibility studies and so on;
- provide debt and welfare advice or support for credit unions;
- bring together a range of activities under one roof to create a Resource Centre or 'one stop shop'.

The trust gives grants for up to 100% of capital and revenue costs, and there are no fixed upper or lower limits.

Applicants are normally community and voluntary organisations, charities, local authorities and similar bodies, but the trust welcomes applications from any group, organisation and agency committed to the regeneration of coalfield areas and their communities.

Some examples of grants given in 1999 are:

- *Amble Development Trust,* for an employment counsellor service (£150,000);
- *Chrysalis Youth Project,* for a learning environment for young people in Castleford (£70,000);
- *Furniture Project,* for providing refurbished furniture to the low waged and unemployed in North Nottinghamshire (£27,700);
- *Moira Furnace Museum Trust Ltd,* for the final development phase of the museum which will provide a visitor attraction (£19,500);
- *Newbiggin-by-the-Sea Partnership Ltd,* for a feasibility study to identify the need for and practicality of a proposed community facility (£7,000);
- *Methodist Church Hall,* Handsacre, for community facilities (£7,000).

Exclusions: The trust does not fund: projects that do not meet the aims and objectives of the trust; retrospective costs; projects exclusively or primarily intended to promote religious beliefs; projects that are properly the subject of statutory funding; grants to individuals.

As the trust is a charity it is unlikely to provide support to established private businesses.

Applications: Because organisations of varying sizes have different requirements, the trust has four different types of application:

- small applications, for less than £20,000;

- medium and large applications, for voluntary and community organisations where the application value is over £20,000;
- medium and large applications, for statutory bodies where the application value is over £20,000;
- partnership applications, for programmes initiated by national or regional charities taking place in several coalfield areas or in several locations within one coalfield area.

The trust does not require applicants to match its funds with support from other funders, although it does encourage this wherever possible. Trust funds can be used to match other funders' contributions, including those of the European Structural Fund.

There are no deadlines for applications; the trust processes applications as and when they arrive.

Community Investment Fund

The Community Investment Fund (CIF) was administered by English Partnerships specifically to support small community based projects requiring between £10,000 and £100,000 funding. It funded projects with social and economic benefits at community level. Assistance was available in the form of capital funding to provide or improve land and buildings; revenue funding was not provided. The fund, which had about £3 million annually, transferred from English Partnerships with the establishment of Regional Development Agencies (RDAs) in 1999.

Applications: Requests for information and guidance about funding should be addressed to the appropriate RDA (see separate listing). The ways in which this funding is being handled varies considerably from region to region.

Regional Cultural Consortiums

These bodies arise from the department's decision to shift more funding decisions on the arts, heritage and sports to regional level. The Consortiums aim to:

- champion the spectrum of cultural and creative industries in each region, including tourism and sport;
- forge links across this spectrum;
- create a common vision expressed in a cultural strategy for the region.

Consortiums promote and speak for all the cultural sectors within a region, and advise and inform central government, Lottery distributors, local government and regional bodies such as Regional Development Agencies. One of their major tasks has been to draw up a cultural strategy for their respective regions, with a common focus drawing together the many threads and identifying priorities for the region. These strategies are expected to be finalised by Easter 2001.

Consortiums will be made up of various interests within regions, which could include voluntary sector organisations. There are eight consortiums with boundaries coterminous with those of Regional Development Agencies and Government Regional Offices. They can be contacted through Government Offices – see separate entry for addresses. Instead of a Consortium, London has a Cultural Strategy Group to advise the Mayor.

Contacts:
Living East (Eastern England Cultural Consortium):
Tim Freathy Tel: 01223 346 748

South East Cultural Consortium: Dan Chadwick Tel: 01483 882 281

East Midlands Cultural Consortium: Geoff Milner Tel: 0115 971 2766

South West Cultural Consortium: Barry Cornish Tel: 0117 900 1839

Culture North East: Jamie McKay Tel: 0191 202 3878

LIFE West Midlands: Liz Charlton Tel: 0121 212 5343

North West Cultural Consortium: Janet Matthewman Tel: 0161 952 4341

Yorkshire Cultural Consortium: Bernard McLoughlin Tel: 0113 283 5452

Regional Arts Boards

Note: *Important restructuring announcements concerning the Regional Arts Boards (RABs) were made just before this guide went to press. The proposals can only be broadly sketched here.*

In March 2001 the Arts Council of England announced plans to unite with the 10 regional arts boards to create a single funding and development organisation for all the arts in all parts of England. The new Arts Council will have a strategic central office that is responsible for national arts leadership and is well connected with the arts nationally and internationally. The regional offices will be responsible for regional partnerships and investment and front-line contact with the arts.

The structure for the new Arts Council is due to be published in July 2001, with the new organisation expected to be established by December 2001. The new arrangements should come into effect from April 2002. It is planned that the regional arts offices should parallel the Regional Development Agencies areas. This will entail a reduction of regional arts offices in the south from three to two. Whether responsibility for Cumbria lies with the northern or with the north west office will also be decided.

The following information was applicable before the restructuring:

Support to organisations: The RABs provide financial support for professional theatre companies, dance and mime companies, music ensembles, literature, arts centres, galleries, community projects, arts education and training and a wide range of local arts bodies which promote arts events. The greater part of RAB funding is allocated to the professional sector, largely because of the greater expenses of professional arts companies and because amateur activities are more generally seen as the responsibility of local rather than regional authorities. Nevertheless some assistance is provided to support amateur work.

Support to individual artists: RABs offer a number of opportunities for individual artists; many of these are aimed at helping artists to reach a new and wider audience. A variety of commissions, bursaries, fellowships and residencies are available to writers, artists, craftspeople, composers, photographers and filmmakers who should contact their own RAB in the first instance as ACE has delegated many of its awards and schemes for individuals to the RABs.

Priorities: Each RAB establishes its own priorities from year to year, in line with a regional strategy agreed with the Arts Council. Generally, RABs are concerned to develop ventures in areas where provision is poor. Obviously chances of receiving a grant increase if activities/projects coincide with current RAB priorities in content and/or geographically. As with the Arts Council the relevant RAB department will want to see examples of work before they decide whether or not to make a grant.

Services provided: RABs employ specialist officers to deal with particular art forms or combinations of these. Other officers provide financial, marketing, PR, publications and administration services. RABs offer a range of marketing services to regional and touring arts organisations and many coordinate with Arts & Business (see separate entry) on advice sessions about how to raise sponsorship or access business skills. Via these staff and reference facilities, the RABs provide funding, information, publicity, planning and guidance to arts organisations and individual artists in their regions.

The Lottery: Since the advent of the National Lottery, the RABs have acted as agents for the ACE in the assessment of applications for awards. In 1999, following the Making a Difference lottery strategy consultation, the RABs have also assumed some direct responsibility in disbursing lottery funds in their regions. They became responsible for administering the small capital projects requesting less than £100,000. The RABs will together handle some £6.5 million a year for capital projects in 1999/2000, an amount probably less than 10% of the total capital spend but accounting for a far higher proportion of the applications. The RABs will continue to be involved in the assessment of larger projects in their regions. In addition the RABs are now responsible for developing the new 'revenue' schemes totalling £13.5 million in 1999/2000. The broad themes for these grants of between £5,000 and £30,000 each for one-off projects are:

- access;
- education;
- production and distribution;
- investment in artists;
- organisational development.

Each RAB has developed its own specific priorities within these areas. The Regional Arts Lottery Programme (RALP) operates regionally on the basis of common rules and regulations.

Local authorities: RABs can be very useful to help locate the relevant arts officer for funding from local authorities and the local arts councils/ associations which are usually funded by local authorities and often help support amateur activities.

Film and video: Not all RABs fund film, video and broadcasting. At the time of writing there were separate organisations in London (the London Film and Video Development Agency) and in the South West (the South West Media Development Agency). With the creation of the Film Council during 2000, further changes are planned.

The entries on the individual RABs which follow indicate the scale of their annual funding. Readers need to appreciate that the funds available for one-off projects are small and in total would usually be between only 10–20% of total grant-aid and are invariably heavily over-subscribed. The New Revenue Schemes of Lottery funding administered by the RABs from 1999 have increased the funding for projects.

The coordinating body for the boards is:
English Regional Arts Boards, 5 City Road, Winchester, Hampshire
SO23 8SD
Tel: 01962 851063; Fax: 01962 842033; E-mail: info@erab.org.uk
Chief Executive: Christopher Gordon; Administrator: Carolyn Nixson

Website: www.arts.org.uk

ONLINE Regional Arts Pages Website: www.arts.org.uk

Regional Arts Boards contacts

East Midlands Arts Board
Mountfields House, Epinal Way, Loughborough LE11 OQE
Tel: 01509 218292; Fax: 01509 262214
Website: www.arts.org.uk

Area covered: Northamptonshire, Leicestershire, Derbyshire (excluding the High Peak district), Nottinghamshire, unitary authorities of Derby, Leicester, Nottingham, Rutland.

Grant-in-aid from Arts Council of England: £6,603,000 (2000/01)

Contact: Deborah Duggan, Information
E-mail: info@em-arts.co.uk

East England Arts
Cherry Hinton Hall, Cherry Hinton Road, Cambridge CB1 4DW
Tel: 01223 215355; Fax: 01223 248075;
Website: www.eastenglandarts.co.uk

Area covered: Bedfordshire, Cambridgeshire, Essex, Hertfordshire, Lincolnshire, Norfolk, Suffolk, and unitary authorities of Luton, Peterborough, Southend on Sea, Thurrock.

Grant-in-aid from Arts Council of England: £6,202,000 (2000/01)

Contact: Ayleen Muir, Information Officer
E-mail: info@eastern-arts.co.uk

London Arts
Elme House, 2 Pear Court, London EC1R ODS
Tel: 020 7608 6100; Fax: 020 7608 4100;
Website: www.arts.org.uk/london arts

Area covered: The 32 London boroughs and the Corporation of the City of London.

Grant-in-aid from Arts Council of England: £28,240,000 (2000/01)

Contact: Chrissie Cochrane
E-mail: chrissie.cochrane@lonab.co.uk

North West Arts Board
Manchester House, 22 Bridge Street, Manchester M3 3AB
Tel: 0161 834 6644; Fax: 0161 834 6969
Website: www.arts.org.uk

Area covered: Cheshire, Lancashire, Merseyside, Greater Manchester and the High Peak of Derbyshire; unitary authorities of Blackburn with Darwen, Blackpool, Halton, Warrington.

Grant-in-aid from Arts Council of England: £14,195,000 (2000/01)

Contact: Ian Gasse, Information Officer
E-mail: info@nwarts.co.uk

Northern Arts Board

Central Square, Forth Street, Newcastle upon Tyne NE1 3PT
Tel: 0191 255 8500 ; Fax: 0191 230 1020
Website: www.arts.org.uk

Area covered: Cumbria, Durham, Northumberland; unitary authorities of
Darlington, Hartlepool, Middlesbrough, Redcar and Cleveland, Stockton;
metropolitan districts of Newcastle upon Tyne, Gateshead, North
Tyneside, Sunderland, South Tyneside.

Grant-in-aid from Arts Council of England: £10,900,000 (2000/01)

Contact: Jo Beddows, Press and PR
E-mail: info@northernarts.org.uk

South East Arts Board

Union House, Eridge Road, Tunbridge Wells, Kent TN4 8HF
Tel: 01892 507231; Fax: 01892 549383
Website: www.arts.org.uk

Area covered: Kent, Surrey, East and West Sussex; unitary authorities of
Brighton and Hove, Medway.

Grant-in-aid from Arts Council of England: £3,662,000 (2000/01)

Contact: Clive Russell, Director of Resources
E-mail: info@seab.co.uk

South West Arts Board

Bradninch Place, Gandy Street, Exeter EX4 3LS
Tel: 01392 218188; Fax: 01392 413554
Website: www.swa.co.uk

Area covered: Cornwall, Devon, Dorset (except districts of Bournemouth,
Christchurch and Poole), Somerset, Gloucestershire; unitary authorities of
Bath and North East Somerset, Bristol, North Somerset, Plymouth, South
Gloucestershire, Torbay.

Grant-in-aid from Arts Council of England: £6,635,000 (2000/01)

Contact: Claire Gulliver, Information Adviser
E-mail: claire.gulliver@swa.co.uk

Southern Arts Board

13 St Clement Street, Winchester, Hampshire SO23 9DQ
Tel: 01962 855099; Fax: 01962 861186
Website: www.arts.org.uk

Area covered: Buckinghamshire, Hampshire, Oxfordshire, Wiltshire south
east Dorset: unitary authorities of Bournemouth, Bracknell Forest, Isle of
Wight, Milton Keynes, Poole, Portsmouth, Reading, Slough,
Southampton, Swindon, West Berkshire, Windsor and Maidenhead,
Wokingham.

Grant-in-aid from the Arts Council of England: £8,026,000 (2000/01)

Contact: Val Brighton, Finance Officer
E-mail: info@southernarts.co.uk

West Midlands Arts Board
82 Granville Street, Birmingham B1 2LH
Tel: 0121 631 3121; Fax: 0121 643 7239
Website: www.arts.org.uk

Area covered: Worcestershire, Shropshire, Staffordshire, Warwickshire; metropolitan districts of Birmingham, Coventry, Dudley, Sandwell, Solihull, Walsall and Wolverhampton; unitary authorities of Hereford, Stoke-on-Trent, Telford and Wrekin.

Grant-in-aid from Arts Council of England: £9,431,000 (2000/01)

Contact: Helen Scott, Information Officer
E-mail: info@west-midlands-arts.co.uk

Yorkshire Arts
21 Bond Street, Dewsbury, West Yorkshire WF13 1AX
Tel: 01924 455555; Fax: 01924 466522
Website: www.arts.org.uk

Area covered: North Yorkshire; unitary authorities of East Riding, Kingston upon Hull, North East Lincolnshire, North Lincolnshire, York; metropolitan districts of Barnsley, Bradford, Calderdale, Doncaster, Kirklees, Leeds, Rotherham, Sheffield, Wakefield.

Grant-in-aid from Arts Council of England: £8,916,000 (2000/01)

Contact: Ian Aspinall, Information Officer
E-mail: info@yarts.co.uk

Area Museum Councils

Total grant to AMCs: £4.05 million (2000/01)

The Area Museum Councils (AMCs) are regional museum agencies whose role is to promote and support excellence in local museums, in caring for their collections, and providing high quality, accessible services to their public.

AMCs are charitable companies funded largely by central government, but also by income from membership subscriptions, fees, sponsorship and donations. They are independent membership organisations, whose elected boards unite people who work in museums with those, like local authority members, who govern them.

Most of the UK's 2,000 museums are members of their AMC. Local and regional museums are run by many different kinds of organisation, including local authorities, universities, charities and local societies. AMCs aim to provide an authoritative overview to guide sustainable development. They maintain information on the museum sector in their regions, enabling them to offer independent expert advice to local authorities, other regional organisations and national government.

AMCs support UK and national programmes, by, for example, helping to implement the Museum Registration Scheme (the UK minimum standards scheme for museums) and promoting other UK-wide standards. They advise funding bodies, including the Heritage Lottery Fund, on grants to museums and galleries in their areas. AMCs work in partnership with other sectors to enable museums to access funding from other government sources and from Europe. AMCs are particularly well placed to advise on proposals to set up new museums or redevelop existing ones. They can also recommend consultants for more detailed studies.

Funding: In 2000/01 the total government grant channelled through Resource, the Council for Museums, Archives and Libraries, to all seven English AMCs was £4.15 million. This is the breakdown:

- NE Museum Service £434,658;
- NW Museums Service £666,978;
- Yorkshire and Humberside Museum Council £648,210;
- SW Museums Council £534,582;
- EM Museums Service £243,882;
- WM Regional Museums Council £379,746;
- SE Museums Service £1,238,484.

Taken as a whole group, AMCs spend on average around 59% of their turnover on their advisory functions; around 30% on development grants; and 11% on administration.

Each AMC determines its grant priorities according to its particular development strategy. Grant support is increasingly delivered as part of wider, targeted development programmes which also include information, advice, and training. Potential applicants should therefore contact their AMC to discuss their plans and how these might fit with current priorities for support. AMCs do not offer revenue funding.

Area Museums Council: Contacts
North East Museums Service
(covers Teesside, Durham, Northumberland and Tyne and Wear)
House of Recovery, Bath Lane, Newcastle upon Tyne NE4 5SQ
Tel: 0191 222 1661; Fax: 0191 261 4725; E-mail: nems@nems.co.uk

North West Museums Service

(covers Cheshire, Cumbria, Greater Manchester, Lancashire and Merseyside)
Griffin Lodge, Griffin Park, Blackburn BB2 2PN
Tel: 01254 670211; Fax: 01254 681995; E-mail: nwms@nwms.demon.co.uk

Yorkshire Museums Council

(covers North, South and West Yorkshire and the unitary authorities of the former county of Humberside)
Farnley Hall, Hall Lane, Leeds LS12 5HA
Tel: 0113 263 8909; Fax: 0113 279 1479; E-mail: info@yhmc.org.uk
Website: www.yhmc.org.uk

East Midlands Museums Service

(covers Derbyshire, Leicestershire, Lincolnshire, Northamptonshire, Nottinghamshire and Rutland)
Courtyard Buildings, Wollaton Park, Nottingham NG8 2AE
Tel: 0115 985 4534; Fax: 0115 928 0038; E-mail: emms@emms.org.uk
Website: www.emms.org.uk

West Midlands Regional Museums Council

(covers Shropshire, Staffordshire, Hereford and Worcester, Warwickshire and the Metropolitan Authorities of the West Midlands)
Hanbury Road, Stoke Prior, Bromsgrove B60 4AD
Tel: 01527 872258; Fax: 01527 576960; E-mail: wmrmc@btinternet.com

South West Museums Council

(covers Bristol, Cornwall, Devon, Dorset, Gloucestershire, Somerset, Wiltshire and the Isles of Scilly)
Hestercombe House, Cheddon Fitzpaine, Taunton TA2 8LQ
Tel: 01823 259696; Fax: 01823 413114;
E-mail: general@swmuseums.demon.co.uk
Website: www.swmuseums.demon.co.uk

South Eastern Museums Service

(SEMS Central Office)
Ferroners House, Barbican, London EC2Y 8AA
Tel: 020 7600 0219; Fax: 020 7600 2581; E-mail: sems@sems.org.uk

SEMS Eastern Regional Office

(covers Bedfordshire, Cambridgeshire, Essex, Hertfordshire, Norfolk, Suffolk)
Manor House Museum, 5 Honey Hill, Bury St Edmunds, Suffolk IP33 1HF
Tel: 01284 723100; Fax: 01284 701394; E-mail: eastern@sems.org.uk

SEMS London Museum Agency
(covers City of London and 32 Boroughs)
Ferroners House, Barbican, London EC2Y 8AA
Tel/Fax: same as for SEMS Central Office; E-mail: london@sems.org.uk

SEMS South East Museums
(covers East Sussex, Kent, Surrey, West Sussex, Channel Islands)
The Garden Room, Historic Dockyard, Chatham, Kent ME4 4TE
Tel: 01634 405031; Fax: 01634 840795; E-mail: southern@sems.org.uk

SEMS Southern Museums
(covers Berkshire, Buckinghamshire, Hampshire, Isle of Wight, Oxfordshire)
Unit 8, Business Centre, Hyde Street, Winchester, Hampshire SO23 8RD
Tel: 01962 844909; Fax: 01962 878439; E-mail: western@sems.org.uk

Committee of Area Museum Councils
The Secretary, Rosemary Ewles, can be contacted c/o South Eastern
Museums Service, Ferroners House, Barbican, London EC2Y 8AA, or on
Tel/Fax: 020 8988 0910; E-mail: rjewles@pavilion.co.uk

Metropolitan Area Grant Schemes

In the late 1980s the metropolitan counties were abolished. There were
provisions which allowed all the constituent metropolitan boroughs of a
former metropolitan county to set themselves up as an association with
the capacity to levy a contribution from all of them for the purposes of
providing common services.

Greater Manchester Grants Scheme

AGMA Grants Unit
Chief Executive's Department
PO Box 532
Town Hall
Manchester M60 2LA

Tel: 0161 234 3364; Fax: 0161 236 5909/5405;
E-mail: agma_grants@manchester.gov.uk

Contact: Lesley Domnitz/Grainne Bradley, Grants Officer

Grant total: £2.8 million (2000/01)

The Association of Greater Manchester Authorities (AGMA) comprises
ten local councils (Bolton, Bury, Manchester, Oldham, Rochdale, Salford,
Stockport, Tameside, Trafford, Wigan). Funding is sharply focused on

strategic countywide services. The grants committee now has two major priorities, either or both of which an organisation must meet:

- to contribute to the recognition of Greater Manchester locally, nationally and internationally as a creative and vibrant county helping to create the conditions necessary to attract potential investment;
- to contribute to an improved quality of life for all its residents through its first priority above and by supporting agencies which assist those who are vulnerable or disadvantaged.

In addition emphasis is placed on organisations which:

- attract significant revenue from other sources;
- provide a countywide service or form part of a countywide service or which contribute to an issue of countywide concern;
- provide coverage over at least the majority of the ten districts.

Funding can cover the following activities – the arts, economic development and job creation, recreation, social and community, education and youth, advice services, racial and other forms of disadvantage and discrimination, environmental conservation and improvement.

Priorities for one-off funding are as follows:

- applications can only be made for finite projects which will not incur ongoing revenue expenditure from AGMA;
- grants/guarantees against loss on events and brief programmes;
- general fixed term project costs;
- applications not more than £5,000.

The amount available for one-off grants is only a very small proportion of total funding and ranges between £80,000 and £150,000 a year. In 2000/01 a total of 40 revenue grants were made ranging between £2,800 and £407,800. The major part of the funding was disbursed to 21 arts organisations. The six largest grants were to:

- *Hallé Concerts Society* (£407,800);
- *National Museum of Labour History* (£399,200);
- *North West Arts Board* (£340,200);
- *Royal Exchange Theatre Company* (£209,500);
- *GM Centre for Voluntary Organisations* (£151,800);
- *Greater Manchester Low Pay Unit* (£127,500).

Other grants included:

- *Community Technical Aid Centre* (£26,300);
- *Cancer Aid and Listening Line* (£11,900);
- *Women's Domestic Violence Helpline* (£7,400).

In 2000/01 one-off grant beneficiaries included:

– *Rathbone Community Industry;*
– *Live Music Now North West;*
– *Whitworth Water Ski and Recreation Centre* for the British water ski championships.

Exclusions: Individuals.

Applications: Full guidelines and an application form should be obtained for the one-off funding. There are three funding cycles a years: January for consideration in May; May for consideration in September; September for consideration in January.

London Boroughs Grants

5th Floor
Regal House
London Road,
Twickenham TW1 3QS

Tel: 020 8891 5021; Fax: 020 831 6903
E-mail: info@lbgrants.org
Website: www.lbgrants.org

Contact: Ian Brown, Press and Public Relations Manager

Grant total: About £28 million (2000/01)

London Boroughs Grants (LBG) merged with the Association of London Government from March 2001. It will move to new premises.

London Boroughs Grants is the largest funder of the voluntary sector in London. Each of the 33 London boroughs contributes to the budget of the scheme on the basis of its population. Its work covers a wide range of voluntary initiatives – housing, social services, community work, legal and other advice centres, employment, arts, recreation and the environment.

Grants are made to non-profit-making organisations which provide a service of benefit to *London as a whole or an area covering two or more boroughs.* The committee's highest priority is tackling poverty and combating disadvantage, discrimination and deprivation. Grants, ranging in size from £2,000 to £700,000, are made to over 500 organisations a year. There are no restrictions on the kinds of grant that may be made. However large-scale capital grants are rarely given and grants are usually for one-off revenue purposes or for ongoing revenue costs. Most are approved for a year at the end of which they are reviewed for renewal.

Examples of recent grants include:

— *Iranian Association*, for an immigration caseworker and a coordinator (£37,995).
— *Apex Trust*, for a London training resource manager. The trust provides employment, education and training support for people with a criminal record (£31,486).
— *The London Connection*, for the salary of an advice worker dealing with young homeless people in the West End from outer London (£21,290).
— *Hackney Asian Women's Aid*, for a coordinator post (£16,305).

Each year the LBG reviews its key priority areas for funding which are published in its business plan. The following criteria applied for organisations seeking renewal of their grants in 2000/01:

- working strategically with partner agencies;
- adding value by levering-in additional money;
- delivering 'Agenda for Action' objectives on single homeless;
- providing pathways out of social exclusion;
- enhancing services in outer London;
- enhancing the black and white voluntary sector;
- enhancing support and infrastructure services;
- enhancing services to refugee communities;
- enhancing support for women experiencing domestic violence;
- enhancing Londoners' access to arts and culture;
- promoting community/service users rights and entitlements.

Each year about £1.5 million is allocated to a New Initiatives Fund. Its priorities are decided annually. Priorities for 2000/01 were:

- the post-Lawrence agenda;
- outer London;
- 'Agenda for Action' on single homelessness;
- Innovation Fund;
- pathways out of social exclusion.

Applications: More detailed guidance is available on these priorities. Applications can be made at any time.

West Yorkshire Grants

PO Box 5
Nepshaw Lane South
Morley
Leeds LS27 0QP

Tel: 0113 253 0241
Direct line Tel: 0113 289 8215
Fax: 0113 253 0311

E-mail: jmitchell@wyps.demon.co.uk
Website: www.wyg.wyjs.org.uk/index.htm

Contact: Janet Mitchell, Grants Officer

Grant total: £1.16 million (2000/01)

These grants are administered by a joint committee of the metropolitan districts of Bradford, Calderdale, Kirklees, Leeds and Wakefield. Priority is given to:

- organisations that make a strategic impact on the social or cultural infrastructure of West Yorkshire, taking into consideration the number of districts served, the funding received from other sources including local authorities, and the level of user support;
- organisations providing support services to the voluntary sector in West Yorkshire.

Organisations must operate in or benefit people from a minimum of three districts. Grants are only offered on an annual basis.

In 2000/01 a total of 31 grants were made ranging between £1,963 and £289,542 with most of the funding allocated to arts organisations. The largest grant was made to Opera North (£289,542). The nine non-arts beneficiaries included:

- *Y & H Money Advice Support Unit* (£83,850);
- *Charities Information Bureau* (£51,250);
- *Federation of Disabled Sports Organisations* (£47,122);
- *Pecket Well College* (£34,353);
- *BTCV* (£12,300).

Applications: Full eligibility criteria are available from the grants officer. The application deadline in the last few years has been 31 October.

International Section

This section covers those departments where support to the voluntary sector is given to organisations working with an international purview.

Foreign and Commonwealth Office

Whitehall
London SW1A 2AH

Tel: 020 7270 3000

Website: www.fco.gov.uk

General Grants to Voluntary Organisations

Grant-in-aid: £6,551,000 (1999/2000)

In 1999/2000 a total of 22 grants were made to organisations in the voluntary sector. Grants are awarded to organisations which help further foreign policy aims and objectives. Many are annual and longstanding. The larger grants were made to:

– *Westminster Foundation for Democracy* (£4,000,000);
– *Commonwealth Foundation* (£692,644);
– *ICRC – International Committee of the Red Cross* (£600,000);
– *Anglo/German Foundation* (£250,000);
– *British Association for Central and Eastern Europe* (£239,755);
– *British Russia Centre* (£230,850);
– *Great Britain/China Centre* (£214,375);
– *Franco/British Council* (£90,228);
– *Encounter* (£57,000);
– *Canning House* (£44,303);
– *Atlantic Council of the UK* (£31,000);
– *UN Association* (£24,000);
– *UK/Canada Colloquia* (£15,470).

Smaller grants ranging between £3,000 and £15,000 included grants to the Joint Commonwealth Council, the Hague Academy of International Law, the Spanish Tertulias and the West India Committee.

Contact: Carol J Varney, Resource Budgeting Department, Room 428, 1 Palace Street, London SW1E 5HE Tel: 020 7238 4027; 020 7238 4004

Department for International Development (DFID)

94 Victoria Street **(94 V St)**
London SW1E 5JL20

Victoria Street **(20 V St)**
London SW1H 0NF

Tel: 020 7917 7000
Fax: 020 7917 0016

16 Abercrombie House **(A H)**
Eaglesham Road
East Kilbride
Glasgow G75 8EA

Tel: 01355 844000
Fax: 01355 843457
Public Enquiry Point: 0845 300 4100

E-mail: enquiry@dfid.gov.uk
Website: www.dfid.gov.uk

Contents
(Grant-in-aid in italics)

Related Agencies

Civil Society Department
Civil Society Challenge Fund (A H)

New funds available: £4,300,000 (2000/01)

Ongoing funding from former Joint Funding Scheme: £15.8 million (2000/01)

The Civil Society Department replaced the Non-Governmental Organisations Unit during 1999 and the first round of the new Civil Society Challenge Fund was launched in October 1999. The fund is open to any UK-based non-profit group, organisation or network/alliance/ coalition, which shares the department's overall objective, which is the eradication of poverty.

The fund's overall aim is to increase the proportion of poor people in developing countries able to understand and demand their rights – civil, political, economic, and social – and to improve their economic and social well-being. The fund supports initiatives which assist this process. A broad range of activities can be supported.

Activities funded should be linked explicitly to the following:

- providing poor and socially excluded people with access to information and networking which enable them to have more influence over decision makers at all levels;
- building sustainable know-how in developing countries;
- strengthening North-South civil society links and alliances.

'Innovation' will characterise many of the activities to be funded and, in all cases, the department will be seeking approaches with potential for dissemination and replication by other organisations, including the department's country programmes. In addition to activities which can be described as 'projects', the fund will support other initiatives, which may be short term or 'one-off' proposals.

Activities proposed for funding must:

- have clear and achievable objectives, and be able to show how these will be assessed;
- include the building of sustainable local know-how or 'capacity';
- demonstrate that learning is an integral part of the project, and how lessons learned will be disseminated;
- be complementary to/not conflict with DFID's agreed strategies for individual countries, where these exist.

'Capacity building' is defined as strengthening groups, organisations and networks to increase their ability to contribute to the elimination of poverty. Activities can include:

- leadership development;

- programme planning and implementation;
- policy research and advocacy;
- information access, use and dissemination;
- building alliances, coalitions, networks, North-South partnerships and inter-sectoral partnerships;
- financial sustainability.

Proposals based on operational activities on the ground should be clearly linked to strategies for strengthening the voice of poor and marginalised people. The fund will support projects with service delivery components where they:

- enable poor people to get essential and quality services to which they would otherwise not have access;
- improve the equity of overall service provision;
- improve cost-effectiveness and community ownership;
- enhance the sustainability of services.

Examples of grants in 2000/01:

- *AIDS Alliance*, promotion of effective and sustainable responses to HIV/AIDS in Ecuador (£1,124,118);
- *World University Service*, to address the need for literacy and continuing education especially amongst women in Uganda (£994,144);
- *ADD*, improving the economic and social well-being of poor disabled people in four areas of Bangladesh (£874,022);
- *Health Unlimited*, developing a culturally acceptable and sustainable community based health care system in Santa Lucia and San Pedro, Guatemala (£833,360);
- *Birdlife International*, for institutional capacity building/community forest management in North West Cameroon (£829,024);
- *Anti Slavery International*, to establish and develop a network of NGOs in six countries in Western Africa committed to eradicating child domestic servitude and cross-border trafficking (£14,290).

Priority themes: These have been introduced for projects funded from April 2001 to tie in with DFID objectives and priorities. These will be revised from time to time. Good initiatives will continue to be funded but preference will be given to those in the priority areas.

For 2001/02 funding these were:

- Initiatives to enhance the capability of poor and marginalised people to participate in public policy formulation at local, national or international levels, including budget processes. They could either be aimed at developing the skills and know-how of poor people to interact effectively with decision-makers, or seek to develop poor people's understanding of local and national policy and budget formulation processes to enable more informed debate.

- Initiatives which build relationships with 'non-traditional' partners in developing countries, i.e. links and closer working with, for example, trade unions, advocacy, and human rights monitoring groups.

Proposals may be accepted for activities in any developing country, though it is expected that the majority of activities will be in countries where DFID has significant programmes.

Funding: The Challenge Fund can provide up to 50% of total costs, with the balance coming from any non-UK government sources. Funding levels for smaller projects and one-off initiatives (up to £10,000) will be flexible and decided on a case by case basis. Funding for activities is limited to a maximum of five years and funding is not available for follow-on phases of projects.

Applications: There is a two-tier application process: concept note submission followed by a full proposal. Full proposals will be considered competitively twice a year, in early April and in early October. Full proposals must be received by 30 November for the April decision round, and not later than 31 May for the October decision round.

Applicants must also be able to demonstrate that:

- they have established links with partners in developing countries, and that their link, in terms of the activity to be funded, adds value beyond simply being a channel through which DFID funds are transferred; though they do not have to be organisations whose primary purpose is overseas development;
- they are legally constituted in UK; though they do not have to have UK charitable status;
- they share DFID's core values of mutual respect, equity and justice, openness and transparency;
- they have the capability to account for any DFID funds received.

For further information contact: Tel: 01355 843583; Fax: 01355 843457

Website: www.dfid.gov.uk

Partnership Programme Agreements (PPAs)

To come into effect from April 2001 onwards:
Total anticipated funding: £48 million (2001/02)

This arrangement replaces the former Block Grant Scheme for which the total funding was some £48 million in 2000/01. PPAs recognise that organisations with international influence and reach, and with established track-records for managing significant human and financial resources, should qualify for strategic funding at the centre and over a useful timeframe, rather than on a case by case, or project by project, basis. DFID seeks to maximise collaboration with such organisations in pursuit of the international development targets, through Partnership Programme Agreements. PPAs link strategic funding to mutually-agreed strategic outcomes.

Examples of funding in 2000/01 under the former Block Grant Scheme:
− *Oxfam* (£5,572,702);
− *Save the Children Fund* (£4,814,815);
− *Christian Aid* (£3,154,596);
− *Worldwide Fund for Nature* (£2,273,662);
− *Catholic Fund for Overseas Development* (£2,016,872).

Grants to Volunteer Organisations (2000/01):
− *VSO* (£22,128,597);
− *CIIR* (£2,078,172);
− *Skillshare Africa* (£1,581,469);
− *UNAIS* (£1,064,762);
− *BESO* (£1,363,917).

Criteria and application procedures for PPAs (2002/03): Any non-profit organisation (or alliance/network) based in UK will be considered for a PPA provided the following criteria are met:

- There is a demonstrated congruence between the organisation's mission and objectives, as defined in DFID's White Paper/s and Target Strategy Papers.
- The applicant has been involved for at least five years in one or more of the strategic areas covered by DFID's Target Strategy Papers. Organisations which have a single issue focus, for example education or health, are eligible to apply, but they will require the endorsement of the appropriate DFID department prior to agreement to start negotiations. DFID's Civil Society Department will be responsible for seeking this endorsement.
- It has experience of working in a range of developing and/or transition countries. Organisations which focus on particular groups of countries or regions will require endorsement by the appropriate DFID overseas office/s or country department/s. DFID's Civil Society Department will be responsible for seeking this endorsement.
- It has demonstrated capacity to link 'grass roots' work with wider policy/influencing/advocacy work.
- It has a minimum of £750,000 funding from DFID as a whole over the three-year period 1997/98–1999/2000.

Most PPAs are likely to be with individual organisations; however the feasibility of PPAs with alliances of smaller organisations working together at the strategic level may also be considered.

For further information contact: Tel: 01355 843583; Fax: 01355 843457

Website: www.dfid.gov.uk

Development Awareness and Education Section
Development Awareness Fund (A H)

Grant total: £5 million (2000/01); £3 million (1999/2000); £1.5 million (1998/99)

Mini Grant Programme: £330,000 (2000/01); £293,000 (1999/2000); £140,000 (1998/99)

The fund's overall aim is to support activities which promote public knowledge and understanding of development issues, of our global interdependence, of the need for international development; and of the progress, both achieved and potential. DFID will consider project proposals which fall within this broad aim, and which explicitly promote the following:

- knowledge and understanding of the major challenges and prospects for development, in particular the poverty reduction agenda; but also of developing countries themselves;
- understanding of our global interdependence, and in particular that failure to reduce global poverty levels will have serious consequences for us all;
- understanding of and support for international efforts to reduce poverty and promote development including the international development targets; recognition of progress made, and that further progress is both affordable and achievable;
- understanding of the role that individuals can play; enabling them to make informed choices.

DFID is particularly interested in supporting projects which engage new audiences. The fund is primarily focused on UK audiences, but it may, in exceptional circumstances, support activities focused on overseas audiences.

Applicants should normally meet a proportion of project costs from their own resources or from other sources but in exceptional circumstances DFID will meet 100% of project costs. DFID will not normally provide general core funding to agencies. However, administrative costs can be included where these are integral to the delivery of a project's objectives. Funding up to a maximum of three years can be considered.

Contributions of up to £100,000 a year towards the total project costs can be considered. In exceptional cases larger projects may be considered.

A Mini Grants Programme for applications under £10,000 a year for England, Scotland, Wales and Northern Ireland is administered on the DFID's behalf, see contact details below.

Exclusions: Projects involving construction works; items of equipment, other than as an integral part of a wider project; scholarships, for full time study even if part of a wider project; initiatives which clearly fall within the criteria of other funding programmes operated by DFID; initiatives which involve direct lobbying of the UK government or of international organisations of which the UK is a member, or which involve lobbying for or against activities of particular companies, individuals or institutions.

Applications: New project proposals can be submitted at any time up until the end of November preceding the financial year in which the project is scheduled to begin (e.g. proposals for a project starting in May must be submitted by the end of the preceding November).

Contact: John Murray, Fund Manager Tel: 01355 843255;
Fax: 01355 843539

Development Awareness Mini Grant Programme
Contacts:
England
Development Education Association, 3rd Floor, 29–31 Cowper Street, London EC2A 4AP
Tel: 020 7490 8108
Contact: Doug Bourn

Scotland
IDEAS, 34–36 Rose Street, North Lane, Edinburgh EH2 2NP
Tel: 0131 225 7617
Contact: Katrin Taylor

Wales
Cyfanfyd, Welsh Centre for International Affairs, Temple of Peace, Cathays Park, Cardiff CF1 3AP
Tel: 01222 757067/228549
Contact: Dominic Miles

Northern Ireland
Coalition of Aid & Development Agencies (CADA), 4 Lower Crescent, Belfast BT7 1NR
Tel: 01232 241879
Contact: Stephen McCloskey

Conflict and Humanitarian Affairs Department

The department can provide assistance in response to natural and technological disasters anywhere outside the UK.

Humanitarian Assistance (94 V St)

Total grant: £100.75 million (2000/2001) comprising
£11.25 million (Conflict and Humanitarian Policy);
£15 million (Emergency Response);
£15 million (Kosovo Humanitarian Policy);
£10 million (Mines Action Initiative);
£37 million (Multilateral Partnerships);
£5 million (Programmed Emergency Response);
£2.5 million (Refugees and Migration);
£5 million (World Food Programme and other food aid).

Agencies seek support from the emergency funds of the department for:

- rapid onset disaster relief;
- DFID's geographical departments and overseas offices are responsible for gradual onset disaster relief and other complex political emergencies; technological, or natural disasters;
- national and technological disaster preparedness, prevention and mitigation;
- post disaster repair and rehabilitation;
- conflict preparedness, prevention, reduction, and mitigation;
- policy and institutional development, including monitoring and evaluation, training and research.

The Head of Department is Dr Mukesh Kapila Tel: 020 7917 0778; Fax: 020 7917 0502; E-mail: M-Kapila@dfid.gov.uk

The department is divided into three teams.

Team One (Global Issues and Institutions):
Humanitarian policy, Red Cross (ICRC, IFRCS), and UN agencies (OCHA, UNHCR, IOM, WFP), interests in other multinational agencies (UNDP, UNICEF, WHO), NGO relations, UN general, ECHO/ European Union.

Team Leader: Sarah Richards Tel: 020 7917 0792; Fax: 020 7917 0502

Team Two (Humanitarian Programmes):
Rapid onset responses, prolonged emergencies (including Afghanistan, and North Korea). Response preparedness capacity building, disaster prevention, military/civil relations, demining.

Team Leader: Matt Baugh Tel: 020 7917 0040; Fax: 020 7917 0502; E-mail: M-Baugh@dfid.gov.uk

Team Three (Conflict and Security):
Conflict reduction, security sector issues, sanctions and arms proliferation issues, human rights in conflict, OHCHR.

Team Leader: Sarah Beeching Tel: 020 7917 0599; Fax: 020 7917 0502; E-mail: S-Beeching@dfid.gov.uk

The largest tranches of funding are given in two areas: humanitarian assistance and conflict policy and projects including human rights and humanitarian policy.

Conflict Policy and Projects (including human rights and humanitarian policy)

Grant total: £6,151,000 (1999/2000)

Grants were committed to 33 projects in 1999/2000. They ranged from £3,000 to £416,000. Grants included:

- *ACCORD*, Preventive Action Programme (£250,000);
- *International Alert*, Business and conflict research (£165,000);
- *International Peace Academy*, to improve understanding of the political economy of civil wars (£343,750);
- *Responding to conflict*, to develop self sustaining, practical conflict handling capacity among practitioners in areas of instability (£200,000);
- *Institute for Security Studies*, for the drafting of legislation on firearms and ammunition in South Africa (£62,475);
- *Saferworld*, to support implementation of the South African Action Programme on light weapons and illicit transfers (£80,796);
- *Media Trust*, to appraise the potential role that Radio Gulu could play in conflict resolution and peace-building (£10,000);
- *INTRAC*, for research on conflict assessment (£103,917).

Humanitarian Assistance

Grant total: £25,563,257 (1999/2000)

A total of 81 grants were made in 1999/2000 to 42 organisations. Examples included:

- *International Medical Corps*, support to Kosovo health sector (£5 million);
- *HALO Trust* demining in Kosovo (£3 million);
- *World Vision*, essential food items for cyclone victims in India (£200,000);
- *Action Aid*, emergency support to flood victims in Mozambique (£160,000);

- *SCF*, food and other essential items for victims of conflict in Kashmir (£150,000);
- *UK Jewish Aid*, trauma treatment in Kosovo (£50,000).

Disaster Preparedness and Mitigation
Grant total: £1,000,000 (1999/2000)

Commitments were made to 12 programmes in 1999/2000. They ranged from under £5,000 to over £300,000. Grants included:

- *Pan American Health Organisation*, to assist Latin American and Caribbean countries adopt disaster preparedness measures (£303,000);
- *World Bank*, for research on the economic and financial impacts of disasters (£252,803);
- *Intermediate Technology Development Group*, for support to the Duryog Nivaran network in South Asia, looking at livelihood options for disaster risk reduction (£60,489);
- *University of Cape Town*, for integration of disaster mitigation practice into ongoing development programmes across southern Africa (£219,181);
- *IDNDR UK Committee*, to support its activities in the last year of the decade for natural disaster reduction (£91,726).

Refugees and Migration
Grant total: £2,500,000 (2000/2001)

In addition to the projects funded through UNHCR, four grants to four organisations have been made in 1999/2000. The grants ranged from £62,000 to £195,000, and have been provided to assist NGOs working in refugee situations worldwide as well as to increase knowledge and awareness of refugee and forced migration issues.

Note: The DFID NGO Refugee Fund and the joint DFID/UNHCR NGO Fund have both ceased to exist. Applications for funding for emergency projects to benefit refugees and internally displaced people (IDPs), as well as strategic and knowledge generation projects relating to refugee or forced migration issues should be addressed to the Conflict and Humanitarian Affairs Department of DFID.

Applications: The booklet *Guidelines on Humanitarian Assistance* covers the areas of funding referred to above. It covers the format for making proposals, reporting, budgeting and appraisal systems, etc. Geographical departments with responsibility for a country or region usually deal with 'predictable emergencies' – long-running complex political emergencies or frequently recurrent natural disaster. Disaster preparedness and conflict reduction projects are also funded by geographical departments as well as from central budget.

If in any doubt as to where to send an application, contact this department for advice: Tel: 020 7917 0379, or the department's Public Enquiry Point Tel: 0845 300 410.

Social Development Department
Innovations Fund for Emerging Thinking and Methodologies (94 V St)

Grant total: £380,000 (2000/01); £380,000 (1999/2000)

The fund is designed to contribute to innovative activities with an element of risk aimed at developing and disseminating new ideas, generating new tools and methods for best practice, system and policy development, building capacity in the South. The following areas of work are most likely to attract funding:

- development and testing of participative methods for information collection and use which involve poor people;
- improving understanding of, and how to support, social institutions which can have a role in tackling poverty, e.g. in areas such as control over land, labour and capital influenced by membership of kinship groups, common property resources, savings and credit mechanisms;
- development of methods for promoting greater autonomy of, e.g., street children, older people, those with disabilities, refugees, victims of violence or conflict;
- development of strategies for strengthening civil society in representing/advocating on behalf of the poor;
- development of methods to enhance poor and socially excluded people's access to information through organisations such as citizens' advice bureaux, community theatre groups, grassroots video, and local media, and by the use of electronic communications;
- development of tools to strengthen women's empowerment, through e.g. gender mainstreaming, participation in decision-making and challenging violence;
- development of good practice in forming/monitoring business codes of conduct and methods to eliminate exploitative and hazardous labour conditions.

Proposals need to cover two or more countries. Most proposals are expected to fall within £5,000 and £50,000 a year and should be planned to achieve their aims within two years, though an extension to three years may be possible in exceptional circumstances.

Examples of recent grants:

- *ITDG UK*, for development of materials on mainstreaming strategy in the UN (£130,000 over 2+ years);

- *Manchester University*, to produce training and information resources in theatre-based participatory development techniques (£50,290);
- *WomenKind Worldwide*, for review of NGO experience in delivering Beijing Platform for Action (£29,000);
- *Overseas Development Institute*, for handbook of good practice in Poverty Participatory Assessments (£22,000).

Applications: Full *Guidance for Applicants* is available from Helen Ireton, Fund Administrator (see contact details below). Proposals are considered competitively twice a year in late spring and early autumn and need to be submitted by the end of May and the end of October.

Contact: Helen Ireton Tel: 020 7917 0627; Fax: 020 7917 0197; E-mail: sdd@dfid.gov.uk

Further information and advice is also available from: Martin Elliot, Head of Policy Coordination Tel: 020 7917 0488, and John Howarth, Desk Officer Tel: 020 7917 0283

Enterprise Development Department (EDD)
Enterprise Development Innovation Fund (94 V St)
Total funding: £600,000 (2000/01); £350,000 (1999/2000)

The Enterprise Development Innovation Fund (EDIF) aims to encourage the development of new and innovative ideas for enterprise development through the funding of action research projects which offer real scope for broader lesson learning and replicability.

For the period September 2000 to August 2001 EDD will be inviting applications for funding within a specific number of research themes. Additional insights into how these specific areas can be best utilised for the promotion of enterprise development are of particular interest to the department. Research themes will be revised annually to reflect new and developing innovations.

Applicants should ensure that they have up-to-date application forms and guidelines before submitting projects for consideration. The EDIF will fund innovative projects which fall within the following themes.

Theme 1: financial services
New microfinance products: Microfinance practitioners have realised the need to look at the full spectrum of financial services required by low-income households. Applications are invited which explore and provide insights into the following areas.

- Micro-insurance. One type of financial service that is gaining increasing attention is a category of products that address client's need for risk management. Insurance mechanisms provide protection by pooling risks across many households. DFID is particularly interested by life, health and property insurance.
- Micro-pensions. Micro-pensions allow informal sector workers/low income households to save a small part of their income over a prolonged period of time, providing them with an income once they are no longer in employment.
- Micro-leasing. Leasing is a contractual arrangement between two parties which allows one party (the lessee) to use an asset owned by the other (the lessor) in exchange for specified periodic payments. Micro-leasing can therefore expand the access of upper strata micro-enterprises and small businesses to medium-term financing for capital equipment and technology.

Post conflict or post emergency microfinance: The experiences of microfinance in post conflict or post emergency situations are not particularly well documented. Applications would be welcomed which are able to add to the body of research on the effective delivery of microfinance in such situations and/or provide innovative insights into appropriate and effective delivery mechanisms for post conflict microfinance.

Mechanisms to support microfinance for agricultural activities: For various reasons (repayment schedules, loan cycles, loan amounts), 'mainstream microfinance' is not suitable for the financing of agricultural activities. The development of financial products tailored to meet the needs of the agriculture sector is of specific interest.

Innovative areas of microfinance provision: This general category invites applications in other areas of innovative provision of microfinance services.

Theme 2: business development services (BDS)

The use of information and communication technologies in the provision of business development services: In particular applications are encouraged which fall into the following fields.

- Encouraging business access to new technologies such as the internet, either individually or in conjunction with traditional media, to improve access to market knowledge and increase business to business communication.
- Exploring the possibilities and opportunities that e-commerce could offer to small producers and service providers in developing countries.

- Examining the use of ICTs for low cost distance and technical training for small producers.
- Exploring the use of new technologies as a means of increasing access and reducing barriers to training for small scale producers.

The use of entrepreneurs as trainers for micro, small and medium enterprise (MSME) development: Using existing entrepreneurs in the development and delivery of training for MSMEs offers real scope to provide cost-effective, flexible services which meet the real needs of businesses. Applications are welcomed in the following areas.

- Encouraging government bodies, training institutes and NGOs to join up and work very closely with private entrepreneurs in the development and provision of training for MSME development. This approach would seek to use the skills of experienced and successful entrepreneurs (as opposed to institutional trainers) to undertake key educational tasks such as training needs analysis; curriculum design; and where appropriate, the actual business-to-business training.
- Encouraging the use of existing entrepreneurs in training for MSME development through the development of apprenticeship based schemes which allow trainees the chance to develop practical skills in a work-based environment.

Innovative approaches in the provision of business development services: This general category invites applications in other areas of provision of BDS.

Theme 3: legal and regulatory environment

Mechanisms for extra judicial business dispute arbitration: Formal legal mechanisms to resolve contractual disputes are often inaccessible to those in micro or small enterprises. Yet access to such services are imperative if smaller players in the market are to be given a fair deal. DFID is interested in exploring the use and development of external agencies (such as chambers of commerce or business associations) as providers of such arbitration services to those in micro and small enterprises.

Engaging the public and private sectors in the development and enforcement of better policy, laws and regulation: This general category aims to examine innovative ways of developing more effective regulation mechanisms for MSMEs.

A number of the DFID's partners have used the fund in the past to facilitate the development of smaller projects which were not able to be financed via the traditional bilateral programme. In light of this need applications from those partners wishing to fund small, innovative projects which fall outside the pre-determined themes will also be considered. Three 'open' categories for projects in business development services, financial service provision and supervision and regulation have been added to the list for this purpose. Partners should note that only a small percentage of funding will be put aside for general projects of this nature. Competition is expected to be quite intense.

The EDIF welcomes applications from a range of institutions including NGOs, consultancy companies, academic institutions, membership-based organisations or organisations representative of business such as chambers of commerce, business associations or industry federations. In most cases, the EDIF will be seeking applications from organisations in the North with clear links to similar institutions in the South. In certain instances, however, applications direct from southern-based organisations will be considered. Projects submitted should fall within a financial range of £75,000 to £200,000 (in total) and should be not more than three years in duration.

Examples of previously funded projects relevant to this guide:

- *New Economics Foundation*, research on international experience of regulating community and microfinance: lessons for the UK and developing countries;
- *Foundation for Small and Medium Enterprise Development*, University of Durham, developing the Small Business Unit with the New Economics University, Hanoi;
- *CARE UK*, capacity building of community based organisations in Jaffna, Sri Lanka.

Applications: The above guidelines are valid for two separate bidding rounds in September 2000 and March 2001. Copies of the full guidelines can be downloaded from the DFID website (see above). The EDIF has a two-stage bidding process. Interested organisations are initially asked to submit a brief concept note, outlining their proposed project and draft budget. Those partners whose 'concept notes' are successfully evaluated will be informed of the decision within two weeks of submission and asked to forward a full project proposal. Successful applicants at this stage will receive feedback and some limited guidance may be given on the development of the full proposal.

Deadlines for submission of concept notes and proposals for 2000/2001:

Submission of CN	Decision	Submission of proposal	Decision
22 Sept 2000	by 6 Oct 2000	3 Nov 2000	by 17 Nov 2000
30 Mar 2001	by 13 Apr 2001	11 May 2001	by 25 May 2001

Applications or queries should be made to the Enterprise Development Department. Applicants are requested to forward hard copies of any applications submitted via e-mail.

For further information contact: Paula Green Tel: 0208 917 0875;
E-mail: edd@dfid.gov.uk

Geographical Desks
(20 and 94 Victoria Street and overseas)

NGOs can also apply direct to each of the geographical desks, or sectoral departments, for funding, This also applies to the countries covered by the former Know How Fund – approaches should be made to the desks within the Central and South Eastern Europe Department (CSEED) and Eastern Europe and Central Asia Department (EECAC).

Contact the Public Enquiry Desk to find location of the desks:
Tel: 0845 300 4100; Fax: 01355 843632; E-mail: enquiry@dfid.gov.uk

Related Agencies

Charity Know How

114–118 Southampton Row
London WC1B 5AA

Tel: 020 7400 2315
Fax: 020 7404 1331
E-mail: ckh@caf.charitynet.org
Website: www.charityknowhow.org

Contact: Andrew Kingman, Director

Funding from the Department for International Development:
£326,091(2000/01 budgeted); £335,823 (1997/98) 50% of total budget

Charity Know How is an initiative funded by a group of grant-making trusts, individual donors and the Department for International Development. It was set up in 1991 to assist the revitalisation of the voluntary sector in Central and Eastern Europe (CEE) and the Newly Independent States (NIS). It aims to enhance the transfer of skills and know how and to form productive and supportive links between NGOs in the region and the UK.

Applications must include at least two organisations from different countries working in partnership. Eligible organisations may be non-governmental organisations (NGOs) in any of the countries covered by the scheme, or registered UK charities.

Kinds of activity funded:

- exploratory work aimed at further activity which includes a significant element of the transfer of know how;
- visits to any eligible countries or to the UK to enable NGO sectoral and organisational learning and development;
- training programmes for NGO staff and volunteers usually in management and funding areas rather than in specific professional skills such as nursing techniques or journalism;
- professional advice visits from charity or NGO representatives to assist with organisational aspects of an individual NGO, coordinating bodies or the sector as a whole;
- translation and adaptation of training or information materials from NGOs.

General Grant Programme

Grants awarded under this programme must include as principal beneficiary an NGO in at least one of the countries listed below. NGOs from other countries in Central and Eastern Europe (i.e. Czech Republic, Estonia, Hungary, Latvia, Lithuania, Poland, Slovenia) may apply as part of an application involving at least one NGO from one of the following countries:

- **Balkans and Carpathians:** Albania, Bosnia-Herzegovenia, Bulgaria, Croatia, Federal Republic of Yugoslavia, Macedonia (FYROM), Romania, Slovakia;
- **Caucasus:** Armenia, Azerbaijan, Georgia;
- **Central Asia:** Kazakstan, Kyrgyzstan, Tajikstan, Turkmenistan, Uzbekistan;
- **Western CIS:** Belarus, Moldova, Russia, Ukraine.

The maximum grant is £15,000. In 1999 more than 50 grants were made which ranged between £1,200 and £14,500. They included:

- *International Planned Parenthood Federation (IPPF)* and the *Family Planning Association of Moldova* for study visit by young volunteers (£13,266);
- *Multiple Sclerosis Society of Great Britain & Northern Ireland* and *Bulgarian National Foundation for MS and MG* for study visit by three Bulgarian MS groups (£11,830);
- *Minority Rights Group* and the *Inter Ethnic Initiative for Human Rights,* for training programme in Budapest (£11,136);
- *Field Studies Council* and *Children's Environmental School* for visit by Latvian teachers to UK schools (£8,053).

Partnership Development Grants

This pilot programme launched in October 2000 encourages the development of lasting partnership between two or more NGOs. NGOs from any CEE/FSU country or the UK can apply. East–East partnerships are particularly encouraged. There is more flexibility in the use of funding under these grants. Funding should be used for the same type of activities as in the General Programme, but in addition applications considering the following may be considered:

- costs of staff member or consultant to coordinate a specific piece of work within the partnership;
- equipment purchase;
- costs associated with staff secondments.

Maximum grant of £15,000 over two years.

Global Grants

Grants awarded under this programme, which was launched in October 2000, encourages the development of partnerships and sharing of skills and experience between NGOs of different regions of the world. Proposals must include as principal beneficiaries NGOs of at least two countries of the following regions:

- CEE/FSU countries;
- Africa;
- Asia;
- Latin America.

Maximum grant of £10,000.

Exclusions: These include: individuals; core and capital costs; costs of transporting humanitarian aid or medical equipment; youth artistic and cultural exchanges; retrospective grants. Full details with the guidelines.

Applications: Full guidelines are available with the application form. Application deadlines for all programmes are on a quarterly cycle, details available on the website or from the office.

British Council Arts Group

11 Portland Place
London W1N 4EJ

Tel: 020 7389 3194
Fax: 020 7389 3199
E-mail: kate.smith@britishcouncil.org.uk
Website: www.britcounc.org

Director of Arts: Susan Harrison

Contact: Kate Smith (Arts)

Total arts expenditure: £13 million (2000/01)

The purpose of the British Council is to promote a wider knowledge of the United Kingdom and to advance the use of the English language. Drawing on the country's intellectual capital and creativity it reinforces the UK's role in the international community through cultural, scientific, technological and educational cooperation. In contrast to the Arts Council of England and the Regional Arts Boards, the British Council is not an 'arts funding body' in a straightforward sense. It does not support artists and companies for their own development, but promotes UK arts abroad in order to fulfil its aims across all sectors, i.e. to enhance the reputation of the UK in the world as a valued partner. The council's work in the arts in a particular country is therefore bound up with its overall aims in that country.

The principal aims of the council's work in the arts, literature and design are as follows:

- to demonstrate the excellence of British arts to overseas publics, media, opinion-formers and successor generations;
- to promote intercultural dialogue and exchange;
- to stimulate the export of British cultural goods and services;
- to create the climate for export promotion in non-arts sectors, e.g. by mounting cultural events allied to trade initiatives, or by providing international opportunities for commercial sponsors;
- to contribute to international skills development and dissemination through arts for educational projects and training programmes.

The council promotes work which is excellent of its type, which reflects contemporary UK achievement, which is palpably in demand or likely to stimulate demand in the target market and which contributes to the council's aims and objectives in the country concerned.

Facts and figures: Spending on the arts accounts for around 19% per year of the government grant to the British Council. Total arts programme expenditure in 2000/01 was £13 million. The rough breakdown is performing arts – 40%, visual arts – 30% and literature, design and films/ TV – 10% each.

For the arts sector the council supports or manages nearly 3,000 events annually, with 70% of these introducing new British work to the country concerned, 30% involving artists from both countries in educational and exchange work, and with 80% of the total cost of this activity globally coming from partner-funding.

The Arts Group consists of five departments:

- Visual Arts;
- Performing Arts;
- Literature (including British Studies);
- Film and Television;
- Design.

There are advisory committees of specialists in the relevant fields. Expenditure for each department varies widely from year to year, depending on whether major exhibitions, tours, etc. are being mounted in any one year. The British Council is also one of seven stakeholders in the Visiting Arts Office of Great Britain and Northern Ireland (see entry below).

Applications: Each department has separate arrangements. There are no application deadlines.

Visiting Arts

11 Portland Place
London W1N 4EJ

Tel: 020 7389 3019
Fax: 020 7389 3016
E-mail: office@visitingarts.demon.co.uk
Website: www.britcoun.org/visitingarts/

Contact: Camilla Edwards

Visiting Arts (VA) is a joint venture of the national Arts Councils (England, Scotland, Wales and Northern Ireland), the Crafts Council, the Foreign and Commonwealth Office and the British Council. It aims to encourage the flow of international arts into the UK in order to develop cultural awareness and positive cultural relations between the UK and the rest of the world. VA's activities include advice, information, training, consultancy, publications, special projects and project development.

Project Development Awards

Total funding: £320,000 (2000/01); £326,000 (1999/2000); £380,000 (1998/99)

These awards cover a wide range of art forms with particular emphasis on contemporary work. They are available to promoters and venues to help them present quality foreign work with a clear country-specific dimension. The work must also demonstrate its contribution to the development of cultural awareness and cultural relations and be able to produce a continuing impact, influence or follow-up. Priority is usually given to first-time presentations of artists or companies.

There are five areas within which grants are given. These are:
- visual, media and applied arts;
- performing arts;
- combined arts;
- film;
- literature.

Examples of grants from 1999/2000 included:
- *The Millennium Mystery Plays,* Poland (promoter: The Belgrade Theatre) £5,500;
- *Meno Fortas Company,* Lithuania (promoter: Theatre Royal, Bath) £4,200;
- *Consolation Service* (various Finnish artists) (promoter: Finnish Institute) £2,000;
- *Al Rafif Theatre,* Syria (promoter: Institute of Contemporary Arts) £2,000;
- *Jaatra:* Bangladesh Folk Opera (promoter: Tagore Arts Promotion) £1,500;
- *Bernard Kabanda UK Tour,* Uganda (promoter: WOMAD) £400.

Eligibility: Applications are open to UK-based arts organisations, promoters and venues proposing projects that take place in the UK and involve presenting or working with artists from any country overseas. Freelance curators and promoters may apply on behalf of the UK venues or organisations they are working with. Artists or arts organisations based overseas or foreign governmental institutions cannot apply directly but must identify a UK host organisation/individual wishing to work with them. The UK host organisation/individual will be responsible for presenting any application.

Funding levels: The scale per single project varies between £500 to £6,000. However, the average award is between £2,000–£3,000 and only in exceptional circumstances will the award be made to the maximum amount of £6,000. VA's contribution to overall costs will normally not exceed 10%. It is assumed that for most projects multiple sources of funding will be required.

Exclusions: capital projects; stand-alone educational projects; publications (unless an integral part of the project); conferences, seminars and symposia; travel costs to attend events overseas; fundraising charity events, amateur art, one-off performances or performances by children's groups; events that are not open to the general public.

Applications: There are no deadlines but applications must be made at least four months prior to the start of a project. An early approach to VA needs to be made as most successful applications are either initiated, encouraged or developed with their help. Applicants should contact the relevant member of staff to give an outline of the project proposal; if it meets VA criteria applicants are asked to send a brief project outline with outline budget. If appropriate, applicants then make a formal application with more extensive information.

Contacts: Performing Arts: Nelson Fernandes Tel: 020 7389 3107
Visual Arts: Camilla Edwards Tel: 020 7389 3018

Connect Youth International (formerly Youth Exchange Centre)

The British Council
10 Spring Gardens
London SW1A 2BN

Tel: 020 7389 4030
Fax: 020 7389 4033
E-mail: connectyouth.enquiries@britishcouncil.org
Website: www.britishcouncil.org/education/yec

Contact: Indra Bahadur, Information Officer

Grant total: £4,733,000 (1999/2000); £3,195,000 (1998/99)

Connect Youth International (CYI), formerly known as the Youth Exchange Centre, is a department of the British Council whose principal funding comes from the European Commission, the Foreign and Commonwealth Office, the Millennium Commission and the Department for Education and Employment. CYI makes grants towards exchanges of young British people aged between 15 and 25 and young people in other countries. Exchanges are intended to widen the horizons of young people and to enhance their skills and confidence. Exchanges take place with countries in all regions of the globe, although the majority are with European countries. They must be for a minimum of seven days and be theme-based. The average grant is around £100 per person.

Exclusions: Tours to several countries, or cities in one country; competitions; purely touristic visits; exchanges that are part of an educational curriculum; youth wings of political parties; individual young people proposing to live, work or study in another country.

Applications: Contact the appropriate Regional Committee, listed below.

Regional Committees

East Midlands
Rosemary Beard, Deputy Principal Youth Officer, Lifelong Learning Services, PO Box 216, John Dryden House, 8–10 The Lakes, Northampton NN4 7DD
Tel: 01604 237442; Fax: 01604 237441

Eastern Region
Karen Williams, Youth Services in the Eastern Region, Regional Office, School Lane, Sprowston, Norwich NR7 8TR
Tel/Fax: 01603 488824

London
Nicci Carter, Youth Officer, Education Department, London Borough of Richmond, Regal House, London Road, Twickenham TW1 3QB
Tel: 020 8891 7502; Fax: 020 8891 77584

North
Tony Halliwell, Senior Development Officer, NRYCDU, Pendower Hall Education Development Centre, West Road, Newcastle-upon-Tyne NE15 6PP
Tel: 0191 274 3620; Fax: 0191 274 7595

North-West
Janet Preece, North-West RYSU, Derbyshire Hill Youth Centre, Derbyshire Hill Road, Parr, St Helens WA9 3LN
Tel: 01744 453800; Fax: 01744 453505

South
Tina Saunders, County Youth & Community Officer, County Hall, Chichester, West Sussex PO19 1RF
Tel: 01243 777066; Fax: 01243 777771

South-West
Dillon Hughes, South-West Association for Education & Training, Bishops Hull House, Bishops Hull, Taunton, Somerset TA1 5RA
Tel: 01823 335491; Fax: 01823 323388

West Midlands
Chris Knapper, Youth & Community Service, Education Department, Tipping Street, Stafford ST16 2DH
Tel: 01785 278762; Fax: 01785 278764

Yorkshire and the Humber
Penny Robson, Regional Youth Work Unit, Al-Hikmah Centre, 28 Track Road, Batley, WF17 7AA
Tel: 01924 511 183; Fax: 01924 511 184

Scotland
Jim Bartholomew, Central Bureau, 3 Bruntsfield Crescent, Edinburgh, EH10 4HD
Tel: 0131 447 5849; Fax: 0131 452 8569

Wales
Jean Reader, Wales Youth Agency, Leslie Court, Lon-y-Llyn, Caerphilly, Mid Glamorgan CF8 1BQ
Tel: 029 20 855700; Fax: 029 20 855701

Northern Ireland
Bernice Sweeney, Youth Council for Northern Ireland, Lamont House, Purdy's Lane, Belfast BT8 4TA
Tel: 01232 643882; Fax: 01232 643874

Commonwealth Youth Exchange Council (CYEC)
7 Lion Yard
Tremadoc Road
Clapham
London SW4 7NQ

Tel: 020 7498 6151
Fax: 020 7720 5403

Contact: Máire Ní Threasaigh, Exchanges Officer

Grant total: £186,000 (1999); £150,000 (1998)

Note: CYEC funds exchanges on a calendar year basis, although it receives funds from the Exchequer on a financial year basis. Its funding from the government for 1999/2000 was £167,000, and for 1998/99 was £147,000.

The CYEC is a charity financed largely by the government through Connect Youth International (see separate entry) and the DfEE via its National Voluntary Youth Organisations Scheme (see separate entry). It promotes two-way educational exchange visits between groups of young people in the UK and their contemporaries in all other Commonwealth countries by providing advice, information, training and grant aid.

CYEC intends exchanges to be both a programme for increasing international awareness and global citizenship and an informal means of personal and social development. Exchange projects require considerable commitment from young people over a two-year period, from planning, preparation and fundraising, through visiting and hosting, to follow-on activities. Emphasis is placed on young people's full participation in the ownership and management of their exchange, and the benefits for them in terms of new attitudes, skills, knowledge and understanding. Young people taking part in exchanges are encouraged to undertake a Personal Record of Achievement based on the skills they are developing.

CYEC prioritises exchanges with countries in Africa, Asia and the Caribbean and young people who would not normally have the opportunity to take part in an international project. Groups should normally number between 5 and 13 participants, aged 16–25, excluding leaders. UK groups must host as well as visit. One-way visits are not eligible for funding. Return visits should take place within two years. Visits must last at least 21 days for exchanges outside Europe, and at least 14 days for Cyprus, Malta and Gibraltar. Grants are given on a per head basis and represent up to 35% of international travel or hosting costs.

Applications: Detailed guidelines and application forms are available on request (SAE required). Potential applicants should make contact with CYEC as early as possible to discuss their proposals. Applications must be submitted during the autumn and at least nine months prior to a visit.

Appendixes

Appendix 1: Other Key Funding Sources

Contents

New Opportunities Fund

Heron House
322 High Holborn
London WC1V 7PW

Tel: 020 7211 1800; enquiries line: 0845 000 0121
Fax: 020 7211 1750
E-mail: general.enquiries@nof.org.uk
Website: www.nof.org.uk

Contact: Lilian Prodromou

The New Opportunities Fund is a lottery distributor formed to distribute grants to health, education and environment projects across the UK. By working in partnership with other organisations, including other lottery distributors and the voluntary sector, the fund intends to support sustainable projects that will:

- improve the quality of life for people throughout the UK;
- address the needs of those who are most disadvantaged in society;
- encourage community participation;
- complement relevant local and national strategies and programmes.

The New Opportunities Fund has six programmes at the time of writing. The programmes share four key values: partnership, consultation, strategic use of funding and the promotion of social inclusion.

NOF Health

Healthy Living Centres (HLCs)
Total funding for England: £232.5 million (2000/01–2006/07)

The fund plans to establish a core network of HLCs across the UK by 2002, servicing 20% of the population and focusing in particular on the needs of disadvantaged communities. There is no blueprint for exactly what a HLC should be, but it is expected that there will be a variety of projects that promote good health in its broadest sense, to help people of all ages improve their well-being and get the most out of life. HLCs could be mobile services, or could build on existing community centres, health services and leisure facilities. Users and local communities are encouraged to play an active role in the design and delivery of the projects to ensure that the focus of the schemes is on the needs of their communities.

Grants are made for capital and revenue expenditure, for up to five years. Large capital grants for new building, renovation or re-design are unlikely to be made. Applications are expected to come from 'robust partnerships', involving the public, private, and voluntary and community sectors. All projects will have to show that they can be sustained following NOF funding.

Two examples of projects funded under the scheme are:

- *St Augustine's Healthy Living Centre* in King's Lynn; the application was headed by the North End and North Lynn Community Trust. A disused sports and social club is being converted into a centre providing a wide variety of services, including child care, adult education, employment advice, access to a GP, a health visitor, family planning clinics, nutritional information, a cafe and fitness activities. The range of services offered by St Augustine's reflects the NOF's vision for HLCs.
- *Chinese National Healthy Living Centre*, which provides bilingual support and guidance to the Chinese community, thereby improving access to healthcare and reducing poor health and disadvantage. Activities include volunteer befriending and schemes to tackle loneliness and depression. Three regional centres, based in London, Birmingham and Sheffield will act as focal points for outreach work (£1.2 million).

Applications: There is a two-stage application process, whereby expressions of interest are received and then full applications worked out with advice from the fund itself. The final deadline for 1st Stage Applications was 21 December 2000. The fund plans to commit all money by September 2002. As grants may be made for up to five years, some projects could be funded up to 2007.

Further advice and support may be obtained via the Healthy Living Project, an independent networking service for organisations starting HLCs.

Contact: Laverne Anderson, PO Box 327, Leeds LS2 7XU
Tel: 0113 244 1210; Fax: 0113 244 1210;
E-mail: lavernea@healthyliving.org.uk;

Website: www.healthyliving.org.uk

Living with Cancer: Palliative Care and Information Projects
Total funding: £23,250,000 for England (2000/01–2001/02)

Living with Cancer is NOF's £150 million-funded anti-cancer programme. Eighty per cent of the money is being spent on equipment for detecting and treating cancer, with the remaining £23.25 million reserved for palliative care and information projects. These projects are targeted at those that benefit black and minority ethnic communities and socially disadvantaged groups as defined by the Index of Local Conditions. The types of projects funded are those aimed at:

- reducing the inequalities in provision of home care;
- supporting carers, including practical, psychological and emotional support and respite care;

- providing locally-adapted or culturally-sensitive information about all aspects of cancer and care services for patients in the target group.

The deadline for applications for palliative care and information projects was May 2000. Projects were expected to begin in early 2001.

NOF Education

The NOF has four programmes in the area of education, three of which involve the voluntary sector. These are as follows.

Out of School Hours Learning
Total funding for England: £158.9 million

This programme aims to create regular activities in half of all secondary and special schools and a quarter of all primary schools in the UK. The range of learning activities to be supported is wide: projects may include music, drama or art activities; sport; key skills assistance; volunteering activities, and so on. At least £25 million has been earmarked for summer school places across the country. Funding for Out of School Hours Learning is available until 2000; for summer schools until 2002. Charitable organisations supported under this programme include:

- *A Space*, for work with nine schools in Hackney including educational support work, contemporary and cultural dance, ICT, theatre and media studies (£114,165);
- *Child and Sound*, for music and therapy workshops for young disabled people in a Southwark school (£25,589);
- *The Little Theatre Doncaster* is working in partnership with a primary school providing drama sessions to improve levels of literacy.

The charity Education Extra has been closely involved with the development and delivery of Out of School Hours Learning.

Applications: The deadline for a request for forms for Out of School Hours Learning was 31 December 2000. Forms were to be in by 1 March 2001. For summer schools the dates were, respectively, 1 March 2001 and 3 September 2001.

Out of School Hours Childcare
Total funding: £170.5 million for England (2000/01–2002/03)

This scheme is for the provision of good quality, affordable and accessible out of school hours childcare in a range of settings. The public, private and voluntary sectors are expected to be involved in providing activities. £20 million is available for integrated childcare and learning schemes.

Funding is only available for 12 months, and is not intended to subsidise childcare places over the long term; all the places funded must have workable plans for sustainability through a combination of government funding and parental contributions.

Projects supported under this scheme include:

– *Playlines Consortium*, for 23 childcare schemes in Cornwall and Devon (£234,600);
– *Liverpool Lister Drive Kids Club*, to extend its facilities (£48,000);
– *PARK Ltd*, for increased provision in Owlerton and Hillsborough areas of Sheffield (£23,000);
– *Birmingham Latchkey Club*, for the creation of 35 childcare places (£15,000).

'Application milestones' are 15 February, 15 June and 15 October every year up to and including February 2003.

Community Access to Lifelong Learning (CALL)
Total funding: £155 million for England (2000/01–2001/02)

This programme supports the development of learning through information and communications technologies (ICT). The programme's three strands are as follows.

- **The development and running of a nationwide network of so-called UK online centres:** with online computer access to information and community resources. The Department for Education and Employment is funding with £252 million the capital costs of the proposed 700 new UK online centres – see separate entry. NOF will provide revenue funding for activities including: marketing and promotion to identify and attract new users to learning centres; training for users and staff; learning support and guidance; supporting and facilitating use of the UK online centre; monitoring and evaluation.
  Learning support and guidance could include the use of new or existing staff to run workshops, demonstrations and taster sessions; assessment of the learning benefits for users; acting as mentors to new users; the purchase of learning materials, such as CD-Roms, disks, books and manuals; advice and guidance on how users of the UK online centre could progress into other learning opportunities, such as the University for Industry.
- **Community Grids for Learning (CGfLs):** A CGfL is, at its most basic, an internet site that hosts information, advice or learning materials of community interest. The prime aim of CGfLs is to encourage more adults into learning. The fund envisions CGfLs to be open networks, enabling access from any part of the UK through the

National Grid for Learning (the national focal point for learning on the Internet). CGfLs can be developed for local or regional communities or to support learning in communities that are not geographically-based.
NOF will support costs to do with: infrastructure, including central server capacity and interconnection costs; software; content design and development, including the use of consultants and designers; initial staffing costs, including training; and marketing. Applications are expected to come from partnerships rather than being associated with a particular UK online Centre.

- **A People's Network of UK online centres in public libraries:** Funding for this component is only available to library authorities.

Applications: DfEE funding for the capital costs of UK online centres is restricted to the 2,000 most disadvantaged local authority wards. The New Opportunities Fund's funding is not limited in the same way, but applicants should be able to demonstrate how they intend to target the socially-excluded among a variety of groups. A joint DfEE/NOF application form is available for projects seeking both capital and revenue funding.

Forms are available from the contact details above. The third application deadline for the CALL programme is 4 May 2001; all grants will be awarded by December 2002.

NOF Environment

The NOF has one environmental programme.

Green Spaces and Sustainable Communities
Total funding: £96,880,000 for England (2000/01–2001/02)

This programme is designed to help urban and rural communities throughout the UK understand, improve or care for their natural environment. Seventy-five per cent of the money has been allocated to green spaces projects that will make better use of existing green spaces and make them more accessible to the public. Projects could include:

- creating or improving space for children's play;
- recreation and playing fields;
- improvements to parks;
- access to the countryside.

The remainder of the fund is given over to 'community involvement in sustainable development'. This covers such activities as waste minimisation, transport, consumption, promotion of biodiversity and energy efficiency.

The programme is administered across the UK via 12 'Award Partners', who run umbrella schemes or delegated grant programmes to deliver funding at a local level. The following is a list of Award Partners operating in England. Figures in brackets refer to the amount of money each partner has to distribute. Names of schemes are in italics.

Barnardos: *Better Play!* (£9,289,000)

This scheme will provide opportunities for children to play safely within their neighbourhood. Grants will be awarded up to £50,000.

Contact: Barnardos, Tanners Lane, Barkingside, Ilford, Essex IG6 1QG
Tel: 020 8550 8822; Fax: 020 8551 6870

BTCV: *People's Places* (£6,493,000)

An England-wide network of 1,200 green spaces will be created or improved in areas where access to open space is limited due to social and economic disadvantage. Grants will be awarded between £3,000 and £10,000.

Contact: BTCV, 36 St Mary's Street, Wallingford, Oxfordshire OX10 0EU
Tel: 01491 839 766; Fax: 01491 839 646; E-mail: information@btcv.org.uk

Sport England: *Playing Fields and Community Green Spaces* (£31,594,000)

This programme has three strands: for projects protecting, providing and improving playing fields and green spaces for the benefit of local communities, especially in deprived areas; to work in partnership with Learning through Landscapes and other organisations to deliver a programme of school playgrounds for children's play; and to work in partnership with other organisations to deliver ten pilot projects for children's play in the community.

Contact: Sport England, 16 Upper Woburn Place, London WC1H 0QP
Tel: 020 7273 5740; Fax: 020 7383 5740

The Royal Society for Nature Conservation: *Social, Economic and Environmental Development (SEED)* (£13,948,000)

Under this programme, grants will be awarded up to £50,000 to support social, economic and environmental sustainable development. The programme will support a wide range of projects including community food growing and marketing, energy efficiency, waste management and sustainable transport projects.

Contact: RSNC, The Kiln, Waterside, Mather Road, Newark, Nottinghamshire NG24 1WT Tel: 01636 670000; Fax: 01636 670001; E-mail: grants@rsnc.cix.co.uk

Sustrans: *Green Routes, Safe Routes* (£7,425,000)

The project will create safe routes to schools, including road safety training, safe routes to bus and rail stations, Home Zone projects in residential areas and green transport corridors to, from and in disadvantaged areas.

Contact: Sustrans, 35 King Street, Bristol BS1 4DZ Tel: 0117 926 8893; Fax: 0117 929 4173

The Countryside Agency: *Grass Roots* (£12,900,000)

This is a scheme to help urban and rural communities to plan, design, create, manage and use their own multi-purpose 'community greens' based on local need. The scheme will proactively target and support disadvantaged communities. Grants up to £150,000 will be awarded.

Contact: Countryside Agency, John Dower House, Crescent Place, Cheltenham, Gloucestershire GL50 3RA Tel: 01242 521 381; Fax: 01242 584 270; E-mail: info/hq@countryside.gov.uk

English Nature: *Local Nature Reserves* (£4,629,000)

EN already has a central government-funded local nature reserve scheme (see separate entry on English Nature), which has been given some more money from the New Opportunities Fund. Grants between £5,000 and £25,000 will be awarded for capital works, land purchase and for the employment of Community Liaison Officers.

Contact: Northminster House, Peterborough PE1 1UA Tel: 01733 455 000; Fax: 01733 568 834; E-mail: enquiries@english-nature.org.uk

Applications: Details of how to apply for the above funds had not been finalised at the time of going to press. Contact the individual partners for details.

In addition, consultation on six new initiatives was announced in November 2000:

- sports facilities for schools and the local community (£750 million);
- outdoor activities for young people (£50 million);
- fighting against heart disease and stroke, extra money for the existing combating cancer initiative, palliative care for adults and children with life-threatening and chronic illness (£300 million);

- provision of childcare places for children from birth to three years old, together with further support for children of the age of three, particularly in deprived areas (£200 million);
- environmental renewal and community regeneration, also promoting recycling and developing renewable energy resources (£150 million);
- small grants, between £500 and £5,000, for community groups to support local health, education and environment projects.

Policy directions are likely to be received by the fund in spring 2001 and the fund expects to launch the new programmes from summer 2001.

Further initiatives from the fund will continue to come on stream in the future and readers should be sure to keep up to date with developments.

Other National Lottery Distributing Boards for England

Arts Council of England
14 Great Peter Street, London SW1P 3NQ
Tel: 020 7312 0123; Fax: 020 7973 6590
Website: www.artscouncil.org.uk

Community Fund – Lottery Money Making a Difference (formerly National Lottery Charities Board)
St Vincent House, 16 Suffolk Street, London SW1Y 4NL
Tel: 020 7747 5300; Fax: 020 7747 5214
Website: www.community-fund.org.uk

English Sports Council (Sport England)
16 Upper Woburn Place, London WC1 0QP
Tel: 020 7273 1500; Fax: 020 7383 5740
Website: www.english.sports.gov.uk

United Kingdom Sports Council (UK Sport)
40 Bernard Street, London WC1N 1ST
Tel: 020 7841 9500; Fax: 020 7841 8850
Website: www.uksport.gov.uk

Heritage Lottery Fund
7 Holbein Place, London SW1W 8NR
Tel: 020 7591 6000; Fax: 020 7591 6001
Website: www.hlf.org.uk

Millennium Commission
Portland House, Stag Place, London SW1E 5EZ
Tel: 020 7880 2001; Fax: 020 7880 2000
Website: www.millennium.gov.uk

National Endowment for Science, Technology and the Arts (NESTA)
1st Floor, Gainsborough House, 34 Throgmorton Street, London
EC2N 2ER
Tel: 020 7861 9670; Fax: 020 7861 9675
Website: www.nesta.org.uk

Landfill Tax Credit Scheme and ENTRUST

6th Floor Acre House
2 Town Square
Sale
Cheshire M33 7WZ

Tel: 0161 972 0044
Fax: 0161 972 0055
Website: www.entrust.org.uk

Landfill Tax contributions: £183 million between 1997 and August 1999

In 1996 the first green tax, the Landfill Tax, was introduced on waste disposal going to landfill sites in the UK with the expectation that the industry would reassess and reduce waste and its associated problems. The aim of the tax is to shift waste to more sustainable methods of disposal e.g. reuse, recycling and energy from waste. HM Customs & Excise collects the tax at variable rates depending on the type of waste. Landfill operators may divert up to 20% of tax liability to environmental projects. They are reimbursed for 90% of the amount contributed. (They are expected to cover the remaining 10% themselves, although in many cases another organisation may do so for them.)

ENTRUST is not a supplier of funds. Funding can only be obtained from a landfill operator and different operators have set up different ways of handling their support.

Before any funding arrangements can go ahead, all groups interested in obtaining funding from an operator must first check with their local operator who will tell them if they need to be enrolled with ENTRUST, the official regulatory body of potential beneficiaries. It is essential for groups to appreciate that registration and project approval from ENTRUST in no way ensures funding from a landfill operator.

The scheme leaves funding decisions entirely to landfill operators. Groups can shortcut this process by approaching the intermediary funding body set up by, or working for a company (see below for examples). These organisations are themselves registered Environmental Bodies (EBs) and are able to disburse funds to other Environmental Bodies and non-enrolled groups. Since enrolment with ENTRUST costs £100 this route presents important savings for small groups.

Organisations applying for funding must be non-profit distributing bodies. They have to meet criteria for approved work under this scheme which includes:

- land reclamation for economic, social or environmental use;
- pollution reduction;
- research into sustainable waste management;
- education on waste issues;
- provision of public amenity facilities in the vicinity of a landfill site;
- reclamation and creation of wildlife habitats;
- restoration of buildings of architectural and heritage interest in the vicinity of a landfill site;
- provision of financial, administration and other services to environmental bodies.

'Vicinity' is interpreted as about a ten-mile radius from the landfill site.

By June 2000 over 2,000 organisations had enrolled and over 3,300 projects throughout the country were either active or completed. The main ways that landfill tax funding is disbursed are detailed below. This information is illustrative and by no means exhaustive.

Landfill Companies Donating Directly
UK Waste Management Limited
Funding: about £3 million p.a.
Eight sites in England, Scotland and Northern Ireland.

Manages its Landfill Tax account in-house. Its funds are split between national programmes and local projects. In addition it has established regionally-based environmental bodies which distribute money generated locally on local projects.

Contact: Barbara Broadhead/Claire Olver, Public Relations, Head Office, Rixton Old Hall, Manchester Road, Rixton, Warrington, Cheshire WA3 6EW Tel: 0161 775 1011; Fax: 0161 775 7291

Environmental Organisations Administering Funds for a Landfill Company
The Royal Society for Nature Conservation
Administers two major national award schemes. The boards of each consist of three members from the company and three from RSNC. Applications can be made by all organisations registered with ENTRUST. These funds are not directed only at local Wildlife Trusts as some people have assumed.

– *Biffaward for Biffa Waste Services* (£6.4 million in 1999 – established 1997);
– *Hanson Environment Fund* (£3.7 million in 1999 – established 1997).

In 1999 the fund introduced a community grants scheme of £250,000 a year to assist small environmental projects of between £500 and £2,000.

Contact: Andrea White, Royal Society for Nature Conservation, The Kiln, Waterside, Mather Road, Newark NG24 1WT
Tel: 01636 670000; Fax: 01636 670001; E-mail: grants@rsnc.kix.co.uk

Website: www.rsnc.org

RMC Environment Fund (administered by the Environment Council)
Funding: about £1.6 million p.a. – established 1999

Contact: Sasha Grigg, Landfill Tax Fund Coordinator, The Environment Council, 212 High Holborn, London WC1V 7VW
Tel: 020 7632 0127; Fax: 020 7242 1180;
E-mail: rmcenvironmentfund@envcouncil.org.uk

Website: www.greenchannel.com/tec

New Trusts Set up by Landfill Companies
The following are companies with single trusts working UK wide.

Onyx Environmental Group – Onyx Environmental Trust CC No: 1064144
Funding: £2.5–£3 million a year – established 1997

Ruthdene, Station Road, Four Ashes, Wolverhampton WV10 7DG
Tel: 01902 794600; Fax: 01902 794646

Contact: Douglas Davis

Five regional panels with local representation meet regularly to recommend projects for approval.

S.I.T.A. – S.I.T.A. Environmental Trust
Funding: some £5 million a year – established 1997

Willoughby House, 2 Broad Street, Stamford, Lincs PE9 1PB
Tel: 01780 753821; Fax: 01780 751556

Contact: John Brownsell

The company has some 40+ operational sites – East Midlands, Shropshire, Dorset, Surrey, Newcastle, Scotland.

Companies Setting up Multiple Trusts Working Locally

Cleanaway

The company has three main sites in the South East and one in Birmingham. Four trusts have been set up in the South East, particularly in Essex where its operations are concentrated.

Cleanaway Pitsea Marshes Trust and **Cleanaway Havering Riverside Trust**, 2 Chiltern Close, Goffs Oak, Waltham Cross, Herts EN7 5SP
Tel: 01707 874 558

Contact: Eric Dear

Cleanaway Mardyke Trust
c/o Cleaning and Greening Department, Thurrock Council, Civic Offices, New Road, Grays Thurrock, Essex RM17 6SL
Tel: 01375 652296

Contact: The Secretary

Cleanaway Canvey Marshes Trust
c/o Castle Point Borough Council, Kiln Road Offices, Thundersley, Benfleet, Essex SS7 1TF
Tel: 01268 882470

Contact: Chris Moran

Cory Environmental

Cory has set up a series of trusts in its main areas of operation. In addition it contributes directly to the Resource Recovery Forum, Thames 21, Trees for London, Wastebusters Ltd and Business Eco Logic Ltd.

Cory Environmental Trust in Carrick District
Funding: about £80,000 p.a. – established 1998

and **Cory Environmental Trust in Kerrier**
Funding: about £10,000 p.a. – established 1998

Both the above contacted at: 32 Henver Gardens, Reawla, Gwinear, Hayle, Cornwall TR27 5LM
Tel: 01736 850984; Fax: 01736 850163

Contact: Shirley Collings

Cory Environmental Trust in East Northamptonshire
Funding: about £50,000 p.a. – established 1999

c/o Environmental Health Department, East Northamptonshire House, Cedar Drive, Thrapston, Northants NN14 4LZ
Tel: 01832 742052; Fax: 01832 734839

Gloucestershire Environmental Trust Company
Funding: about £750,000 p.a. – established 1997

Moorend Cottage, Watery Lane, Upton St Leonards, Gloucs GL4 8DW
Tel: 01452 615000; Fax: 01452 613817

Contact: Lynne Garner, Secretary

Essex Environment Trust
Funding: about £650,000 p.a. – established 1998

Mackmurdo House, 79 Springfield Road, Chelmsford, Essex CM2 6JG
Tel: 01245 265555; Fax: 01245 495427

Cory Environmental Trust in Colchester
Funding: about £120,000 p.a. – established 1998

c/o Colchester Borough Council, PO Box 331, Town Hall, Colchester
CO1 1GL
Tel: 01206 282918; Fax: 01206 282916

Contact: Sue Warrener

Cory Environmental Trust in Rochford
Funding: about £90,000 p.a. – established 1998

c/o 53 Westbury, Rochford, Essex SS4 1UL
Tel: 01702 541413; Fax: 01702 543654

Cory Environmental Trust in Southend-on-Sea
Funding: about £80,000 p.a. – established 1997

589 London Road, Westcliff-on-Sea, Essex SSO 9PQ
Tel: 01702 340334; Fax: 01702 338282

Contact: Les Barker

Cory Environmental Trust in Thurrock
Funding: about £1 million p.a. – established 1997

Civic Offices, New Road, Grays Thurrock, Essex RM17 6SL
Tel: 01375 652485; Fax: 01375 652784

Contact: Geoff Howell, Secretary

Western Riverside Environmental Fund
Funding: about £250,000 p.a. – established 1998

c/o Groundwork, 1 Kennington Road, London SE1 7QP
Tel: 020 7922 1230; Fax: 020 7922 1219

Environmental Body Set up by a Landfill Company to Administer Funds

Waste Recycling Group

Operates in Cambridgeshire, Cheshire, Derbyshire, Lincolnshire, Nottinghamshire, Norfolk, Suffolk, Yorkshire. Set up WREN – Waste Recycling Environmental Ltd – registered as an Environmental Body which administers its funds via the advice of a series of county committees.

WREN, Waste Recycling Environmental Ltd
Funding: £9 million p.a. – established 1997

Wren House, Manor Farm, Bridgham, Norwich NR16 2RX
Tel: 01953 717165

Contact: The Administration Team

Website: www.wren.org.uk

Intermediary Organisations

Enventure Limited

Enventure acts as professional fund managers for companies contributing to the tax credit scheme. 'Enventure was approved as one of the first enrolled environmental bodies in the country and accounts for a significant proportion of the total Landfill Tax Money being spent on the environment.'

Contact: Maggie Bignall, Chris Jones, Bank House, Wharfebank Business Centre, Ilkley Road, Otley, West Yorks LS21 31P
Tel: 01943 850089; Fax: 01943 462075

Website: www.enventure.demon.co.uk

Essex Environmental Trust

Funding: about £1 million (1999) – established 1998

Mackmurdo House, 79 Springfield Road, Chelmsford CM2 6JG
Tel: 01245 265555; Fax: 01245 495427

Contact: Keith Derry, Trust Secretary

This trust was set up as a county council initiative and receives funding from six landfill operators in the county.

South West England Environmental Trust (SWEET)

Bridge House, 48–52 Baldwin Street, Bristol BS1 1QD
Tel: 0117 929 7151; Fax: 0117 904 6001

E-mail: sweet@lyonsdavidson.co.uk

Contact: Sally Campbell or Paul Verniquet

The trust is set up as a limited company. Its title is misleading as it apparently assists projects throughout the UK. It provides services for landfill operators and for environmental bodies seeking funds.

To find out about landfill operators in your area, ring:

- The Environment Agency general enquiry line: 0645 333111. The local offices of the agency maintain a public register of waste disposal and treatment sites and operators. The agency has 26 areas and a greater number of offices.
- Landfill Tax Register available from Customs & Excise Landfill Tax Help desk 0645 128484
- ENTRUST Regional Offices:
  Northern Office: 0141 561 0390
  Central Region: 0161 973 1177
  Wales & the West: 01222 869 492
  Southern Area: 020 8950 2152

Research Councils

The research councils are funded and coordinated by the Office of Science and Technology (OST) and support scientific, medical, economic and social research. They also receive funding for commissioned research from government departments, industry and other agencies. All but two are based at Polaris House (see below). Funding takes the form of grants for large research projects and 'small grants' for smaller projects, usually based in university departments. The councils do not put any money aside for the funding of research by voluntary organisations, but voluntary groups are not excluded per se.

Biotechnology and Biological Sciences Research Council (BBSRC)
Tel: 01793 413 200; Fax: 01793 413 201

Economic and Social Research Council (ESRC)
Tel: 01793 413 000; Fax: 01793 413 001

Engineering and Physical Sciences Research Council (EPSRC)
Tel: 01793 444 100; Fax: 01793 444 010

Medical Research Council (MRC)
20 Park Crescent, London W12 4AL
Tel: 020 7636 5422; Fax: 020 7436 6179

Natural Environment Research Council (NERC)
Tel: 01793 411 500; Fax: 01793 411 501

Particle Physics and Astronomy Research Council (PPARC)
Tel: 01793 442 000; Fax: 01793 442 002

In addition to these councils, the new **Arts and Humanities Research Board** provides funding and support for advanced research and special funding for museums, libraries and galleries. It was set up in response to the Dearing Report recommendation that an Arts and Humanities Research Council be established. A decision on whether to upgrade the board into a council was pending at the time of writing.

The board has two addresses. The Chief Executive and Postgraduate Division are based at:

10 Carlton House Terrace, London, SW1Y 5AH
Tel: 020 7969 5256; Fax: 020 7969 5413

The Advanced Research Division is based at:

Northavon House, Coldharbour Lane, Bristol BS16 1QD
Tel: 0117 931 7417; Fax: 0117 931 7157

Appendix 2: Main Guides to Government and the Civil Service

Civil Service Yearbook, now available annually as a book and CD.

Order from: The Stationery Office, PO Box 276, London SW8 5DT
Tel: 020 7873 9090; Fax: 020 7873 8200

Price: £35.00, plus a mail order handling charge of £2.94

Vacher's Parliamentary Companion, a reference book for Parliament, Departments of State, senior civil servants and public offices. It is corrected quarterly.

Subscriptions: Vacher Dod Publishing Limited, 113 High Street
Berkhamsted, Herts HP4 2DJ
Tel: 01442 8761325; Fax: 01442 876133

Also available from The Stationery Office.

Appendix 3: Short Glossary

Non-Departmental Public Bodies (NDPB) – a body which has a role in the process of national government, but is not a government department or part of one, and which operates to a greater or lesser extent at arm's length from Ministers. This term is now widely used, particularly by the Civil Service, to cover a great range of governmental bodies, most of which have been commonly referred to as 'quangos'.

Quango – semi-public government financed administrative body whose members are appointed by the government; Qu(asi) A(utonomous) (N)on-(G)overnmental (O)rganisation.

Other funding jargon

Many of the following terms are not found in contemporary English dictionaries but are common usage in any number of funding programme documents, funding reports and spoken exchanges between officers. The meaning of such words is often slightly skewed from customary usage which leads to comprehension difficulties for the newcomer to these verbal games.

Every walk of life develops its own forms of jargon, sometimes as a convenient shorthand but more often just as a way of seeming one of the 'club' or someone 'in the know'. Its effect can be to deter the newcomer, to make them feel unconfident and ignorant.

Do not be put off by words you don't understand, it's no failing. Just ask 'Can you explain in other words, please?'

Added value/Additionality – activities supported by funding which are additional to, more, over and above, those directly funded.

Benchmarks – a criteria by which to measure something; reference point.

Capacity building – assisting organisations to develop their resources, both human and physical, in order to meet their aims more effectively.

Complementarity – activities funded under different grant-aid programmes must complement each other and not duplicate provision, neither should they represent a divergent policy.

Exit strategy – not how to get out, but a plan, made in the early stage of developing a funded project which sets out how the work will carry on after the start up funding has come to an end.

Leverage – strategic advantage; power or influence; the increased potential ability to raise money – the confidence that success with one funding source generates within other sources considering whether to fund.

Match funding – additional funding from separate funding sources to make up the total funding needed; sometimes, but not always, infers that the contributions are equal or 'match' in size.

Non-statutory grants – grants from sources other than government, i.e. charitable trusts and companies.

Outcomes/Outputs/Outturns – all refer to the results of a project; 'outcomes' is used in a more general sense whilst 'outputs' and 'outturns' are used about the measurable, quantifiable achievements of a project – the results of the 'inputs'.

Pathfinder projects – recent jargon for pilot schemes to test approaches.

Pump-priming – support to a new initiative to get it going; long-term funding to be secured elsewhere.

Targets – outputs agreed at the beginning of a grant or funding cycle which need to be met to qualify for further funding- the profile of groups identified as being in need.

Transparency – openness with information.

Appendix 4: Using the Web

The websites of departments and non-departmental public bodies are given with the addresses in this guide. Further references are made to specific websites within entries for particular funding programmes. These usually contain detailed criteria and often downloadable application forms. Although the quality of information and regularity of updates varies, they contain information on government policy, recent press releases, transcripts of speeches and consultation papers.

The following are good starting points and have links to other sites:

www.open.gov.uk

This government information service site provides an index of sites including departments, councils, NHS Trusts and non-departmental public bodies.

www.coi.gov.uk

The central office of information site for English departmental and non-departmental public bodies' press releases, updated daily.

Most sites are now easy to use even for the internet novice and can allow access to a wealth of information which will only increase in the future.

Subject Index

Alphabetical Index